# DECOLONIZING BHARAT
## *The Balu Way*

# INDICA

# DECOLONIZING BHARAT
## *The Balu Way*

### An Interpretation of the Works of Prof. Balagangadhara & the Ghent School

## PINGALI GOPAL

ISBN
Paperback 979-8-89610-959-4
Hardcase 979-8-89610-961-7

**Dedicated to**

Dr. SN Balagangadhara
and
all the present and future scholars of the Ghent School

# CONTENTS


*Acknowledgements* . . . . . . . . . . . . . . . . . . . . . . . . . . . . . . . . . . . . . . . . . . . . . . . . . . *9*

*Foreword* . . . . . . . . . . . . . . . . . . . . . . . . . . . . . . . . . . . . . . . . . . . . . . . . . . . . . . . . *13*

*Introduction* . . . . . . . . . . . . . . . . . . . . . . . . . . . . . . . . . . . . . . . . . . . . . . . . . . . . . . *15*


## I. RELIGION


1.    Do All Roads Lead to Jerusalem? . . . . . . . . . . . . . . . . . . . . . . . . . . . . 33

2.    Religious Conversion-Indian Disputes and Their European Origins . . 51


## II. SECULARISM


3.    Europe, India, and the Limits of Secularism . . . . . . . . . . . . . . . . . . . 67


## III. CASTE


4.    Western Foundations of the Caste System . . . . . . . . . . . . . . . . . . . . 87

5.    Caste: Some Alternative Narratives . . . . . . . . . . . . . . . . . . . . . . . . . 117

6.    On the Impossibility of Refuting or Confirming the Arguments
     About the Caste System . . . . . . . . . . . . . . . . . . . . . . . . . . . . . . . . . . . 133

7.    Continuous Distortions in Discourses of Indian Social Systems . . . . 147

## IV. CULTURE


8.   Reconceptualizing India Studies . . . . . . . . . . . . . . . . . . . . . . . . 177

9.   What Does It Mean to Be Indian? . . . . . . . . . . . . . . . . . . . . . . 193

10.  Cultures Differ Differently . . . . . . . . . . . . . . . . . . . . . . . . . . . . 207

11.  India in the Eyes of Europeans . . . . . . . . . . . . . . . . . . . . . . . . 223

12.  Magic between Europe and India: On Mantras, Coercion of Gods, and the Limits of Current Debates . . . . . . . . . . . . . . . . . . . . . . . 239


## V. GENERAL: COMPILATIONS AND SUMMARIES


13.  Colonial Consciousness – A Widespread Phenomenon Trapping Our Country . . . . . . . . . . . . . . . . . . . . . . . . . . . . . . . 259

14.  The Unity of India . . . . . . . . . . . . . . . . . . . . . . . . . . . . . . . . . . 291

*References and Additional Readings* . . . . . . . . . . . . . . . . . . . . . . . . .307

*About the Author* . . . . . . . . . . . . . . . . . . . . . . . . . . . . . . . . . . . . .317

# ACKNOWLEDGEMENTS

First and foremost, I would like to thank *Indiafacts, Indica Today,* and *Pragyata* online magazines for the chapters that were previously published in their magazines.

*Indiafacts* online magazine first published:
1. Caste: Some Alternative Narratives
2. Continuous Distortions in Discourses of Indian Social Systems
3. Colonial Consciousness: A Widespread Phenomenon
4. The Unity of India

I thank Nithin Sridhar (the previous editor of Indiafacts and presently Chief Curator, Indica Moksha) and Dr. Ramesh Rao (the present editor of India Facts) for so graciously supporting me. Nithin Sridhar deserves special recognition for being my initial supporter and the driving force behind my passion for writing on Indic-related subjects.

*Pragyata* online magazine first published:
1. On the Impossibility of Refuting or Confirming the Arguments About the Caste System
2. What Does It Mean to Be an Indian?
3. Cultures Differ Differently
4. India in the Eyes of Europeans

I am grateful to Ashish Dhar (CEO of Upword and Pragyata) for the constant encouragement in my writing endeavours.

*Indica Today* online magazine first published:
1. Religious Conversion: Indian Disputes and Their European Origins
2. Magic between India and Europe
3. The introductory Chapter (modified from the original article, *Wanted Urgently: New Discourses for Caste, Religion, and Secularism)*

Yogini Deshpande (editor of Indica Today) has been a great support, and I stay in awe of this extremely dynamic lady, a busy civil engineer who shows the best path to managing divergent passions. I am grateful for her assistance.

I began exploring the world of Balu a few years ago, and that exploration will continue for at least this lifetime. Being outside the academic domain, in the strict sense, has its advantages and disadvantages. The advantage is that I can pick and choose which articles to read without getting too bothered by voices of criticism or disagreement about the Ghent School's ideas. The major drawback is that there will always be questions about my authority, and there is a danger of misrepresenting the ideas of the Ghent School. Fortunately, Balu himself allowed me to go ahead with the compilation of these articles without becoming too worried about possible distortions or misrepresentations. My perspective is purely as a concerned citizen of the country, and this school makes the best sense of my lived experiences as an Indian. I was and still am scared of other scholars, who might see me as a bit of an incongruity. In my summaries, I have generally stayed close to what the authors are saying. To the best of my knowledge, I have clearly marked the individual ideas or thoughts.

Perhaps the trickiest are the last two chapters—or grand summaries, as I call them—where I look at India through the eyes of the Ghent School. The scholars of the Ghent School might disagree at times, especially in the last two chapters. I apologise in advance for any deviations from Balu's or the Ghent School's ideas. However, contrary to my apprehensions, the few I know have been extremely kind to me. Special thanks go to Sarika Rao, Prakash Shah, Dunkin Jalki, Sufiya Pathan, Martin Fárek, and Jakob De Roover for their sweet words of encouragement (and perhaps gentle silence on transgressions, if any).

I would also like to acknowledge the support of other scholars, such as MS Chaitra (Director Founder of the Aarohi Foundation in Bengaluru),

Rohith Krishna, and Aravind Kaushik. Wholehearted thanks to all of the scholars at the Ghent School for quietly doing such extraordinary work, which we can only applaud. I am firmly convinced that a harmonious India (and even the world) can only happen in the future if scholars and laypersons understand their work.

Public intellectuals and writers like Saumya Dey, Nagaraj Paturi, Srinivas Udumudi, GV Shivakumar, and Raghav Krishna have amply supported my writing efforts in trying to understand what the greats have already said. I remain grateful to all of them. I have the privilege of knowing some extraordinary people who are doing outstanding work for Indian culture, and I seek their blessings in my humble efforts. These inspirations include Vishwa Adluri, Joydeep Bagchee, Michel Danino, Bharat Gupt, and Chittaranjan Naik.

I am also fortunate to have a vast network of schoolmates, college friends, professional colleagues, walking companions, family, and extended family (following my daughter's marriage) who consistently offer their claps and whistles to my writing endeavours (sometimes even without reading!). Space constraints prevent me from listing all of their names, but I want to thank them all from the bottom of my heart.

There are many whom I consider my gurus and who guide me on my life's journey. However, three hold a special place in my heart. The extraordinary discourses of Brahmasri Samavedam Shanmukha Sarma, a boon to Telugu people, have helped me immensely understand the traditional texts of India and Advaita. Sri VV Sridhar Guruji of the Sri Jwala Trust epitomises what Balagangadhara says about rituals and performative ability being the foundational basis of our culture. A 'Prayogi' of the highest order, whom mere mortals like me cannot understand, effortlessly connects the highest philosophy of Advaita with matters of the world. In addition to conducting elaborate Vedic rituals for the benefit of all living and non-living beings, he also delivers wonderful discourses. Sri Sri Ravi Shankarji, of the Art of Living, is famous worldwide, and his Sudarshan Kriya is an integral part of my life. In all my endeavours, I will forever seek the blessing of these legendary gurus.

I thank, most importantly, Hari Vadlamani of the INDICA, who is always a phone call away to answer my queries. After I submitted my proposal with some trepidation, it took him exactly five seconds to arrange for a brilliant editor and sponsor the entire book project. I am indeed a big beneficiary of Hariji's passion for promoting and perpetuating Indic-oriented themes and authors. I am deeply appreciative of his assistance and kindness. Whatever good a reader may find in the book is only because of Balu, the scholars at Ghent School, and Hari Vadlamani. No words can suffice to express my gratitude to Michael Thorn, based in the UK, for his thorough editing and proofreading of the entire document. His work was meticulous and elevated the project to another level.

I am deeply indebted to the inputs of Hari Vadlamani and my dear friends Uday Nandan and Karthik, who helped with perhaps the most taxing process of a book: designing the book cover! I am grateful to my publishing manager, Kavya Reddy, and her team at Notion Press for a thorough professional job in designing the final book for publication.

After reading the articles, I hope to inspire the reader to go to the original sources. The book's references and additional readings section lists the primary sources for the chapters and some additional readings. It is always a possibility that I might have missed some of the key aspects while doing the summaries and reviews. On a lighter note, I am solely responsible for any small and irrelevant issues like spelling mistakes and grammatical errors, but for the larger issues and ideas, I am standing behind the shield of Balu and his scholars!

I am grateful to my wife, Ratna, who has been a huge supporter in all my writing endeavours, an activity that adds nothing to the family balance sheets. Her willingness to manage the household on her own mostly keeps me free enough to spend time on the laptop when not engaged in professional duties. My daughter Samyukta, my son-in-law Abhinav, my brother Shankar, and my father Ramana Rao play a very important role in making all this worth it. I lost my dearest mother, Annapurna, recently, and I am sure she is smiling from the heavens and blessing me from the realm of the ancestral world. And finally, everything moves in the universe by the grace of Mother Bhadrakali of Warangal, the protector of all, and I humbly place this effort at her feet.

**Dr. Pingali Gopal**
Hanamkonda-Warangal

# FOREWORD

Dr. SN Balagangadhara, affectionately known as Dr. Balu, is one of Bharat's most significant 20th-century scholars and intellectuals. His post-independence scholarship is groundbreaking, offering profound insights into historical understanding and reconceptualizing the social sciences for India, grounded in indigenous perspectives. Dr. Balu's work critically exposes Western misinterpretations of India, rooted in Western concepts, and enables a reverse analysis of the West using its own frameworks. This approach has guided scholars in rethinking the colonial impact on Indian civilization and has enabled the imagination of a new paradigm for the social sciences. His insights have helped reinterpret history through an Indic lens, strengthening the social sciences on our terms.

Dr. Balu is the author of several books, including the popular *The Heathen in His Blindness*, as well as other significant works like *Reconceptualizing India Studies*, *Cultures Differ Differently*, *As Others See Us* and *Do All Roads Lead to Jerusalem?* His paper "Secular State and Religious Conflict", co-authored with Dr. Jakob De Roover, is a foundational critique of secularism. As director of the India Platform and the Research Centre for Comparative Science of Cultures at Ghent University, Dr. Balu's legacy is carried forward by numerous scholars.

Dr. Pingali Gopal has furthered this work with dedication, creating accessible stepping stones for deeper understanding. Dr. Gopal, a devoted student of Dr. Balagangadhara, has studied his work and engaged with like-minded scholars. His summaries, published on IndiaFacts and INDICA Today, have garnered much appreciation and sparked interest among scholars and general readers. This book is the culmination of those efforts, weaving together essays that integrate knowledge and perspectives into a cohesive body of work. Dr. Gopal has organized the essays into four parts: Religion, Secularism, Caste, and Culture. These sections explore how modern social sciences have problematized our civilization, the influence of Western perspectives on our self-understanding, and the distortions brought about by colonial consciousness and secularism. These essays provide stepping stones to understanding Dr. Balu's work. Dr. Gopal, a medical doctor from Warangal, draws from the works of key figures in this field and this book reflects his deep commitment to decolonization studies, making Dr. Balu's work accessible to a broader audience. Additionally, as an ardent advocate of Indian Knowledge Systems, he continues to champion this cause as a public intellectual.

INDICA began its engagement with Dr. Balu and his work in 2020 when we organized a retrospective symposium. Subsequently, we published his book *What Does It Mean to Be an Indian?* We also had the privilege of supporting his research for three years under our Legacy Grant scheme. INDICA is now proud to present this introduction to the seminal work of Dr. SN Balagangadhara as a tribute to Bharat, and we wish Dr. Pingali Gopal continued success in his scholarly journey.

**Shivakumar GV**
Director, IKS Changemakers, INDICA

**Hari Vadlamani**
Founder INDICA & NICE

# INTRODUCTION

*"What I have sought is to understand what has been said."*
*Ananda K. Coomaraswamy*

This is a paraphrasing, reviewing, and a summarising of the many books and articles of the now popularly known Ghent School of Belgium, initiated by the legendary philosopher-academic Dr. SN Balagangadhara (Balu), now retired from the University of Ghent. He was the director of the India Platform and the Research Centre on Comparative Science of Cultures. The books and articles authored by him, and his group, hold the key to understanding India better. They may even lead to solutions for our problems related to distorted social discourses, especially on caste and religion.

Why should a non-academic, scalpel-holding medical doctor be compiling this book? Would it not be more appropriate for such a project to be undertaken by a respected academic scholar? What, the reader might ask, is the *adhikara* (loosely competence) of Dr. Gopal Pingali, a very ordinary citizen of the country? The answer is precisely that: he is indeed a very ordinary citizen; but one with an extreme concern for the country, just like millions of others. While growing up in different parts of the country, I imbibed certain narratives about India, which certainly did not make me feel proud of my identity as belonging to a certain state, caste, language, or religion.

Growing up as an Indian, however, made me aware of a severe mismatch with what I was reading in the books and articles. My experience dealing with people across all faiths and communities contrasted severely with the imbibed theoretical frameworks. I was confused for almost four and a half decades of my life until I came across *Western Foundations of the Caste System*. Suddenly, a lot of things fell into place, and I went deeper into the world of Dr. Balagangadhara. The Balu school framework certainly gave more sense to my lived experiences as an Indian.

A realisation came that there was every reason to be proud of being an Indian and of my every single identity without the need to put anyone else down, either in my own country or in the West. A general disdain towards the West was replaced with an understanding that we are equals. The Balu school characteristically shows that there is a huge unity across India that academics, intellectuals, politicians, and the media seem to have completely missed. Not only that, but Indian culture also has solutions for pluralism. In recent years, pluralism and multiculturalism have packed into smaller and smaller geographical areas.

The lived values of our tradition and civilisation have the power to transform the world and dissolve borders. Our pluralism and multiculturalism are models that the world needs to replicate. Balu always insists that the East and the West should meet each other as equals and learn from each other. There is no purpose in either hating the West or driving a guilt complex into the West for all their past 'sins', especially their colonial enterprises. Understanding history is important, but not for the purpose of extracting revenge.

To understand the solutions, we need to unpack many of the ideas we have grown up with in the first place, and this is where the Ghent School comes into play. It also shows a direction to proceed forward. The present understandings bring only strife, confusion, anger, and violence. The little I understand of the Ghent School's writings gives me a lot of hope for the future of India. It is with this hope that I have humbly collected all the summaries and reviews and present them to the reader.

It is my sincere hope that, by reading this collection, concerned Indian citizens and perhaps even serious academicians gain a better understanding of what the school is trying to say. Some may be inspired to explore more deeply into the world of Balagangadhara and the Ghent

School. Even though their writings appear to be critical of Christianity, they are extremely respectful towards all communities and faiths. The intention is never to denigrate or abuse the West as a superficial reading might suggest. The problem is never with Christ or Christians but with the secularised and political Christianity of Europe, which is responsible for the setting of many narratives in India. And neither are they Hindu fundamentalists, as others might construct. Both are false descriptions and reductions and, hopefully, a careful reading of this book will dispel such naïve conceptions.

Balu presents ideas in a simple language without resorting to the technical terms available in the social sciences. Without dumbing down or simplifying anything, his wonderful style of writing is equally accessible to the specialist academic and the common citizen who knows English. The only thing required is time for a careful and slow reading. The same applies to the writings of the other scholars. The burning issues of the country today relate to caste, religion, secularism, and Indian culture. Critics, both here and abroad, use these as punching bags to shame India and Indians on a large scale, almost daily.

The summaries and reviews of the books and articles began a few years ago. These were published in various online magazines. An idea was formulated to collect all these in one place in the form of a book for the interested reader. I divided them broadly into four parts: caste, religion, secularism, and Indian culture. The fifth part is made up of compilations that bring many of the Ghent School ideas together. These chapters were written at different times over the last decade, and inevitably there is some repetition. I have edited many such repetitions, but key ideas do keep recurring in the chapters. Perhaps this is beneficial, as it could highlight and fix firmly some critical concepts.

### Religions in India: Do They Exist?

The first part on religions consists of summaries of two important books: Dr. Balagangadhara's *Do All Roads Lead to Jerusalem?* (co-authored by Divya Jhingran and a simplified version of his classic *The Heathen in His Blindness*) and *Religious Conversion: Indian Disputes and Their European Origins* by Sarah Claerhout and Jakob De Roover. The first is Balagangadhara's powerful thesis on religions. This is a paradigm-changing understanding of India, in which he argues that Indian phenomena like Hinduism, Buddhism, Jainism, or Sikhism are *not* religions but may be best described, for lack of a better word, as traditions.

India is a traditional land with rituals as its essence. He writes, "If the point of reference that provides meaning to the word 'religion' are the Semitic religions (Judaism, Christianity, and Islam), then Indian culture does not have any indigenous religions (Hinduism, Sikhism, Jainism, and so on)." He then details the creation of religions, as experienced by colonial scholars. The colonials experienced plenty of practices in the alien land they were ruling and, in order to make sense of them, they bound all the different practices into a single religion: Hinduism, Buddhism, Sikhism, or Jainism. The belief that religion is a *cultural universal* and that it is impossible for cultures not to have a religion was rooted in the religious configuration of Western culture.

Balu says that the starting point of any cultural study is its religion. Religion as a cultural universal is a presupposition that has never undergone a serious examination. Unfortunately, the experience of a small segment of humanity in the West has become universal enough to describe all humanity. India is a land of traditions, not religions. Applying the same definitions of religion in the Indian context (a book, a god, a doctrine, a temple) leads to severe problems in understanding Indian culture.

In Western religious cultures, the truth value of scriptures, doctrines, or beliefs plays a vital role, and frictions arise frequently. The learning configuration of religious culture is the 'why' question, and hence the West is the fertile soil in which both rejections of religion and scientific enterprise flourished. In contrast, India, with a huge number of traditions (*sampradayas* and *paramparas*, broadly where lineages are more important), has a learning configuration based on the 'how' question or the performative ability. Rituals form the foundational basis of traditional cultures. It is a fact of history that rituals unite people and religions divide people. The defining aspect of any traditional culture is indifference to differences that go beyond the standard tolerances or mutual respects of solutions for harmony across diverse belief systems.

Europe understood religions in India in their own framework. Missionaries and intellectuals approached India with a poor stock of concepts, including 'heathen', 'pagan', 'idolaters', 'devil worshippers', and 'zoolaters'. Hinduism was a 'false religion' a priori without any attempt to understand such concepts. Enlightenment criticisms of Indian religious beliefs were in fact based on unsophisticated missionary and travel reports. The source of beliefs had to be textual, and thus began a search for a single book. Indian tradition confused the intellectuals with its many texts and stories. They finally zeroed in on the 'Vedas'. Upanishads or Puranas became the other 'holy books'; anything explicitly not religious, like 'grammar', became non-holy. Despite this, as Balu says, frustratingly, most Indians were oblivious to most of the doctrines. Commentators like David Hume and James Mill characterised Hinduism as something loose, non-canonical, vague, wavering, illusory, obscure, and inconsistent. The apparently amorphous nature of Hinduism is simply because 'Hinduism' as a religion did not exist. It was an imaginary entity, conjured up in the minds of Europeans due to their absolute conviction that *there had to be a religion* among the natives.

Why does this matter? Here is the most powerful idea of Balu when he says that the standard understanding of religion has only given us wars, strife, conversions, and inquisitions. To understand 'religion' as tradition, allowing for a variation of practice, will build up harmony and understanding in a world still in the grip of religious frictions. The biggest problems in the world (colonial, post-colonial, modern, post-modern, and so on), cutting across all ideologies, stem from the stubborn misunderstanding of Indian traditions as religions.

Sarah Claerhout and Jakob De Roover explain in their book *Religious Conversion: Indian Disputes and their European Origins* that it is precisely the different configurations of Western and Eastern cultures that lead to conflict on the issue of conversion. In Indian society, two groups of a different nature coexist: the Hindu, Buddhist, Sikh, and Jain traditions on the one hand; and Christianity, Islam, and Judaism on the other. The former group lacks all the characteristics that allow us to recognise Christianity, Islam, and Judaism as religions: a fixed body of doctrine, an ecclesiastical organisation or central authority, or a single holy book. Barring a few exceptions, most intellectuals, both for and against proselytization, debate from the standpoint of three basic assumptions: a) Indian cultural traditions are religions; b) these religions are rivals; and c) they are rivals because 'truth predicates' apply to them. Problematically, these 'common-sense' facts are a set of claims of both theological and secularised Christianity that assume all cultures *must* have a religion.

In a mutually exclusive view, the Semitic religions look at the diversity of Indian society as a *rivalry of religions,* and the Indian culture sees it as a *coexistence of traditions.* Thus, conversion becomes a vital problem of diversity only if one looks at the world the way Christianity and Islam do. The secularisation of Christian theology translates into the importance of the absolute right to profess, propagate, and change one's religion. However, in traditional cultures, the significance shifts to the freedom to continue one's tradition without aggressive interference from the outside. Thus, the dominant principle of religious freedom in the Indian Constitution privileges Christianity and Islam because it involves the freedom to propagate or proselytise. It implicitly endorses the assumption that religion revolves around doctrines and truth claims.

## Secularism in India: Is It Paradoxically Increasing Fundamentalism?

The second part deals with the issue of secularism in India and how inappropriate it is to deal with the faith-based frictions in India. Jakob De Roover's seminal book *Europe, India, and the Limits of Secularism* analyses the deeply flawed secularism in the Indian context. For centuries, India handled pluralism far better than Europe. We should study our own mechanisms instead of inappropriately importing Western solutions. On a broader scale, notions of secularism arise from a poor understanding of religions and traditions. Secularism was a solution for the European Christian world at a specific time in its history. Making it a universal solution for all cultures and across all times is a recipe for disaster, as is evident in India.

In Europe, the Papal Reform, the Protestant Reformation, and the Enlightenment formed a sequential continuum of theological and political principles. This firmly established the two kingdoms of the secular and the religious—the realm of the public and the private, respectively, as De Roover explains. The opposition between the secular and the religious clearly made sense in Christendom. In Europe, the separation of politics from religion resulted from a specific understanding of confessional strife, which divided Christendom into various factions, each claiming to be the true religion, leading to conflicts. The separation of religion from politics for the smooth functioning of a nation-state worked well in a society where, in the background, everyone knew what Christ, Christianity, or religion meant.

Huge problems arose when a solution for a Western non-plural society at a specific time in its history became a universal solution for all societies. Today, the influx of Islam into Europe and the problems in India when secularism tries to handle a pluralistic traditional country highlight the severe stresses and loopholes in this model. Secularism became a solution for the problem of 'communalism' in India. In India, however, there is no clarity in defining what constitutes the sphere of religion needing separation from public life. No state or court possesses an impartial, uniformly applicable scientific criterion for identifying and delimiting religion.

For post-independent Indian thinkers and politicians, the material prosperity of the West was proof positive that they had better solutions to our problems. The entire reasoning of thinkers remained that the absence of liberal secularism implies a negation of liberal secularism, which leads on to religious politics and religious intolerance. The peculiar idea of secularism propagated by politicians, intellectuals, and the left-oriented, influential academia amounted to appeasement. One of the exercises of such secularism was to whitewash Islamic history of its brutalities while reducing Hindu contributions to Indian historical narratives to footnotes. To please or protect, our thinkers in all relevant fields inappropriately associated the present-day Muslims with past Islamic invaders, when it was quite unnecessary.

As Roover shows elegantly in the book, secularism becomes an intense attack on Indian culture when traditions are forced into the straitjackets of religions. There is a desperate attempt to find some core set of doctrines, principles, or books of such religions and, as a major consequence, paradoxically gives rise to fundamentalism. The rise of 'Hindu fundamentalism' or 'revivalism' is an inevitable outcome of this secularism. Roover puts it simply: "Secularism breeds fundamentalism."

Pagan traditions are still a living force in India. For the Abrahamic religions, conversion is a requirement; for the pagan traditions, conversion is almost illegal and unethical. In a society where these two viewpoints clash, there is bound to be a hardening of the stances of both sides. The state's concept of secularism—which applies only to religious societies and not to traditions of the kind existing in India—enhances religious strife. The core mantra of Hindu liberals who go around proclaiming "Hinduism is good, but Hindutva is bad" stems from a deep ignorance of the nature of Indian culture and the problematic nature of secularism on Indian soil.

In a 1994 Supreme Court judgement, each of the seven judges gave separate versions of secularism. The Assembly debates between 1946 and 1949 show how westward we were in trying to set the basis for the Indian secular state. No one knows the doctrinal core of the Hindus, which has multiple texts, multiple philosophies, and multiple teachers. Today, our courts have taken on the role of past Christian churches in assessing pagan rituals, which decided on *the truly religious, the secular, and the idolatry (or the false components of religions)*. The judges now talk about 'essential' and 'non-essential' practices, and these are inherently theological ideas.

Historically, Indian society has been far more tolerant and liberal than any society thus far. We accommodated a much greater variety of religious, ethnic, and cultural groups than Europe at any point in history. Indian society never disintegrated despite its diversity; hence, it must have known successful practices and mechanisms of coexistence. This surely needs better study. As De Roover says, for reasons we cannot grasp now, Christianity and Islam took the character of traditions like other traditions in India; they lost the fixation on distinguishing between the true and the false and the resulting proselytising drive. Syncretism with Hindu thought also grew in India, with some fine examples all over the country. These aspects need deeper and urgent explorations.

There has been no deep study of Hindu-Muslim conflicts. Unlike the religious conflicts between Islam and Christianity in the West, these conflicts have been more socio-economic and political. Inappropriate secularism ends in converting traditions into religions. A flexible, absorbing mass of traditions slowly converts to religion in trying to define holy books, principles, and ideals. A rich mass of pluralistic traditions stringently defines itself, crystallising into 'Hindutva', which the critics want to eagerly label as the almost oxymoronic 'Hindu fundamentalism' or even 'fascism'. Secularism is flawed to the core and will continue to fail in this country. Perhaps we always had better solutions for dealing with multiculturalism and pluralism, which need a rediscovery. The answer might be in traditionalising religions rather than religionising traditions.

## The Caste System of India: Does It Exist?

Unfortunately, the strongest divisions in Indian society today concern religion and caste, and both are the result of Western colonial narratives. This book's third section on caste consists of summaries of the book *Western Foundations of the Caste System* and various papers from the Ghent School. The 'caste system', the Brahmins, and the hierarchies are responsible for almost all our evils, forever holding society to ransom. Every single social understanding has undergone radical alterations with new knowledge, but the core idea of 'Brahminism'—an exploitative, divinely sanctioned system—remains permanently etched into Indian society.

There are *Varnas* and *Jatis*, no doubt, and there is no denying the practices or elements that go into the construction of the so-called 'system'. However, to talk of an overarching caste system as a uniting framework is not to reference a reality but an *experience* of a Western culture, as Dr. Balagangadhara's group strives to show. The present discourses on the caste system make it a point to show that it is almost morally obligatory on the part of all Indians to be immoral.

The census officials of the nineteenth century found it impossible to distinguish between caste, tribe, occupation, and nationality, and so often incorporated all these categories as variations of caste in their data collection. It was impossible to map the innumerable caste divisions in any coherent fashion along the line of the four divisions of principal castes or *Varnas*. Things have not much improved as we still debate and try to understand concepts like caste, *Varna, Jati,* and *Biradari. Ad hoc* explanations seem to be the order of the day. We need new paradigms for discussing caste for the sake of harmony. The distorted ideas regarding caste lead to emotions in each one of us ranging from pride to extreme shame and anger — and the irony is that most of these ideas have Western roots.

*Jatis* represent the lived reality of Indian social systems. Thousands of them exist across the country based on occupation, language, ethnicity, customs, traditions, and even gender, with their own rules of marriage, food, clothing, belief in gods, and so on. *Jatis* have their own rules of endogamy (marriage), commensality (eating practices), and other practices. They evolve over time, either dissolving or going up and down on the social-political-economic scale. Ancient scriptures started with a description of a few of them and, across centuries, these have grown into many thousands. Sometimes, they have merged together into a common *Jati*, and at other times a single *Jati* has split into two or more. The individual customs have been wide-ranging, fluctuating, and flexible.

On the other hand, the four *Varnas* have remained constant across centuries. *Varnas*—consisting of Brahmanas, Kshatriyas, Vysyas, and Sudras—are perhaps a normative ideal for the proper functioning of society. The *Varna* categorisation has been based on still-contested ideas like birth, *guna (nature), swadharma,* and *karma.* Nobody knows the rules of the caste system, and nobody is aware of any central organisation that enforces these rules throughout the country. We still debate the correct basis for *Varnas,* each one being a huge conglomeration of many practices and traditions.

One of the most confusing discourses on social structuring in India has been to correlate the *Varnas* and the *Jatis.* There has never been a one-to-one correlation, neither with the individuals nor with the authorities trying to decide the *Varna* of each *Jati.* Perhaps the *Varnas* were more of a category.

The scriptures were inconsistent in the hierarchical ordering, but selective quotations and cherry pickings from the vast corpus of literature by the colonials (the *Manusmriti* and the *Purusasukta*, the all-time favourites) and academics constructed a contrived hierarchical ordering with exploitation as its base, as in slavery. One aspect on which the scriptures always insisted was that the achievement of the highest ideal of the individual, *moksha*, was accessible to all four *Varnas*.

Three important colonial ideas played an important role and laid the basis for consolidating the narrative of a 'caste system' in India: 1) the Portuguese origin of the word '*casta*'; 2) the Protestant criticism of Jewish and Catholic priesthood, which was the background of the colonial criticism of the Brahmanical priests; and 3) the Aryan theory with its racial connotations. The word caste, most surprisingly, has no equivalent in any of the Indian scriptures. It was a Portuguese import applicable to their world when they landed on the shores of Goa. In the Iberian Peninsula, with the dominance of the Christian rulers, the existing Jews and Muslims either converted or emigrated. The '*casta*' based on the purity of blood ideas divided the population into the *New Christians*—the recent converts—and the *Old Christians*—the older ones with pure blood. A whole new word came into India to describe our social systems.

The British, like the current social sciences, without understanding the nature of *Jatis* and the social systems, put across meta-theoretical claims of a coherent structure called the caste system. As Balu writes:

The horror stories of 'caste discrimination'; the social humiliation of groups; the phenomenon of 'untouchability'; the presence of poverty, and such became the routine evidence for this. This discrimination is neither unitary nor monolithic. If its presence is evidence of the existence of 'the caste system', then the latter is present everywhere in the world. Discrimination, poverty, and social humiliation of groups are in slavery, in the feudal societies of Europe, in the capitalist societies of today, and so on. These are compatible with multiple social structures. On their own, these phenomena are not evidence of one specific social structure, namely, 'the caste system'.

*(Reconceptualizing India Studies)*

Untouchability, in some of its forms during a certain period of our history, was certainly a weed. However, many intellectuals (colonials, missionaries, and modern thinkers) have called for the dismantling of the entire structure of Sanatana Dharma to tackle the issue of untouchability. Thinkers like Sri Aurobindo and Ananda Coomaraswamy condemned untouchability forcefully too, but without needing to dismantle the structure of society. Savarkar and Gandhi, like Dr. Ambedkar, made innumerable efforts to eradicate it from society. However, there were many nuances to untouchability that none of our intellectuals or parliamentarians could understand or articulate.

Without understanding or specifying what untouchability actually means, the entire segregation of 65 million people and 1200 *Jatis* into the *Scheduled Castes* is based on the single but tenuous criteria of an 'ex-untouchability' status. Importantly, as Pathan and Jalki show, the data for caste atrocities simply does not exist. The definitions are narrow; discriminations are studied only in isolated groups; and the whole narrative of 'caste discrimination' is, in the end, a case of data manipulation, statistical cherry-picking, and making macro claims based on micro evidence. There are sensational media claims in anecdotal reports. The media and intellectuals use data from the National Crime Records Bureau to project an alarming picture of India. However, the same data in a deeper study shows that, on average, the Scheduled Castes population faces roughly 30 times *less* crime than the general population.

Ananda Coomaraswamy said that the caste system needs an explanation and not an apology. Today, the understanding of caste is a confusing and contradictory mix of three distinct strands. The first is the actual *Varna* and *Jati* arrangement of society, the rules of which nobody clearly understands. Indian texts identified this arrangement, but there was no theorisation of the rules. Sri Aurobindo called the three intricately linked quartets (the four *Varnas*, the four *Ashramas*, and the four *Purusharthas*) the bedrock of Indian civilisation, responsible for withstanding constant onslaughts and preventing a collapse of civilisation. For Coomaraswamy and Aurobindo, teasing out *Varnas* from the other quartets and studying them in isolation, without considering other metaphysical aspects, such as *karma* or rebirths, commits intense violence to an understanding of the culture. The second is the colonial understanding and theorisation of the caste system, which had mainly hierarchy and exploitation as its main struts. The third is the post-independent political handling of the issue, which solidified the social system into some hard categories—like Forward castes, Backward castes (with further subclassifications like A, B, C, and D), Scheduled Castes, Scheduled Tribes, and so on—purely for political and administrative purposes. The three have mixed only to give rise to strife and division.

As the Ghent School scholars formulate, hierarchy, purity, pollution, endogamy (marriage concerns), and occupational communities have been and continue to be properties of several human social systems across the globe in multiple social settings. There is no unity in the sets of phenomena clubbed together and described as either component parts, causes, or effects of the Indian caste system. The dominant western story about the caste system is false if taken as an explanation of Indian society.

### Indian Cultural Studies

The fourth part contains summaries of important books by the Ghent School dealing with Indian culture, of which *Reconceptualizing India Studies* is arguably the most important. As Balu writes, colonial education gave a scientific status to the coloniser's account of the culture and society of the colonised. The all-pervasive Hindu religion, evil Brahmins, the tyranny of caste, and secularism as the only solution became true descriptions of our world. Educated Indians and our social sciences adopted theories and ideas of Western cultural experiences to describe Indians as deficient variants of the West.

The colonials had a purpose: to understand and rule our society, perhaps requiring them to even bring about great internal fissures either by ignorance or mischief. But why did our own humanities or political and social sciences fail us after independence? We need new theories to understand Hindu traditions and alternatives to secularism to bring peace and harmony across the country. We absorbed and assimilated every culture from across the world for thousands of years, and yet we are in the dock for the 'ugly caste system' and 'Hindu fundamentalism'. We need a great revival and great unity. It is time for us to dissipate the anger and start fresh narratives.

Balu carefully develops the thesis of "colonial consciousness" which is at the root of almost all our problems, while trying to understand ourselves. These are the Western lenses that both foreign and Indian scholars wear while studying India. The social sciences the West employed to study itself and the non-Western cultures remain unchanged. Hence, when Indians use these social sciences, they study India the way the West studied them. The most important project today would be to decolonise our social sciences. Balagangadhara writes in *Reconceptualizing India Studies*: "It (colonisation) is finally about denying peoples and cultures their own experiences; of rendering them aliens to themselves; and actively preventing any description of their own experiences except in terms defined by the colonisers."

Today, where does colonial consciousness operate? The simple answer—everywhere: the Aryan-Dravidian story; understanding Indian traditions as religions; accepting secularism as the best solution for harmony; rejecting the ideas of *Varna, Ashrama,* and *Purusharthas* developed in our texts and superimposing caste, a Western idea, into the *Varna* and *Jatis* of India; the inferior view of Ayurveda; blanking out the most profound Indian philosophies (or Darshanas) from schools by calling them religion; rejecting Sanskrit and making English the language of culture, prosperity, and social mobility; a historical reading of our texts and scriptures causing immense violence; making the Western conflict between science and religion our own; understanding our rituals from a scientific perspective and making them irrational; accepting the political ideologies of the left-right- centre; the story of the revolt of Buddhism against Hinduism; the disbelief in a golden period of India; the story that we were never a nation; the discourse on corruption, which makes most Indians immoral because of a faulty religion and social system... And so on, *ad infinitum*. It is a huge work for decolonisation.

### *Summing Up Articles*

Indian culture and traditions have formed an unbroken continuity for thousands of years. We are one people and one land. Every person on this land is a part of and an inheritor of this great culture, irrespective of what faith they may be following, what Jati they may belong to, or what language they are speaking. The last two chapters do not refer to individual works by scholars of the Ghent School. They are written from the perspective of an ordinary, concerned citizen of India and are intended as a summation of the many articles and books of the Ghent School. There is no claim to original scholarship.

The most important thing to learn from this school is that there is a grand unity in this great country called India, or Bharat. We also need to study the West from our perspective to understand why they are asking a variety of questions about us. In the whole journey of Balu's writings, there is never a denigration of the West, and he places both the East and the West as equals. This has been the overwhelming message of all our previous thinkers, like Ananda Coomaraswamy, Sri Aurobindo, and Swami Vivekananda. I sincerely hope that readers are stimulated to explore further the world of the Ghent School and make some serious efforts for the well-being of the country.

A gentle disclaimer here. It is entirely possible that the Ghent School academicians and other scholars who follow them keenly may not completely agree with my way of looking at the Ghent School thoughts and ideas. As a layperson handicapped by a lack of academic credentials, I apologise in advance for any such interpretations that may be inconsistent with their original ideas. Secondly, the ideas may appear new and 'radical' to some readers, who may range from a gentle disagreement to a vehement rejection in their response. My conviction about this school is not required, but I would like them to keep an open mind and understand that there is an alternative view of the country that contradicts the dominant narratives. It's possible that they could provide a more constructive approach to finding solutions. Personally, I believe that Prof. Balu and the Ghent School finally promise to bring harmony and unity to the country, an elusive dream at the moment.

Part I

# RELIGION

*"The wise say, my Lord, that they are forever lost, whose ancient traditions are lost."*

**– Bhagvad Gita, Chapter 1, Verse 44**

## Chapter 1

# DO ALL ROADS LEAD TO JERUSALEM?

*SN Balagangadhara and Divya Jhingran*

Written in collaboration with Divya Jhingran, this book simplifies Balu's classic, *The Heathen in His Blindness*, a work that scholars have found challenging to comprehend. This book outlines Balu's basic thesis about religions. Balu says that it is an unexamined presupposition that all cultures have religions. If Christianity, Islam, and Judaism define 'religion,' then Indian culture does not have religions. It would be more accurate to refer to Hinduism, Buddhism, Jainism, and Sikhism as 'traditions', given their distinct characteristics in comparison to other major religions.

The West looked at all Indian practices through its own lenses and frameworks. The West's specific cultural configuration, deeply rooted in religion, allowed them to see religion in all the cultures they studied. Balu's thesis provides a better understanding of India and explains many things, including the failure of secularism as a solution for harmony. Unfortunately, the experiences of a small segment of humanity in the West have come to represent all of humanity. Our own lenses provide a different view of Indian phenomena.

Balu states that modern writers find it difficult to define what constitutes religion in other cultures, yet they are simultaneously convinced of the existence of such religions. A central prophet, church, holy book, and revelation, along with belief in one God, are necessary properties for religions (Judaism, Christianity, and Islam). These are absent from the ancient Greek polytheistic religions, from Hinduism, and from Buddhism (even God is absent here), and yet they are religions.

According to Western-Christian thinking, there is metaphysically one true God and many false gods, as well as separation between the creator and creation. Understanding Indian culture, with multiple equal gods and no such separation, becomes an impossibility. Why insist on the existence of a religion when other cultures lack one, defined solely within the framework of Christianity? Western writings often ambiguously define creeds as either necessary or not necessary to qualify a tradition as a religion. Thus, if Semitic phenomenon are religions, other cultures do not have religions, and if other cultures have religions, Semitic phenomenon are not religions.

### Christian Encounter with the Romans: Redefining Religions and Traditions

Christianity grew in a Greco-Roman world against the backdrop of the Judaic community. What was *religio* to the Romans? The ancient Roman world had an extraordinary variety of philosophical schools, ritual practices, and gods. The characteristic tolerance (bordering on indifference) between a diversity of beliefs and practices illustrated the human ability to entertain multiple perspectives. In pagan Rome, individuals such as Cicero—a priest as well as a poet, philosopher, and orator—penned a vast body of literature that disregarded gods. Cicero's *De Natura Deorum: On the Nature of the Gods* inspired Enlightenment thinking against religion. Western thinkers reconciled this ambiguity by writing that either the writers, consciously compromising, were hypocritical (writing something different from personal belief out of fear of persecution) or the citizens were illiterate and could not read what the public personalities were writing in private.

Balu says that, oddly, Greco-Roman intellectuals, although intellectually on par with Enlightenment thinkers in their arguments against gods and religions, did not become atheists. Enlightenment thinkers were unable to comprehend the distinct cultural matrix of the Greco-Roman world. Theological debates about gods in the Roman world were unrelated to rituals dedicated to various deities. The Romans were proud that their religion allowed for the worship of all deities. Rituals were not dependent on the status of the gods—real or unreal. For the Romans, *religio* simply meant ancestral practices transmitted over generations. They required no other theoretical justification. Enlightenment thinkers thought that pagan rationalism never reached its logical conclusion of rejecting traditional practice.

The Romans persecuted the Jews and Christians on the basis that they did not have traditions and hence were not *religio*. Jews responded by claiming great antiquity and, therefore, *religio*, exempting them from following others' traditions. Christians found it challenging because they were neither Romans nor Jews and had no antique history, language, or tradition. The Christian writers transformed the question by appropriating both the Old and New Testaments, claiming to be true because they contained the most ancient doctrines or scriptures. Christianity fulfilled the prophecy of not only the Jews but of all people, articulated from a position of increasing power.

Christianity, the religion of humankind, thus made pagan traditions obsolete and prototypical of false religions. Christian writers brought about a fundamental shift: *religio* became counter to tradition rather than synonymous with it. Religion became today's definition of a belief based on doctrines. Christian authors, in appropriating the Old Testament, also created a unified story of humanity. There was a true and universal religion corrupted over time by idolatry and devil worship. Then God spoke to Abraham, Isaac, and Jacob to lead the dispersed and 'lost' tribes back on the true path. The absence of tradition led Christianity to place extraordinary value on written doctrines, their purity, and correct interpretations, creating a single path from the start. For the pagans, the truth value of traditions was not considered necessary. The Christians thought it was a necessity.

## *European Encounter with India: Writings of the Early Christians, Protestant Reformers, and Enlightenment Intellectuals*

The Greeks, first encountering India, were respectful in their writings. The European writers of the fifteenth and sixteenth centuries, lacking this respect, ventured into new realms of morality and religion. The Europeans expected India to be an exotic and rich land, with Christian communities for reconnection and pagan communities (descendants of Noah) whose souls needed saving. The constant descriptions from travellers and missionaries did not distinguish between geography (flora and fauna) and ethnology (people). European readers enthusiastically lapped up the gross misrepresentations describing the most ethically and morally depraved practices by Indian kings, citizens, and priests. In the early sixteenth century, an imaginative Ludovico di Varthema described India's sexual excesses vividly. As late as 1984, a scholar named Stephen Neill writes that the naiveté of Varthema's accounts is a reason to believe that he is not inventing! Instead of questioning whether a religion truly existed, the European writings simply assumed false religions, heathens, and idolaters were populating India.

Simultaneously, in the sixteenth century, the Protestant Reformation movement erupted and severely questioned Catholic practices. Ironically, Reformation intellectuals used the same pagan intellectual critiques of Christian religion, such as Cicero's, to criticise the priest-driven ritualistic practices of Catholicism. The innate divinity in humans made the allegedly corrupted priests redundant. They contrasted the true and superior Christian religion with the false pagan religions. The pagan societies had nothing to teach.

In this context, Europeans saw the Indian subcontinent as populated by heathens, idolaters, and false religions. Crucially, Christianity established a link between belief and practice. Thus, knowing about the natives' external actions meant finding out what the natives internally believed in. In its mission to convert and eradicate erroneous beliefs, Christianity engaged in persecution, such as the Goa Inquisition. When this approach proved unsuccessful, it resorted to severe criticism of native beliefs. The latter step began the creation of religions and 'isms' like Hinduism, Buddhism, Jainism, and Sikhism. Intellectual criticisms poured in—focused on the disordered philosophies, gods, and texts—as Europeans tried to make sense of Indian cultures.

Balu's important thesis is that the Enlightenment consisted not in the doing away of religion but simply continuing the same Christian discourse in a secularised form. For example, instead of calling religion *God's gift* to humanity, the Enlightenment made it *nature's gift*. The Enlightenment thinkers finally merged ancient Greco-Roman paganism with Asian paganism and divided the world into Christians, Jews, Muslims, and Heathens. It also ensured a developmental ordering of human history, where paganism represented man's childhood with its 'concrete' ideas of God, while Semites advanced with their 'abstract' conceptions. 'Concrete' and 'abstract' now acquired a secular mantle, with applications in fields such as psychology and anthropology. Strangely, traveller and missionary reports were the basis for deciding the primitiveness of pagan societies. Theories of religion came into existence, and finally, it became impossible to conceive of a culture without religion. Religion thus became a cultural universal.

### The Search for the Holy Texts and the Polemics on the Caste System When Creating Religions

'Heathen,' 'pagan,' 'idolaters,' 'devil worshippers', 'zoolaters', and 'false religions' were the key descriptors for missionaries and European writers when describing India. Without protest, these reports formed the theoretical basis of the Enlightenment. Finally, Europeans created Hinduism as a set of fixed doctrines modelled on contemporary European religious theories. As is typical of Semitic religions, the idea of a single book finally led them to the Vedas after a confusing search through many texts, sub-texts, stories, and Puranas.

Vedas, Upanishads, or Puranas became the 'holy books'; anything not religious, like grammar, became non-holy. Frustratingly, Indians were indifferent to both the doctrines and the internal differences in the texts. For polemical writers like Hume and Mill, this amorphous Hinduism was a deficiency of Indian people and culture. Balu argues that people were unaware, both then and now, that Hinduism is 'amorphous' because it does not exist as a religion. Indian 'holy' books discuss the totality of social life and human existence. If religion means *everything*, the word itself loses its meaning. This European project also separated "philosophical" Hinduism from "popular" degenerate Hinduism, which was filled with Sati and other shameful practices.

The nature of Hinduism, the caste structure, and the Brahmins were the great obstacles to large-scale conversions to Christianity. Unlike the 'blacks' (enslaved) and the 'reds' (decimated), the 'whites' could only colonise the inferior 'yellow or brown' without converting. In India, the equally prevalent European socio-economic inequality became a caste and religious issue. Regarding caste, scholars and missionaries speculated that either the holy books or Brahmins sanctioned the system, and their anger fell on both. Since the Brahmins proved resistant, the missionaries targeted the lower strata. The hatred against priestly Brahmins, cultural ignorance, and arrogance generated charges of immorality against the Brahmins. Today, social scientists, in a secularised form, continue to critique the Brahmins and the caste system for all the evils in society.

### The Creation and Discovery of Hinduism and Buddhism

The British first called Indians 'Gentoos.' The Persians referred to everyone on the other side of the Sindhu River as Hindu. In the nineteenth century, the religion of the Gentoos became the religion of the Hindus, and finally Hinduism. William Jones and his associates founded the Asiatic Society in Calcutta, initiating an Oriental second 'Renaissance' by rediscovering Sanskrit literary texts. The Renaissance merged a living culture with an antique paganism. The Romantic thinkers referred to India as the 'cradle' of civilisation, which was hardly a compliment given that a living culture, including its religion, had become characteristically primitive and innocent. From Hegel to Marx, India was described as being in a state of stagnation since antiquity because of the caste system and an all-pervasive religion.

After Hinduism, the Europeans created Buddhism. The latter evolved into a reformist, Protestant-like attack on Hinduism, just as Buddha became a Martin Luther. Buddhism, with its clearer texts, crystallised rapidly as a proper religion in a short span of seventy years. Similar to Hinduism, the authors created two versions of Buddhism: a corrupted "popular" version and a pure "philosophical" version. By the beginning of the twentieth century, Buddhism had originated and matured in the libraries and institutes of Paris and London as a distinct religion in Indian culture.

Missionaries, travellers, and scholars worked on previous reports and projected a similar image of Indian culture throughout. To understand a culture meant studying its texts and finding out what the people believed in. Ridiculously, Europeans were judging a living culture based on ancient texts like the Laws of Manu. It was like assessing present-day European culture based on gibberish vernacular translations of the Bible. Sadly, the present Indian intellectuals accept all these narratives about Hinduism and Buddhism as unquestionable truths.

### Definitions and Paradigms of Religion: Shifting Sands

Religion, an established fact, has been extremely difficult to define. Yet, an inability to define has not prevented scholars from comparing prototypical religions (Judaism, Christianity, and Islam) with other cultural traditions. The many varied definitions, whether large or small in scope, rarely shed light on the perplexities that necessitate a definition of religion, such as whether devotion to science qualifies as religion. The disputes reflect problems with either classification or our knowledge. For various authors, the huge literature about Indian traditions is adequate to claim Hinduism or Buddhism as religions. Today's definitions are simply a linguistic and historical intuition of a secularized Christian culture. Balu writes, "Unless we establish what religion is and what properties make Christianity a religion, we cannot make comparisons with Christianity to claim the existence of religion in other cultures."

Scholars like Hume presupposed the truth of the claim that religion is a cultural universal, just as religious studies presuppose the truth about Biblical themes, but in a secularised language. The *naturalistic paradigm* gained ground in the eighteenth century, starting with Hume. This paradigm, disagreeing with a supernatural account, asserted that primitive man created religion as a means of bringing order to the chaotic world of births, deaths, and disasters around him.

Balu says this is a flawed argument, since the primitive man might have instead been *impressed* with the order of the cosmos and the expected unexpectedness of natural disasters. The postulation of gods does not make the world orderly, since pagan gods have many moods of caprice, benevolence, anger, and love. The idea that God creates order is a characteristic assumption of religions based on the Old Testament. The projection of our psychology onto the primitive man is true if cultural evolution has not had any impact on human emotions. The primitive man might have been much more accepting than us of the vagaries of nature, says Balu. The origin of religion in fear is doubtful since theologians (like Leonardus Lessius) also theorise the same fear as the cause of atheism!

David Hume's theory gives religion five psychological properties: 1) it postulates invisible powers; 2) it acknowledges human dependence on such powers; 3) the invisible powers are unknown causes; 4) the causes are of the same kind; and 5) humans are models for these causes. Now, even scientific theories have the first four of the above properties, and modelling is important in developing scientific theories. Hence, in trying to explain the unknown in terms of the known, the primitive man may have been extremely rational. Balu explains that the Enlightenment explanation of humans attempting to transform divinity into a human form is characteristic of Semitic traditions, not Asian traditions such as Hinduism or Buddhism.

According to Balu, religion has never answered the question of what life means. Religion, in fact, raises the question of meaning in life. Christianity then posits degrees of faith, with pagan cultures showing an absence of it. Balu says that, unfortunately, one cannot have faith without an inbuilt intolerance. The religious person may not be a persecutor or a missionary, but he would never accept that other religions are equally true. Religion is thus the truth in a specific sense, independent of the truth of any other belief we may hold. *Thus, the adequacy of one religion against another is only within the framework of a religion and can never be scientifically neutral.*

Balu argues that many theories on the origins of religion, including the religious 'experience' definition (whose experience?), are useless. These simply transform Semitic theological ideas into the characteristic properties of religion, and all along they presuppose that religion is universal in all cultures. The naturalistic paradigm has never challenged the supernatural explanation of religion.

## Contingent Properties of Religion

Balu says that the five contingent properties of religion are:

1. God.
2. Humans to fulfil a purpose of God.
3. A relationship between God and humans.
4. An intelligible and understandable cosmos.
5. Core doctrines.

The means are the worship of the true God. These properties which make a religion also divide them unfailingly since a belief exists that conversion implies going to a better religion. These concepts, specific to Judaism, Christianity, and Islam, mean that followers cannot understand why pagans should bow to cows, monkeys, and serpents. The simple explanation for Christian scholars was a blind Heathen. A specific type of faith, religious experience, and worship set religions apart from each other, but the pagans did not accept these descriptions.

## Protestant Response to Atheistic Movements and the Problems Generated

At the end of the 1890s, a German Protestant religious school at the University of Göttingen emphasised the unity of religions and studied the relationships between religions. They believed that all religions form a continuum of the human response to divine revelation. The adequacy of responses determined the differences among religions. They had a significant impact on later scholarship, shaping the progression of religions from primitive to the most perfect and advanced, specifically the Protestant form of Christianity. Revelation is everywhere, but it is pure in higher religions and takes a degenerate form through dogmas and priestly rituals in primitive religions.

The focus now shifts from doctrines and structure to an individual religious experience, typically referred to as 'sacred' or 'holy'. In response to Enlightenment atheism, Christianity shifted its focus from Christ to a more universal God. Religious subjective individual experience emphasises intuition and feelings to distinguish religion from non-religion and guide inter-religious study. However, problematically, "intuition" loses its validity when one has clarity on the object and type of experience in question. This also became a Christological dilemma. The claim of an exclusive Jesus led to problems with accepting Christianity, and the claim of many revelations in theism decreased the importance of Jesus Christ as the central figure.

Protestants could allow secular values like tolerance and pluralism in their discourse, but only after presupposing that traditions like Hinduism and Jainism were religions and fitting them into a developmental ranking. No author who popularised the experiential aspect of religion spoke of this experience among Hindus or Buddhists without presupposing the truth of the Bible. The future writers used similar arguments, though in secular terms. Thus, a single religion and its secularised form become the framework for describing other cultures.

## Category Mistakes and Domination of a Single Discourse

A category mistake occurs when terms and concepts appropriate to some domains are applied elsewhere. Asking a Belgian priest, "Are you a Brahmin?" is a category mistake, just as it is to ask about 'religiosity' in Indian traditions. Being a Brahmin or a non-Brahmin makes sense in Indian traditions only, and the category of religion similarly applies to Christianity only. Today, anthropologists, philosophers, and religion theorists continuously make category mistakes because Christianity has become the universal language of humankind.

For pagan philosophers like Cicero, religion meant ancestral traditions transmitted through generations. Christian philosophers redefined religion to include God as well as the relationship between God and man. Religion is a word best suited for the intra-traditional world of Christians alone. When religion attempts to define or understand other traditions, it makes a category mistake. In the first place, Buddhism and Jainism have no gods, and many Hindu philosophical schools give no particular importance to God.

Secularisation does not lead to the rejection of religion; it simply continues Christian ideas in a different language. Thus, "God gave religion to humankind" becomes "all cultures have religion"; "God gave one religion to humanity" becomes "all religions share something in common," and so on. We freely use words like prophetic, revelatory, soteriology, eschatology, sacred, sacrament, blasphemy, and apocalyptic to describe various traditions and cultures. However, these words make sense only in the Christian tradition. The vocabulary and concepts appear neutral, but they have a strong theological basis. Unfortunately, today, there is no other way to conceive of religion except as handed down by Christian theology, says Balu.

Throughout history, the colonials made numerous category errors while attempting to comprehend the foreign cultural world they ruled. This resulted in the conversion of India's diverse traditions into the 'proper' religions of Hinduism, Buddhism, Jainism, and so forth. Their understanding created some more distortive narratives, which became dominant in public perception. Thus, Buddha rebelled against Hinduism, which was patently false, says Balu.

In the *Dhammapada* and the *Sonadanda Sutta,* Buddha describes a true Brahmana and puts Kshatriyas at the top of caste hierarchy while explaining the evolution of varnas in society. A rejection does not try to define the perfection of the rejected. Marx rejected capitalism, but he did not define a true capitalist. Buddha criticised corrupt Brahmins, but he intended to define a true Brahmin and never rejected the varna arrangement. His path was open to all of society's varnas. Shramanas (the origin of Ajivikas, Buddhists, and Jains) or Bhaktas, described as revolutionary movements by scholars, were renunciating traditions. The renunciating traditions were outside of the caste system since they had given up the caste (Varna and Jati) practices and left society on their own. They were not "outcastes" or "untouchables," shunned by society, as popularly described or conceived by the scholars.

### *Understanding Religion from an Indian/Heathen Perspective*

Intolerance and proselytization are the keys to understanding religion. In the many fights of Christianity with others and amongst themselves, we clearly know which were religious and which were not. Christianity, Judaism, and Islam hold similar ideas, which binds them together as a single category. Once we grasp their view of religion, we can understand why they saw religion wherever they went, despite contradictions. For Semitic religions, doctrines, beliefs, and actions form the crux, and differences in these led to frictions. Conversion meant rejecting the previous as false and the new as true. Religious explanations, unlike natural sciences and social sciences, include themselves as part of the explanation of the universe. Thus, religion need not prove the existence of God; the existence of religion is proof positive of God and his creation of the universe.

Indian pagans could accept Christianity, Islam, or Judaism because they understood religion as another form of tradition, where all are equally true. Semitic religions, inherently intolerant, label other traditions as religions and classify them as true or false. Political power propagated these Christian ideas. Religion then demands that the stories and generational traditional practices have justification and purpose. Importantly and disconcertingly, when it turns into religion, tradition begins a search for a 'deeper' foundation, something that was previously absent.

Regarding idolatry, Balu demonstrates that idolatry is a religious concept that originates in Christian theology and aids in expansion. Idolatry became a superimposed issue in Indian traditions, even among Indian reformers. Religious expansion reduced the categories of Christian (or sacred), secular (or civic), and pagan (or profane) to a simple dichotomy of Christian and pagan. Political and army power first absorbed or removed the secular (New Year celebrations, circuses, and so on). The pure pagan world then vanished. Idolatry and devil worship were potent methods of creating the 'other', attacking them virulently, and then absorbing their culture. India has been resilient till now, but for how long?

## *A Culture Without Religion: Metaphysical and Sociological Impossibilities of a Religion in India*

Balu, in the final sections, explains in detail the absence of religions in Indian culture. He says that if we encounter a culture that uses different mechanisms for experiencing divine or social integration, then our standard definitions of religion are wrong or inadequate. Oddly, Balu says, no religious theory explains the consequences of a culture's absence of religion. However, if we assume that not all cultures have religions, then the consequences of this assumption would obviously be that the universality of religion is a non-empirical claim.

'Worldview' is a set of fundamental beliefs that bind a community. Thus, a religious framework that asserts religion as a cultural universal assumes a secular tone when it advocates for a universal worldview across all cultures. Till 1600 CE, before secular ideologies and scientific theories, worldview meant only religions. Balu asks, "Do all cultures have or need a worldview, and could we define a community and its boundaries by describing their worldview?" In the framework of these questions, Balu says that there simply cannot be a religion in India.

Metaphysically, religion must make a claim about the origin and purpose of the world (in terms of One True God), and this message must be as true as other 'true' knowledge claims like gravity. Indian traditions and texts (Vedas, Upanishads, Brahmanas, Puranas, and Itihaasas) never properly raise the issue of the origin of the Cosmos. They contain a wide variety of 'origin' stories, all of which an individual in Indian traditions can either equally accept or reject. Some would say that the origin question is illegitimate because it always existed. Buddhists and Jains have no God in the first place. Again, unlike the West, the truth or falsity of the books is irrelevant in Indian intellectual traditions. Rama or Krishna may have never existed, but the Ramayana and Mahabharata are eternally true. In Indian intellectual traditions, literature investigating texts' truth claims (like for the Bible in the West) is conspicuously absent.

The absolute sociological conditions required for guaranteeing the identity of religions across time and space are: 1) a worldview codified in a 'holy book'; 2) a standard worldview with clear boundaries that cannot change across generations; 3) a central authority to settle disputes of interpretation; 4) a source of excommunication; and 5) an organisation to transmit and propagate the worldview. These do not exist in India with respect to Hinduism, Sikhism, Jainism, Buddhism, and so on.

The metaphysical position and these sociological conditions are religion's two defining properties. Thus, in metaphysical and sociological terms, Balu stresses that it is an impossibility that Indian culture knows of religions or their secularised version—a worldview.

## Universalization or Secularization of Religion

Universalization implies that religion's form and structure become so well-entrenched that its specific doctrines fade into the background while the main cognitive structure remains intact. According to Balu, Christian doctrines must spread in two distinct ways: the conversion of people to Christianity and the widespread acceptance by non-Christians of their account, which spread in a secular, de-Christianized form. Importantly, this double movement expresses itself in the double relation that religions have towards each other: they are intolerant of each other, yet there are attempts for inter-religious dialogue because of the intuitive feeling that "all religions are one" writes Balu. The final result of the two phenomena of Christianity (proselytization and secularisation of its vocabulary) is belief in the universality of religions across all cultures. Religion is an important element in Western culture's identity, ultimately leading to the belief that religion is the constitutive element of all cultures.

## A Comparison of Cultures—Differences in Learning Configurations

Exclusive Western frameworks do not allow for a comparative science of cultures, where each culture describes itself and others in their own contexts. For example, a single framework (including early Christians and modern writers) that assessed the beliefs of other cultures based on the actions they performed does not understand how pagan priests performing complex rituals could write texts questioning the existence of God. Balu, in the important section on configurations of learning in various cultures, says that humans need to adapt to both nature and society (by socialisation) equally. The critical socialization process entails knowledge transmission from the group's reservoir. The reservoir comprises the customs, myths, and traditions of the culture, while the mechanisms of transmission (intended or unintended discoveries) include child-rearing practices, schooling, texts, and so on.

Numerous frameworks exist for the acquisition and dissemination of these socialization practices. The most crucial point of Balu's thesis is that differences in social environments and diverse ways of learning processes determine differences between cultures. Each culture has a specific configuration of learning, which is an outcome of the dynamic interaction between the main and subordinate learning processes. Balu says that the *configuration of learning in the West is religion,* where the 'why' question becomes the dominant learning process.

Religion, the ultimate example of an explanation, generates an orientation for guiding the culture's intellectual and practical energies. Religion, in relating and explaining unconnected phenomena through an invisible ordering force, was the foundation for developing a scientific attitude. Later, an unimpeded growth of science leads to a clash and finally an indifference to religious doctrines. Religion and the 'why' question, as the root model of learning, explain both the Christian Church's hostility to science and the growth of atheism in the West.

## *Learning Configurations in the Pagan/Heathen World*

In certain cultures, such as India, the dominant learning process revolves around the 'how' question or performative ability. Such a culture demonstrates incredible social stability, cohesion, and order. Rituals, which define this performative ability, have generated a configuration of learning that has built a stable Indian society, resisting attempts to dismantle it for centuries. Christianity viewed pagan rituals as inferior but, historically, religion has always divided communities, including wars, while rituals have mostly united them. A dominant mode of learning becomes a subordinate mode in another culture. The relationship between the dominant and subordinate learning processes determines a culture's 'learning configuration.' Hence, though rituals and religious elements are present in Western and Indian cultures, respectively, they play a subordinate role.

The West struggles to understand karma, reincarnation, and Atman, which make sense only in the Indian context. Western culture has a single view that all cultures must have a religion of various grades, while pagan cultures accept multiple ways of going about the world. This makes Semitic religions intolerant, while Asian traditions are tolerant and accepting. The West, in its search for order, produced theories that broke away from practical life. Indian or Asian cultures, in contrast, invested their energies in creating, sustaining, and continuously modifying a social or practical order. Balu says that, unfortunately, the two cultures met where the Asians were willing to learn, and the West thought they could only teach.

### Final Thoughts of SN Balagangadhara

In summary, Balu's thesis asserts the following propositions:

1. Religion, by its nature, generates the belief that religion is a cultural universal.

2. Religion is not a cultural universal, despite all Western-trained intellectuals, social scientists, anthropologists, sociologists, and neuroscientists believing it to be. There is no empirical foundation for this belief.

3. Jews and early Christians understood traditions in terms of 'true' or 'false' religions. Later Europeans understood traditions within the frameworks provided by the schisms in Christianity between the Protestants and the Catholics.

4. The finest libraries and intellectuals in France, England, and Germany crafted Indian religions, conceptualising any culture solely through religious lenses.

5. Anthropological facts are merely secularised terms from the Bible.

6. The standard understanding of religion has only given us wars, struggles, conversions, and inquisitions.

7. Understanding religions as traditions, rather than the other way around, will foster greater harmony and understanding in the world in the grip of increasing religious frictions.

8. Traditions have a characteristic *indifference to differences* that far transcends the tolerance and mutual respect that secularism (which historically was a solution only for a Christian European world at a specific time in its history) can achieve.

9. Religion and its secular offshoots used force, language, and a sense of superiority to erase the otherness or reduce the sheen of all other cultures to a monochromatic dullness.

10. Balu calls this a scientific proposal that is open to debate and falsification. Despite much disagreement amongst scholars, arising mostly from a lack of understanding or a refusal to engage deeply with the ideas, Balu's thesis remains unrefuted to date.

## Chapter 2

# RELIGIOUS CONVERSION-INDIAN DISPUTES AND THEIR EUROPEAN ORIGINS

*Sarah Claerhout and Jakob De Roover*

## *Introduction*

Religious conversion is a vexing problem in all plural societies. How can the concept of accepting the 'new' while totally rejecting the 'old' apply to non-Christian, non-Islamic cultures that have profoundly different approaches to belief, practice, and membership? In India, intellectual debates since colonial times remain fuzzy with problems generated by religious conversion. Why is a conversation between those who support and oppose proselytization just not possible?

*Sarah Claerhout* and *Jakob De Roover* are brilliant scholars at Ghent University in Belgium whose articles and books clearly explain why the issue of conversion is so contentious. Typical of their school, their language, always neutral, is easy and fluid, and reaches out not only to university professors but to every concerned citizen of India. It is also helpful to the Westerner when attempting to study Indian culture. At the core of the Comparative Science of Cultures programme initiated by the legendary SN Balagangadhara, the West and the East face each other as equals, and this makes any reading from their group illuminating without arousing anger. The present book, edited by another doyen, D. Venkat Rao, at the English and Foreign Languages University, Hyderabad, is no exception.

The authors trace the phenomenon of religious conversion from its roots (mainly from the Christian perspective) and show how intellectuals across time have grappled with the idea of religious conversions.

Balagangadhara's core hypothesis about religions explained in *The Heathen in His Blindness* (or in its simplified version, *Do All Roads Lead to Jerusalem?*) is the first step to understanding the problem. In Indian society, two groups of a different nature coexist: the Hindu, Buddhist, Sikh, and Jain traditions (evolving from a single tree broadly termed Sanatana Dharma) on the one hand, and Christianity, Islam, and Judaism on the other. The former group, clumped together as 'Hinduism' by the Constitution, lacks all the characteristics that allow us to recognise Christianity, Islam, and Judaism as religions: *a fixed body of doctrine, an ecclesiastical organisation or central authority,* or *a single holy book.* Barring a few exceptions, most intellectuals, both for and against proselytization, debate within the framework of three basic assumptions: 1) Indian cultural traditions are religions; 2) these religions are rivals; and 3) they are rivals because 'truth' predicates apply to them. Problematically, these 'common-sense' facts are a set of claims of both theological and secularised Christianity that assume as a first step that all cultures *must* have a religion.

### The Problem

Ordinary citizens and the highest echelons of parliament and the judiciary hotly debate the issue of conversions and proselytization. However, it is still unclear why the issue arouses such passions. As the authors write, these debates consist of a bewildering tangle of themes of varying importance: violence against Christians and Muslims; Hindu nationalism; the oppression and liberation of Dalits; upper-caste concerns about losing control; the rights of minorities; the need for, and threats to, a secular state; foreign funding to Indian NGOs; attempts to undermine India's national integrity; patriarchy and its treatment of women; the legacy of British colonial rule; the hidden agendas of missionaries; Western imperialism and its derogation of Indian culture; demographic changes in post-Independence India; the desirability or otherwise of 'inter-religious marriages'; and so on.

Today, conversion is fundamentally a clash between the 'Hindu nationalist' forces on one side and the 'secular-liberal-minorities-religious-rights activists' on the other. The former looks at 'freedom of religion' in the Constitution as a right to practise one's faith freely *without fear of interference* from missionaries pulling people away from their traditions and causing social disruption. For the other group, 'freedom of religion' implies a freedom not only to choose one's own religion but also a *state-protected right to convert*. The 'social' aspect involves the argument that conversion allows an individual to move away from the oppressive caste-based and other practices in the Hindu religion. One group wants legislation to ban conversion, and the other group views such legislation as a pretext for harassing Christians, Muslims, and potential converts.

The major response of the Indian population to proselytization since the seventeenth century up to the present day has essentially been *incomprehension* along with anger at the need for conversion to another religion. The distinction between 'genuine' and 'fraudulent' conversions is another area of confusion. Hence, objections to missionary activity in India often focus on attempts to convert minors or the ignorant, illiterate, and uneducated. Obscurity pervades the legislation and the intellectuals through the use of many words like 'force', 'fraud', 'allurement', 'inducement', 'threats of divine displeasure', 'conversion', 'religion', and 'propagation'. The social sciences offer a limited view since they continue working on a set of assumptions concerning Indian traditions as outlined previously.

### *Conversion, Reform, Education in Colonial India*

Following the Charter Act of 1813, Christian missionaries, colonial officials, and Orientalist scholars worked on an unprecedented scale for the purpose of conversion using direct and indirect means. The nineteenth century also saw intense resistance by Indians to conversions. The Europeans approached Indian traditions using self-evident theological terms embedded in Christianity: 'idolatry', 'superstition', 'error', 'heathenism', 'gods', 'priests', 'religion', 'worship', etc. The Indian response also used the same English terminology but without understanding the background theology, frequently leading to incoherence.

Missionaries wanted to convert a 'land of idolatry and superstition' to the true religion of Christianity. Orientalists and colonials, applying caution, attempted to show that Indian scriptures were of human origin. With immoral deities, they were incoherent, inaccurate, and thus false. A demand for 'scientific', 'factual', or 'empirical' proof of the divine origin of the Indian texts (especially the Vedas) would dissolve the trust placed in these texts, if it is found to be absent. This would prepare a fertile soil for seeing and accepting the truth of Christianity.

The vigorous Indian responses repeatedly took various forms: one religion cannot be true for the whole of humanity; since each is good for its practitioners with no internal conflict, there is no need for conversion; there were no clear records of Jesus Christ; the inspiration to become a Christian could only be for base desires and a lack of reflection, and so on. At times, the Indians preferred silence or simply an attitude of indifference.

What looked significant and sensible to one appeared trivial and unreasonable to the other. There was much mutual incomprehension, characteristic of the disputes about religious conversion in India. For British missionaries, officials, and Orientalists, the conflicts about true religion between Catholics and Protestants in the post-Reformation era, between Christians and Jews during the Middle Ages, and about heresy and apostasy formed the framework for understanding Indian traditions. However, they summarily rejected the Indian explanations because Indians *could not think* rationally, logically, or morally about their traditions, deities, and texts.

An important idea crystallised and seeped into Indian intellectuals too: that the deficient situation of Indians was related to their 'religion' and needed remedy through education and reform. A range of practices and attitudes rooted in Hindu religion became immoral. A missionary debate started in the 1820s about whether caste was really a civil or a religious institution. This was an intra-Christian issue formulated in terms of Christian theological conceptual distinctions between the *civil* (acceptable), the *religious* (acceptable if true; rejected if false), and the *idolatrous* (needing rejection). After decades of dispute, the Madras Missionary Conference of 1850 declared that caste was essentially a false religious institution and not a mere civil distinction. Thus, caste became immoral and idolatrous. Conversion entailed emancipating oneself from the hold of this religious institution and its Brahmanical oppression. This shows how Christian Europeans saw Indian culture and how many of their views became facts.

Hindus needed to either reform such practices or simply convert to Christianity. Despite a strong education policy focusing on the evils of Hindu religion, conversions to Christianity did not occur at any significant scale. However, there were other results on a gradual scale, amounting to a different way of approaching Indian traditions: criticism and exegesis of texts; a search for historical evidence in those texts; seeing a need for a scientific temper that should replace superstition; and so on.

All these discourses spill over into twentieth and twenty-first century India. Today, Indian secularists and Western commentators agree that religious conversion in India is a way for Dalits or lower-caste members to escape from the oppressive caste system. For Dr. Ambedkar, destroying the religion of the *Shrutis* and *Smritis* was the only way to bring about a breach in the caste system. Mutual incomprehension remains intact as one group insists on conversions as a true path and the other questions the need for conversion. On the Hindu side, both secularists and nationalists seek reform and purification of traditional practices; however, the former defend proselytization as freedom of religion while the latter oppose it.

### Conversion in Christian Europe

As Balagangadhara's hypothesis about religions says, Christianity spreads or 'universalises' itself in two ways: *proselytization* (or direct conversion) and *secularisation* (where Christianity generalises its religious ideas in apparently 'non-religious' forms, leading to the emergence of 'secular' institutions in the social world). Western culture today is a child of Christianity, shaped by this twofold dynamic of religion. 'Conversion', a theological term, denotes the transition of an individual or group from one religious confession or denomination to another. As a next step, it refers to the internal process of transformation whereby the believer becomes a true Christian. It is here that the Christian imperative to evangelise plays a central role: as God's revelation of His will, the Bible should come to all of humanity; the good news of salvation through Jesus Christ must reach all people.

Medieval theologians divided the clergy and the laity into two distinct 'estates' within the church. The Protestant Reformation, changing all that, viewed the Christian citizenry of their time as degenerate, the clerical institutions and their ceremonies as corrupt, and social life as depraved. The process of conversion is now open to all Christians. Hence, anticlericalism took centre stage. The message of Christian spiritual freedom and freedom of conscience was central to the Protestant Reformation, and one of its central charges against the Roman Catholic Church was that it had taken away this freedom and established a spiritual tyranny of the priests.

The Reformation determined the way in which nineteenth century British missionaries and colonial officials described Indian traditions. It strongly provided the framework for their conceptions of religion and idolatry and of the need to convert the people of India to true religion. 'Idolatry' was any practice identified as a human fabrication falsely presenting itself as necessary for religion. British missionaries and officials explicitly represented the traditions of the Hindus as a 'false religion' full of superstition and with evil Brahmin priests indulging in false ceremonies and establishing a tyrannical caste system. Thus, in a generic form, the Reformation's conception of the Catholic Church and society served as a model for these accounts of Indian culture and society. The need for conversion to the true God and religion was obvious.

The secular descriptions, which tried to weed out the secular from the religious (which, after plenty of debate, included 'caste') in Indian traditions justified the duty to reform Indian culture and society through secular education. Even those British who were not convinced Protestants or Christians embraced a framework that transformed Indians into deficient, immoral, and corrupt beings, needing reformation, education, and civilisation.

Throughout Christian history, debates about conversion required terms like: 'sin', 'the fall', 'regeneration', 'salvation', 'repentance', 'mercy', 'renewal', 'contrition', 'confession', 'penitence', 'satisfaction', 'will', 'grace', 'Christ', 'the

Holy Spirit', 'righteousness', 'faith', 'charity', etc. Indian conversation partners faced great difficulties in making sense of the discussed matters of 'religion' and 'conversion' since the language and the concepts used were totally alien to them. The superimposition of these terms on Indian concepts led to gross distortions from both sides. This unfortunately continues to date.

## The Coherence in The Incoherence of Gandhi

Gandhi, though appreciative of the humanitarian missionary work, spoke extensively and strongly against proselytization, again expressing an incomprehension about the need for conversion. 'Topos' (plural 'topoi') refers to commonplace ideas and words that occur as clusters of interrelated ideas specific to a culture. For example, both while discussing Christian theology and in common language, the West uses words and ideas with self-evident meanings like 'belief', 'faith', 'doctrine', 'conversion', 'religion', and so on. 'Conceptual distortion' occurs when *topoi* originating from one cultural setting interpret *topoi* from another culture. Gandhi's apparent inconsistency arose from the fact that he was adopting typical ideas and phrases from Western and Christian thinking but mapping them onto Indian settings.

Sketching Gandhi's position, he regarded all religions as equally true. He did not accept Jesus Christ as the only Son of God. Gandhi suggests that one should draw upon one's ancestral religion and immediate religious surroundings to live a fulfilling life. One can surely draw the good points from other religions, but a conversion to another religion amounts to immorality and an unnecessary shaming of one's ancestral religion. No religion is perfect, and it is important to bring reform from within (like untouchability). Conversion, however, means a process of change where there is spiritual and ethical growth.

This fundamentally clashes with the central doctrine of Christianity that Jesus Christ is God incarnate or the only Son of God; Christianity is the only way for all humanity; and conversion is the only method for the salvation of a non-Christian. But substitute the word 'traditions' for 'religion' and suddenly there is absolute coherence in what Gandhi was describing. He was characterising the traditions in fair detail, but by trying to map the traditions of India as equivalent to religions, there was a 'conceptual distortion'.

When Gandhi speaks of 'faiths' or 'religions', he refers to the traditions of different groups or communities. 'Religion', if consisting of the traditions of a particular community, does not have a foundation in doctrines, beliefs, or truth predicates. As ancestral practices, they provide *action heuristics* that instruct the individual on how to become a better human being. Traditions are thus of equal value in providing action heuristics to pursue spiritual and moral growth. Thus, there can be a rich mutual interaction between traditions. Since each tradition has adequate resources to reform from within, there is no requirement for wholesale conversion. It is thus an impossibility that one tradition can be true for all of humanity.

However, there were inconsistencies too when he reproduces the typical understanding of religions as belief systems and praises Hinduism for its belief systems (like oneness of all lives, transmigration of souls, varnashrama). Despite these, Gandhi had a deep understanding of Indian traditions, but putting these as equivalent to religions and then using the language and ideas of Christian theology made him look incoherent when, in fact, he was not.

## Religious Freedom and the Limits of Propagation

For the Hindu, Jain, Sikh, and Buddhist traditions, the assumption of rivalry is simply alien. In a mutually exclusive view, one side looks at the diversity of Indian society as a *rivalry of religions*, and the other sees it as a *coexistence of traditions*. Thus, conversion becomes a vital problem of diversity only if one looks at the world the way Christianity and Islam do. The secularisation of Christian theology translates into the importance of the absolute right to profess, propagate, and change one's religion. However, in traditional cultures, the significance shifts to the freedom to continue one's tradition without aggressive interference from the outside. Thus, the dominant principle of religious freedom in the Indian Constitution privileges Christianity and Islam because it involves the freedom to propagate or proselytise. It implicitly endorses the assumption that religion revolves around doctrines and truth claims.

Article 25(1), at the crux of the debate on religious conversion, says: "Subject to public order, morality, and health, and to the other provisions of this Part, all persons are equally entitled to freedom of conscience and the right freely to profess, practise, and propagate religion." The major controversy is the usage of the word 'propagate' in all forums (constitutional debates, legal judgements involving the courts, state-level legislation banning conversions, or intellectual discussions).

After extensive (but fruitless) debates, the Constitution seems to have approved 'propagate' as freedom to convert. Indian courts, however, have interpreted Article 25(1) very differently and denied that it grants any fundamental right to convert people from one religion to another. Hence, one side (Christians, Muslims, and seculars) argues that any state legislation to ban conversions is simply unconstitutional and discriminates against Christian and Muslim minorities. The other (Hindu 'nationalists', traditionalists) insists that conversion itself constitutes a violation as it involves aggressive intrusions into a community and its traditions through force, fraud, or allurement.

Balagangadhara's thesis that India has traditions and not religions is important in understanding the mutual incomprehension across time to understand each other's viewpoints. Hinduism, Buddhism, Sikhism, and Jainism, by definition, are different phenomena from the religions (Christianity, Islam, Judaism, and Zoroastrianism). However, most arguments construct Indian traditions as religions, resulting in incompatibility. Some of the intuitive properties of traditions do not make sense when viewed as religions.

Tradition refers to the ancestral customs and practices of different communities. The fundamental property of traditions is an *indifference to differences*. Traditions do not have some core set of 'true' beliefs. They are conservative because practices generally stay intact across time. They are flexible too, allowing reform or rejection of some practices after reasoning. Dissemination of ideas and intense debates between various traditions have been a part of Indian society, but without the need for mass conversion or physical violence.

The Constituent Assembly members then and traditionalists today understand 'propagation' as education concerning its ideas and practices, as is typical of all Indian traditions. In this sense, though one can appreciate or absorb good points from other traditions, there is no need to 'convert'. This cluster of intuitive ideas about the nature of traditions is widely present in Indian society. Thus, for this group, Article 25 of the Constitution of India does include the freedom for Christians to continue their practices, but within the limits set by the Indian conception of tradition and its notions of dissemination.

On the other side, the core of the Christian religion is God's revelation of His will in Jesus Christ, which spreads because of His intervention rather than purely by human transmission. Therefore, the freedom of conscience and the right to 'propagate religion' always entail the freedom to convert, perhaps the most fundamental of Christian rights. Generally, the Indian 'anti-conversion' legislation meets with moral indignation at the intolerance generated by Hindu nationalism or majoritarianism. Secular intelligentsia concur with this position as if it were self-evident and rational while ignoring concerns generated by an Indian conception of tradition.

There is a deep conflict between an Indian conception of the dissemination of tradition and Christian claims about the process of conversion. Surprisingly, the Pew Research Centre (2021) found in its detailed study that, contradicting popular perception, a majority of Indian Christian and Muslim adults felt they were free to practice their religion, while a majority of Hindus felt that conversion was not a major threat. This is surprising but takes away nothing from both the facts of violence against Christians and the aggressive proselytization methods of the missionaries. Thus, the authors feel that a deeper understanding of Indian traditions rather than slogans and anecdotes would help us better resolve the issue.

### *The Deadlock*

In their illuminating and related paper, "Conversion of the World Proselytization in India and the Universalization of Christianity, 2008," the authors describe a current deadlock between a group of secularists, Christians, and Muslims who insist that religious freedom entails freedom *of* conversion, and another group of Hindu thinkers, who view religious freedom as freedom *from* conversion. Is there a way out because neither anti-conversion laws nor the principle of religious freedom to convert will do the job, since both privilege one of the two sides of the controversy? The former favours the Hindu majoritarian position and restricts an essential freedom for Muslims and Christians, while the latter disrupts the social fabric of Indian traditional land.

The authors write:

> What is the alternative? We can only be brief here. Looking into the history of the subcontinent, it is striking that, in several regions, the Hindu traditions and Indian Islam and Christianity succeeded at living together in a relatively stable manner. There is a risk of romanticizing the past here. Still, many scholars have pointed out that local Islamic and Christian traditions lost their aggressive proselytizing drive in India. Hindu attempts to impose anti-conversion legislation also seemed to be absent. The answer, then, consists of a question, or a set of research questions, to be precise: How have the Indian traditions succeeded at alleviating the problem of religious conversion in the past? Which mechanisms and dynamics were at play here? To what extent do these live on today? How could they be rediscovered and revived so that we can work towards a vibrant pluralism in India?

### *Personal Concluding Remarks*

All enlightened spiritual gurus of India, like Ramana Maharishi, Ramakrishna Paramhansa, or Chandrasekhar Saraswati, discouraged any Muslim or Christian devotees from converting to Hinduism by saying that each religion had 'enough material' to reach *moksha*. They were only reaffirming the traditional structure of the land, where each tradition is true for practitioners on its path and leads to the same destination. In this idea of traditions, all paths are equally valid.

The authors end the book with a promise for the next part in the future. The reader certainly expects solutions from the authors after laying a strong foundation for understanding the problem of religious conversions.

For the present, we must wait. However, from some awareness of their works to date, it is possible to sketch the way forward.

Their school writes that India, despite having greater multi-culturalism than any other part of the world, has known more harmony and peace than any other culture. When alien religions came to India, they met with an already-existing, well-formed culture. India could absorb the alien religions that came with the ideology of *My One True God* and *Your False Many Gods*. India's practical solution was to traditionalise the religions so that they lost focus on proselytization and made some genuine attempts at cultural syncretism. This adoption and adaptation to Indian culture allowed the different religions to merge into society and yet keep their belief systems intact. And this adaptation is what the Islamic clergy, or Christian evangelists, fight against.

The entire process reversed, starting with colonial understandings, when traditions came to be seen as religions and inappropriately, secularism became the solution for harmony. Secularism was a solution for European Christendom at a specific point in its history. Transferring it wholesale to Indian soil by Indian intellectuals and politicians fascinated by the West has been a recipe for disaster and is ironically resulting in the hardening of stances. As Hindu traditions started modelling themselves after the Semitic religions by searching for common doctrines, among other things, intolerance and 'Hindu fundamentalism' are unsurprisingly on the rise. An indifference goes beyond 'tolerances and mutual respects' achieved maximally by secularism.

Both sides continue to debate in the framework of colonial scholarship which assumed that Indian phenomena are religions. Hence, the same colonial consciousness colours both sides of the debate. The conversion of traditions (*I am true, but you are not false*) to religions (*I am true, and you are false*) and then applying secularism has been the biggest mistake in our understanding. Harmony now is in the direction of understanding these two phenomena as separate and continuing the old process of traditionalising our religions.

The West has studied us for centuries and continues to do so. Indians follow the West in their study of both India and the West. It has been an amazing aspect of Indian knowledge systems that, despite a prodigious amount of knowledge output in Sanskrit and all Indian languages, they have never engaged in the study of alien cultures or religions. In this aspect of indifference, we have not been able to study the West from our perspective. Such an enterprise, the Balagangadhara school promises, would benefit all of humanity. The present understandings spell only collapse and disaster for the world with its multi-culturalism packing into smaller geographical areas.

# Part II

# SECULARISM

"Hinduism has left out no part of life as a thing secular and foreign to the religious and spiritual life."

**– Sri Aurobindo**

"The sacredness of all things—the antithesis of the European division of life into sacred and profane… In India…religion idealises and spiritualizes life itself rather than excludes it."

**– Ananda K. Coomaraswamy**

## Chapter 3

# EUROPE, INDIA, AND THE LIMITS OF SECULARISM

*Jakob De Roover*

## *Introduction*

The author of this book, Dr. Jakob De Roover, is professor of India studies and Comparative Science of Cultures at Ghent University, Belgium. This book is important in understanding how secularism has failed in our country to achieve harmony and will continue to do so. There are alternative mechanisms to achieve this elusive harmony amongst diversity, and there is no better place than India to discover them. Secularism evolved in the Western world as a reasonably successful solution for its predominantly Christian culture. Transferring it as a solution for dealing with non-Western cultures, especially India, which is a mix of many religions and pagan traditions, became inappropriate. It became even more dangerous because, paradoxically, secularism in India seems to be a *cause* of religious friction rather than a solution.

For over a millennium, we had our own effective mechanisms for dealing with pluralism and multi-cultural diversity. Instead of studying and offering alternative solutions, Indian intellectuals strangely chose to look through Western lenses and see India in a distorted framework, continuing the Western themes. As a result, even 'Hindu revivalism' speaks in the same conceptual language as secularism. De Roover also delves into the debates in post-colonial independent India, where colonial consciousness stays firmly intact amongst our leaders and intellectuals. The mantra of secularism is all-pervasive, but it is a conceptual mess.

## The Crisis of Liberalism and Secularism

Secularism, in the public sphere, believes in religiously neutral state policies and legal systems. Liberalism, in the private sphere, makes religious freedom and mutual respect paramount. Today, normatively, civilised countries should be liberal-secular democracies abiding by neutrality, toleration, religious freedom, and the separation of politics from religion. However, liberal secularism, a reasonably successful Western model, fails in non-Western cultures and also faces stress from the influx of Islam into Europe. There are also conceptual problems in separating the secular from the religious sphere.

The dominant Western frameworks transform non-Western cultures into deficient variants. The Western way is the only alternative to all non-Western forms of life. However, historically, Indian culture has had a wider diversity of religious, ethnic, and cultural groups than Europe at any point. The absence of a disintegrated society, living mostly in peace, points to alternative mechanisms for dealing with multiculturalism. Regrettably, liberal secularism entangled itself with narratives of a primitive 'Hindu religion' or an evil 'caste system'. This prevented looking towards India for solutions to harmony, writes De Roover.

Today, multiple forms of secularism exist in various countries, pointing to an inherent clash between a state's conception of equality and the individual freedom of its citizens. France vigorously bans any public religious display, while the UK has reserved seats in the House of Lords for bishops. Indian secularism intervenes in temple management and Hindu law, simultaneously giving special rights to some minorities. The differences among secular states are due to the difficulties in distinguishing between the spheres of 'public political' and 'private religion'.

Liberal political theory proposes a state-governed public political sphere and a private sphere of individual freedom. The *harm principle* is an important dividing line where, if individual freedom harms others, the state steps in. However, unlike physical harm, psychological harm remains vague and obscure in its definition. On an individual basis, the state can coerce, but a generalised theoretical standard for defining the two spheres is difficult. De Roover writes that, while applying liberal secularism, we are not only unaware of the boundaries but also what constitutes the *inside* of the public and private spheres.

The debates about the headscarf and beard in Muslims or the cross in Italian schools have shown that what is symbolic to one may not be for another. If symbolism is an individual perspective, it is impossible for states to determine from a neutral, secular, or legal perspective the religious nature of symbols. Strangely, secular courts today decide the essentials and non-essentials of religion, as the Christian church did in regard to pagan practices in the past.

Homogenous traditions can apply a uniform interpretation of religious symbols, but that is an impossibility in multi-religious cultures. To prevent the tyranny of the majority, we need some authority to interpret religious symbols, but the trend of judges becoming theologians is disturbing. De Roover writes that even in America the courts, when defining the scope of religion, show bias towards the majority religion. However, if religious freedom rules supreme, every person would become a law unto themselves. Thus, there are confusions about implementing secularism and religious freedom.

### The Troubled Dream of Indian Secularism: A Distinctive Secularism?

Secularism has been an enigma to intellectuals in independent India, where it generates constant controversy and confusion. In a 1994 Supreme Court judgement, each of the seven judges gave a separate version of secularism. Hence, secularism seems to be an elastic term in the Indian context, where some feel it should address even caste discrimination apart from religious diversity.

Between 1946 and 1949, the complex Constituent Assembly debates for a secular state saw Muslims reject the Uniform Civil Code. Dr. Ambedkar, repeating the European cliché, wanted Hinduism (concerning everything from life to death) limited to only beliefs, rituals, and ceremonies, which are essentially religious. It was a circular reasoning since he used the term religion to define religion, Hinduism in this case.

Hinduism defies a clear definition with its many rituals, myths, and philosophies. When a lamp lights up at an official function, it is difficult to define the boundary between the religious and the secular. With multiple texts, philosophies, and teachers, no one is aware of the doctrinal core or the essence of Hinduism. In this matter, our judges, as per their own training and biases, now yield chaotic power to decide the 'essentials' and 'non-essentials' of religious practices. Christian churches, colonials, and Indian reformers also did this when assessing pagan practices in the past.

India collectively thinks of secularism as anything that allows people to live together. Instead of examining how diverse traditions lived harmoniously for hundreds of years, one indulges in the obscure language of secularism. The distinction between the two spheres is unclear, yet our political theorists and jurists take it as a given. Secularism, applicable to the homogenous West at a certain time and place, when transferred to the plural world of India, is a recipe for disaster.

## Classical Evolution of Secularism: Straight-line Accounts from a Savage to a Modern Liberal

The Enlightenment viewed religion as an ordered progression from a savage state (venerating nature), through polytheism and monotheism, to finally outgrowing religion. The modern West was, of course, at the peak of human development. However, this depiction of straight progress was made by cherry-picking hundreds of quotations removed from their historical contexts. The West has been relatively free of violent religious clashes in the previous century, but rising anti-Semitism, Catholic and Protestant encounters in Ireland until the 1990s, the shunning of communists to hold office in Germany till 1985, and the present influx of Islam into Europe stress the secular model for toleration. 'The rise of the modern West' is anomalous when one considers Europe's inability to accommodate genuine diversity, its violence and inhumanity during the colonial period and World Wars, and the increasing unhappiness among its citizens.

Even modern Western thinkers presuppose that all plural societies consist of conflicting religious doctrines trying to gain dominance. They place non-Western cultures at lower stages of development, where pluralism inevitably generates persecution and oppression based on comprehensive doctrines. This was clearly false in India. De Roover writes that modern Westerners thought they had reached the other shore, where they successfully separated politics from religion. However, this is based on the Western understanding of its own history as the benchmark for all cultures.

### *Secularization: Specific to the Western-Christian World*

De Roover writes that today's secularism is intimately related to Christian religious doctrine. The moral, intellectual, political, and social history of the West is to some extent Christian, yet it dissolves religious thought by applying Christian principles to secular matters. Some philosophers think that the continuity between modernity and Christianity is not a secularization, but rather a process of inheriting a set of questions originally solved by theology.

Christian secularisation happened within a specific Western cultural framework. Secularism, among its various connotations, refers to the split between an 'immanent' factual world and a 'transcendental' normative world. This is structurally similar to Christian theological ideas of a transcendent and an immanent God. If religion is ubiquitous, we can talk of a religious age shifting to a secular age in all cultures. However, if the phenomena in diverse cultures are not religions, then the transcendent-immanent distinction (between *what is* and *what ought* to be) makes sense only in Christendom and not in Asian or Indian cultures. As a result, secularisation is a Western-Christian self-description that only transforms other cultures into inferior variants. There are theorists who argue that separating superficial religion from the common secular core of all cultures leads to harmony. The author strongly disagrees, saying that religion is never an add-on but significantly shapes a society's core cultural form.

### A Culture Without Religion: Metaphysical and Sociological Impossibilities of a Religion in India

De Roover then discusses Balagangadhara's most significant claim, which is that *there are no religions but traditions in India*, thus rejecting secularism as a solution for multiple religions. European scholars, missionaries, and Indian counterparts successfully converted traditions into religions. Do all cultures have or need a religion, or its secular equivalent, a 'worldview'? Balu responds negatively.

Metaphysically, a religion must make a claim about the origin and purpose of the world, and this message must be true. The Vedas, Upanishads, Brahmanas, Puranas, and Itihaasas have multiple stories of the creation and purposes of the universe, saying just about everything about everything, including even the absence of God. As Balu says, in Indian culture, a person can equally believe or reject all the stories, making the 'origin' question and the place of God irrelevant or even illegitimate. The Western world, gripped by historicity, always tries to find the 'truth value' of its scriptures. This attitude of assigning a truth value to texts hardly disturbs Indians. To ask whether texts are true or false is a profound ignorance of the culture whose stories they are.

Similarly, Indian religions (Hinduism, Sikhism, Buddhism, and Jainism) do not have the sociological conditions that are absolutely required for guaranteeing a religion's identity: a codified 'holy book,' a standard worldview that cannot change, and a central authority to settle disputes, propagate worldviews, and excommunicate when interpretations collide. According to Balu, in metaphysical and sociological terms, it is an impossibility for Indian culture to have religions or a worldview.

### Balu's Thesis of Learning Configurations of Different Cultures

Socialisation consists of transmitting knowledge from the group's reservoir (customs, myths, and traditions) through various mechanisms, such as child-rearing practices and schooling patterns. Balu's important thesis is that in diverse cultures there are multiple frameworks for learning to socialise, and this is the basis for cultural differences.

*Religion* is the dominant mode of learning in the West, and the 'why' question is important. The dominant learning process of seeking 'knowledge about' resulted in the generation of theoretical knowledge, sometimes away from experiential order, which in turn led to the development of secular sciences. Trying to provide an explanation for unconnected phenomena by appealing to an invisible ordering force makes a scientific attitude contiguous with a religious attitude. The growing understanding of this culture ultimately leads to a conflict with religion, manifesting as atheism, which attempts to surpass religion completely.

Indian culture has an alternate *ritual-based* configuration of learning where the performative ability or the 'how' question is important. Such cultures (Indian or Asian) invest in creating, sustaining, and continuously modifying a social or practical order. Both Western and Asian cultures have the 'why' and 'how' components, but a specific combination of dominant and subordinate learning processes determines a culture's learning configuration.

Religious cultures see religions in all societies and, placing them on a developmental scale, tend to convert or colonise other cultures. They are thus inherently intolerant and necessitate secularism. On the other hand, Asian or Indian traditions do develop theoretical explanations, but they are based on performative ability. They create stable societies, are more tolerant, and rarely require expansion. Secularism becomes an inappropriate solution here. As the Ghent School authors reiterate, it is a fact of history that religions divided people while rituals united them. The West and Asia met in an unfortunate set of circumstances, writes Balu, where the latter were willing to learn, as is typical of their cultural configuration, and the West thought it could only teach, again typical of their cultural configuration.

### Evolution of Two Kingdoms: Transforming Theology into Political Theories

The two secular and religious kingdoms have their roots in Christianity. The Papal Reform, the Protestant Reformation, and the Enlightenment were a continuum of theological and political principles. Faith, as a process of conversion to God, entailed a division between the soul (spirit) and body (flesh), which corresponded to the spiritual and temporal components of human life.

The initial monastic Christianity conceptualised the carnal and spiritual realms. The twelfth-century Papal Reform distinguished between the spiritual estate of clerics and the temporal estate of laypeople. The later Protestant Reformation rejected priestly authority, making all followers have the treasure of Christian liberty. This enabled the twofold division of the spiritual kingdom (or sphere of liberty) and the temporal kingdom (in the grip of secular authority and coercive laws).

It is evident that the contemporary liberal-secular model has a strong foundation in previous theological ideas. In the *political* sphere, secular laws hold supreme, while in the *liberal* sphere, individual freedom reigns supreme. Like the previous models, this is also a normative model (an ought to model). The secular and religious separation are clearly internal Christian discourses that make sense in European Christendom with shared theological ideas. An absence of theological background, as in non-Western cultures, makes secularism supremely unintelligible. Though secularism appears to be a neutral solution, it simply runs into intractable problems without understanding the background from which it arose. However, presently, secularism is a pre-theoretical way of achieving universal harmony.

### The Confessional and the anti-Confessional Movements

In the Protestant Reformation movement, which basically started as a revolution against papal tyranny, several churches with different but extensive and strict doctrines arose. In the quest for uniting the factual world (what 'is') to the normative heavenly world (what 'ought' to be), new churches and doctrines evolved—like Lutherans, Calvinists, Presbyterians, Baptists, Quakers, and Puritans. To keep the flock together, the individual denominations codified, made stricter doctrines, and encouraged increasing intolerance towards other groups. A non-believer in an individual doctrine among the many divided confessional groups would fail to achieve salvation, as claimed by each doctrinal group.

Intolerant confessional groups with strict doctrines paved the way for Europe's anti-confessional movements. These equated God's will with the universality of toleration and the liberty of conscience in rejecting church laws. The anti-confessional thinkers argued that a true Christian was duty-bound to tolerate heresy and idolatry. Humans have no right to interfere with other modes of worship. The civil magistrate should avoid religion. According to the anti-confessionals, the individual internalises the norms of belief and behaviour. One's internal conscience guides external behaviour, rejecting the role of any external authority.

## The Enlightenment and the Secular: Were They Against Religion?

Enlightenment thinkers' secular ideas about the separation of the private religious sphere and the public political sphere are self-evident to contemporary liberals. However, De Roover demonstrates that, despite the Enlightenment's seeming rejection of God and religion, it did not renounce the conceptual theological baggage of Christianity. In the Protestant version, as God had revealed, no human institution had the authority to bind others to its understanding of religion. In the Enlightenment version, humans are never certain about the truth and therefore ought not to impose their beliefs on others. The point remains the same, but the distinction between the 'norm' and the 'fact' also remains. Catholics, Jews—and later Islam—were negations of the model of liberal toleration, writes De Roover.

Theological beliefs like these served as the foundation for the Enlightenment.

- Religion is a universal domain in all societies.

- Human beings have a conscience.

- Religion and politics are two distinct spheres of human social existence.

Problematically, in some societies, religions may not exist in the definitional sense, and there may be no belief that every individual has a moral conscience guiding his private actions. In a traditional and ritualistic culture like India, there is an intimate intertwining of public and political life. How can the Enlightenment ideas be true for all of humanity when Christian theology provides the basic conditions of intelligibility for normative ('ought to') liberal theories of toleration and secularism?

De Roover writes that, in the double dynamic of secularisation and proselytization of Christianity, these clusters of ideas shifted from explicitly theological settings to common-sense reasoning in Western societies. The variable expressions of secularism in Europe today are a result of an interplay between concerns about state toleration in religious matters and limiting public expressions of religion. However, without the background framework of theological understanding, secular language is impossible and leads to intractable problems. To evaluate this hypothesis, De Roover looks to India.

### Religious Toleration and Reform in British India

The British Indian model of religious toleration was the result of many factors. The British consistently believed that Hinduism and the caste system constituted 'religious tyranny.' The rulers, mainly Protestant believers, agreed on the Christian duty to convert others to the true God. However, this clashed with the official policy of toleration, which Orientalists also supported and which prevented large-scale conversions.

The official toleration policy was either a prudential decision to prevent a fight with a united India or a power-knowledge nexus in which the British desired knowledge of Hindu laws to secure power. As a result, there were no British civilian settlements, and a ban existed for evangelization. De Roover demonstrates how the British used Hindu texts to morally justify their laws.

An important question for the colonials was whether the detestable Indian social practices fell into the category of civil crime or whether they were approved by sacred scriptures as a necessary practice. This was an important question. Colonial scholars sought scriptural justification for 'abhorrent' Indian social practices in order to ban or allow them. If there were scriptural sanctions, it would be a moral obligation to accept them. They could ban female infanticide, but it took a few debates before they could abolish Sati. Thus, the British attitude, as a morally superior religious community, was to detect detestable Hindu practices and tolerate them if found to have a scriptural sanction.

Some early colonial scholars, obsessed with the idea that devils and priests deviate souls from God's revelation, tried to discover corruptions in the pure Hindu core. They had the task of cleaning up the superficial practices and rituals covering the original core. Both evangelicals and Orientalists conceived of paganism as the equivalent of 'popish idolatry.' However, as De Roover writes, the colonials struggled to balance the Christian principles of tolerating 'false' religions with the task of granting Christian spiritual liberty to the ruled.

Instead of leaving the traditions untouched, the toleration policy began reforming and codifying the allegedly deficient ancient 'dharmashastras', or law manuals. Many of these were specific to a certain time and place, but they became sacred laws applicable to all Hindus at all times. Problematically, it was unclear what exactly constituted Hindu law. "Religious" (to tolerate), "secular" (to allow), and "idolatrous" (to ban because false) were Christian distinctions to assess pagan practices. Protestant theology spoke about false religions; the secularised version spoke about impure human additions to a pure sacred core.

In the absence of a single book on Hindu law, the British could either create a new code altogether based on general principles or create a consistent code from the mass of previous fragments of tradition. They chose the latter. However, despite a vast variety of customs emerging from different parts of the country, they were convinced that all of these were degenerations of an original Hindu code. Hindus themselves have now internalized this discourse of religion's *truly religious, secular, and idolatry (false)* components. The judges now discuss the Hindu religion's *essential* practices and *non-essential superstitious* accretions.

### The Consequences of Toleration: Transforming Traditions into Religion and Generating Hindu 'Fundamentalism'

Colonial toleration introduced a *coercive mechanism* for scriptural justifications. Reformers like Raja Rammohun Roy propagated the original Vedas and Upanishads as the core of Hinduism and banned rituals and idol worship in the quest for 'pure' Hinduism. In his fight for Sati abolition, he demonstrated the absence of scriptural sanctions. Hinduism modelled itself on a monotheistic religion, especially Protestant themes of fighting the priestly tyranny. The Arya Samaj movement exemplified Hindu traditions taking on an institutional shape. Even the counterarguments (like Deen Dayal), in trying to justify idol worship, took recourse to scriptural injunctions. Thus, finally, the colonial policy of toleration transformed a tradition into a scripture-dominated religion.

'Hindu fundamentalism' or 'Hindu revivalism,' as a common set of principles, was a search for a discrete core that would separate the united Hindus from Christians and Muslims. Paradoxically, the lack of dogmas gives rise to the claim of common principles of 'tolerance' (traced to some Sanskrit aphorisms). These apparently contrast Hinduism with the theocratic nature of Islam and Christianity. *According to De Roover, Hindu tolerance, as a principle, becomes a ground for intolerance in the demand for other religions to accommodate religious equality.*

Hindu nationalists reproduce the transformation of Indian traditions instigated by the liberal state. The toleration policy in colonial India, as a final consequence, shows that liberal secularism and religious fundamentalism reinforced each other in transforming India's indigenous traditions into variants of the Book religions. This straitjacketing explains the growth of so-called 'Hindu fundamentalism.' In India, liberal secularism might not be an antidote but may, in fact, be generating religious fundamentalism, writes De Roover.

### Post-Colonial India: Either Secularism or Religious Fundamentalism

A majority of Europeans saw Indian traditions as an inferior version of Christianity. Influential writers like Charles Grant (1746–1823) and James Mill (1773-1836) used the Protestant critique of false religions to rigidly describe Indian culture. Such writings established an asymmetry of cultures that made the Hindus morally flawed and Hinduism false. These derive from the opposition between true and false religion, the opposition of clerical (Brahmin) tyranny to spiritual freedom, and a fixed hierarchy (caste system) denying equality. Today's secularism talks about the same deficient Hindu character because of superstitions, rituals, and caste systems, but without the background of Christianity. According to the theology model, the absence of a true religion implies the existence of a false religion. In the secular transformation of the theological model, the absence of a secular liberal model implies intolerance and tyranny.

Thus, discourses on Hinduism or the caste system ultimately revolve around the alleged negations of Christian freedom and equality norms, either in theological or secularised form. In India today, a policy either follows the norms of liberal toleration or embodies its negation. The secularists, in a colonial consciousness mode, simply transpose Western ideas as Indian solutions. Unfortunately, anti-secularists use the same conceptual language when referring to traditions as religions. Both fail to stem the growing religious intolerance.

Liberal secularism, based on toleration, state neutrality, and religious freedom, are contemporary unconditional principles for a harmonious society. Any government policy either accepts these principles or rejects them, dangerously mixing religion and politics. However, this has failed in India because, despite secularism being a universal political guiding principle, communal polarisation is increasing.

Historically, Indian and Greco-Roman societies were far more tolerant and liberal than the West at any given time. Critics, however, point to the absence of liberal values, even though societies were accommodative and pluralistic, based on the oppression of certain groups. This closes the mind on all alternative modes of existence. This reasoning is faulty, says De Roover, because past societies could have been accommodative and pluralistic because they had principles other than liberal secularism, and there may have been intolerance due to factors other than the absence of liberal values.

After independence, Nehru propagated a scientific temper to break the superstitious hold of religion. Nehru, culturally disconnected from India, absorbed Enlightenment values through his colonial education. As a result, for Nehru there was either a progressive secular state or a backwards religious one. The public and private spheres should stay separated. Dr. Ambedkar, more critical, believed, like the colonials, that the central flaw of Hinduism was its representation of caste as a sacred order. For him, Hinduism, a set of prohibitions and commandments, equalled the caste system, which equalled untouchability. To address untouchability, he wanted to finally annihilate Hinduism. This critique is a straight theological discourse on true and false religions. Nehru and Ambedkar did not advocate Christianity or colonialism but argued for secularism, liberty, and equality in addressing communal oppression and caste tyranny.

### Colonial Consciousness

Balu formulated the important idea of 'colonial consciousness', which Jakob De Roover briefly discusses as a three-step process. The first step presupposes that the Western narrative is correct and ideal for everyone. As a result, Indian descriptions of a tyrannical religion and caste were both true and scientific; the second step describes non-Western societies as deficient variants, a presupposition based on indoctrination and violence; and the third seeks to implement Western ideas for reforming non-Western cultures.

The liberal secularism model in India follows these steps. First, missionaries and colonial scholars developed a normative idea based on theology. Next, in post-colonial India, Indian reformers and secularists agreed that this model was the only ideal for a harmonious society. The theological background disappears as the descriptions of religious and caste tyranny take help from modern European theorists. The last step ends in a concerted reform attempt: missionaries with a true religion; colonials with scientific education and liberal values; and Indian reformers and secularists with secularism and a scientific temper.

Adopting Western lenses (essentially seeing things from the point of view of secularised Christianity), Indian intellectuals described themselves and made an alien world their own. In the absence of an alternative framework, they described themselves as deficient variants of Western culture. The social sciences, our education system, and intellectual analysis all lost access to indigenous cultural experiences. Today, the framework of understanding India remains the same for both secularists and anti-secularists. An alternative theory of harmony which is a lived fact over thousands of years, fails to develop in India.

## *The Tragedy of Secularism and Anti-Secularism in India*

The European separation of politics from religion resulted when the various Christian denominations, each claiming to be true, found themselves in conflict with one another. The colonials used the same framework to understand the communal problem in India, and they proposed secularism as a solution, just as they had done in the West. The assumption that all conflicts stem from the 'ultimate ideals' and 'truth value' of individual groups, such as those between Christian confessions or between Christianity and Islam, is incorrect when considering Hindu-Muslim conflicts. These conflicts have primarily been socio-economic in nature, rarely involving religious principles, and there has never been an attempt to study this phenomenon.

De Roover asks: If there is no attempt to understand the nature of conflict between Hindus and Muslims, then how can one apply all-encompassing secularism as a solution? The word secularism loses its meaning. Colonials understood Indian society as having different religions competing with each other—Hindus, Sikhs, Jains, Buddhists, and so on. Their inadequate understanding, which persists to this day, mistakenly identified the various traditions as religions.

The tragedy of anti-secularism stems from a colonial consciousness that views Hindu, Buddhist, Sikh, and Jain traditions as manifestations of religion (similar to Christianity, Islam, and Judaism), involving clerics, doctrines, sacred texts, and faith. This framework includes caste. Religion defines the community of believers and the correct doctrines. Traditions are plural and flexible, involving the inherited practices of the community rather than doctrines. The Ghent School group strongly claims that, for reasons we cannot grasp now, Christianity and Islam took on the character of traditions like other traditions in India. They lost their fixation on distinguishing between the true and the false, as well as their drive to proselytize.

Secularism becomes a solution only if it transforms traditions into religions. The Hindu nationalists suffer from the same 'either-or' dichotomy of secularism or its absence. Secular nationalism or religious nationalism stay intact, and both narratives fail to develop alternatives. De Roover says,

"Today we have a model of either secularism with separation of religion and politics or its normative negation—communal violence and caste discrimination. It is unthinkable that the framework of secularism is flawed to the core."

### Alternative Solutions

We urgently need alternative theories to cope with cultural diversity. This, most importantly, necessitates an independent study of Indian and other Asian cultures without Western theories. No theory, including liberalism, has been successful in distinguishing the two spheres of public 'political' and private 'religious.' We cannot universalize an understanding of a specific culture and its solutions to all cultures without causing contradictions and strife, as we are witnessing in India.

Normative or 'ought to' frameworks are intolerant as an inherent dynamic. Liberalism rejects other traditions, political Islam, and Hindu nationalism as negations of its principles. Intolerance is as intact as with regards to all religions by the Enlightenment. An alternative model cannot take the same intolerant form. De Roover writes, "It would be far better to study a society factually to see how well it has dealt with pluralism. India is perhaps the best example. Then we develop instructions for action that aim to incrementally improve the situation for peaceful coexistence. This is better than the approach of first building a model based on normative axioms and principles and then implementing it forcefully in society."

The search for doctrinal and scriptural proof for all practices inappropriately transformed traditions into religions. Hindu nationalists, caught in the same trap, scoured the scriptures for the 'Hindu principle of tolerance' or the equality of religions. Other religions do not accept this, hence breeding intolerance towards Islam and Christianity. This doctrine of Hindu tolerance conflicts with the Indian cultural modes of pluralism that have existed for centuries. Indian culture has the striking capacity to accommodate diversity, but to attribute this to some doctrine of Hindu tolerance is to miss the power of its pluralism, writes De Roover.

Balu's theory of cultural difference says that human coexistence is the domain of *practical knowledge,* and there is no foundation in reason, theoretical knowledge, or doctrines. Reason plays a role in reflecting on human practice and improving it wherever possible. We should embrace this approach instead of implementing top-down strategies based on theories and doctrines.

De Roover ends this powerful and thought-provoking book by writing:

The world is in crisis today. Cultures need to meet on an equal footing where there is mutual give-and-take. Each one must learn from the other. The moral, intellectual, and ethical sense of superiority while dealing with other cultures and civilizations must go. It has caused havoc for a long time, and only if we dismantle the previous paradigms and develop alternative themes and dialogues can we hope for a better future for humanity.

# Part III

# CASTE

"It is not, then, to apologize for the caste system, but to explain it, that we write, in the hope that the reader will put such questions as these to himself. "

— **Ananda Coomaraswamy**

## Chapter 4

# WESTERN FOUNDATIONS OF THE CASTE SYSTEM

## (2017)

*Edited By Martin Fárek, Dunkin Jalki, Sufiya Pathan, Prakash Shah*

*Western Foundations of the Caste System* is a paradigm-changing collection of essays based on Dr. SN Balagangadhara's pioneering research, written and edited by Ghent School scholars. Caste is one of the most pervasive issues in the social, political, economic, and cultural life of the country. Today, the understanding of caste is complex, encompassing three interconnected narratives: 1) the original Varna and Jati arrangement of Indian society, which dates back centuries; 2) the colonial imposition of a European understanding of a caste system on the Indian social systems; and 3) the caste understanding of post-independent India's academics and intellectuals. The various essays in this book delve deeper into Balu's main thesis, which posits that the caste system served as a meta-narrative explanation for their experiences with the Indian social systems. This construction was shaped by their own Western narratives and Christian themes, presented in a secular manner. The present caste discourse is a cause of deep strife and social discord in this country, generating emotions ranging from extreme pride to extreme anger in individuals. This extremely important book addresses many of these issues and gives a direction for potential solutions.

The summaries differ slightly from the original book's Chapter sequence. After the introduction, three sections deal in sequence with the

Western roots of the caste system. The next two discuss issues involving the caste system in India, followed by a section on caste problems in the United Kingdom. The final section is the original book's concluding chapter.

## CASTE STUDIES AND THE APOCRYPHAL ELEPHANT

The editors, in the introductory chapter, explain the difficulties in describing the caste system in India. Despite the challenges in understanding the exact nature of the system, contemporary caste scholars are unequivocal in their assertion that it is an immoral system that has persisted throughout India for centuries, despite numerous attempts to eradicate it. However, there are some pertinent questions about this story. Firstly, how different is this caste system from other social groupings across the world? Exploitation, discrimination, and other negative social practices exist in all societies in the world, but what makes the caste system special in propagating these social evils? Are the prohibitions on temple entry, physical beatings, and other social evils an inherent property of the caste system or a necessary consequence? Studies that will answer such questions do not exist.

The indigenous social descriptions were based on the four Varnas and the innumerable Jatis. The second important question is how the word 'caste' correlates to the Varnas and Jatis. It has been a near-impossible task to establish whether caste refers to Varna or to the Jatis. 'Jatis' refers to groupings based on profession, hereditary occupation, language spoken, religion, geographical affiliation, gurus followed, and even gender. Sometimes these groupings are based on birth, and at other times they are not. They have also been constantly evolving, from the initial description of about fifty in Manushastra to the official recognition of thousands today. On the other hand, the four Varnas, which have endured over centuries, still lack a clear explanation. The notions of karma, reincarnation, birth, guna, and dharma all come into play, even as we still struggle to say whether birth is an exclusive cause of Varna. More importantly, the one-to-one correlation between Jatis and Varna has been one of the most difficult exercises since colonial times, with Jatis frequently disagreeing over which Varna they belong to.

All agree that the caste system is an ancient system but remain clueless about its mysterious origin and propagation. Balu says it is sociologically impossible that it burst upon the scene simultaneously in all parts of the country with the same names and groupings, or that it emerged at different places and converged later. The only logical thing would be to assume that the caste system originated in one place and propagated widely across India. However, the widespread distances, diverse languages, and the absence of any centralized political or administrative body for a major part of Indian history would make such a mechanism implausible. Current scholars, without questioning the inconsistencies in the narratives of the spread of the caste system, state that it somehow originated and somehow propagated everywhere.

It is also unclear what constitutes the primary basis for the caste system: birth, endogamy, hierarchy, purity-pollution concerns, or occupation. The caste system appears to have no unique properties. Field data concerning Jati and community practices has falsified every single criterion that serves as the theoretical basis for caste. Scholars also overlook the prevalence of similar social groupings in other religious communities in India. To address the diversity of Jatis, scholars use terms such as sub-castes or sub-sub-castes. Scholars are still uncertain about the proper unit of caste. Is it caste or sub-caste? Some claim that the Indian caste system is the only one that brings them all together. Yet, even when they come together, some elements may be absent. This is a typical *ad hoc* or cafeteria approach of caste scholars, says Balu.

Hence, the properties of caste are unclear, the understanding of Varnas and Jatis is unclear, and its alleged properties and associated evils exist equally in many other social systems as well. However, the caste system is clearly visible in Indian social systems and nowhere else, and it is the root cause of all social evils in the country. Such are the confusions and contradictions when scholars discuss the caste system in India.

## THE WESTERN ROOTS

## WERE SHRAMANA AND BHAKTI MOVEMENTS AGAINST THE CASTE SYSTEM?

### Anomalies of the Uniting Anti-Caste Hypothesis

Scholars and activists describe the Shramana (ascetic) and Bhakti movements (like Chaitanya Vaishnavism) as revolts against the caste system. These egalitarian movements, allegedly a long conflict of lower castes against Brahmanism or the tyrannical caste, form the "uniting anti-caste hypothesis." Martin Fárek, in this illuminating chapter, has a detailed look at these movements and strongly refutes the claim. Fárek also proposes that the 'caste system' originated in the Portuguese transposition of their own problems in the Iberian Peninsula between the Christians on one side and the Jews and Muslims on the other.

According to the textbook story, Buddha, the first reformer like Martin Luther, opposed the complicated but empty ritualism of the Brahmins while fighting the caste system and preaching equality. Many scholars, like HH Wilson and Basham, disagree and say that Buddha and Buddhists neither rejected the Brahmanas nor the caste arrangement. Buddhists established an ascetic tradition outside the community (the Shramanas), which did not advocate for social reform or revolt against the existing social system. In fact, Buddha discussed the characteristics of a spiritually mature 'true Brahmin.'

The author cites extensively from Buddhist texts such as *Aganna-sutta, Sonadanda, Dhammapada, Kassapa Sihanada-sutta, and Vajra-suci* to show that Buddha and Buddhists not only accepted the Varna divisions as dharmic but also put the Kshatriyas at the top of the hierarchy. Buddha called some Brahmins corrupt, but his overriding question was, "Who is a true Brahmana?" Similarly, the *Uttaradhyayana sutra* in Jain traditions, which discusses the qualities of a true Brahmana, does not provide evidence of Jain rejection of the caste system or a revolt against Brahmins.

Fárek delves deep into the writings and speeches of Bhaktivinoda and Bhaktisiddhanta Sarasvati, important teachers of the *Chaitanya Vaishnava* traditions, and establishes that *Bhakti movements* were never rebelling or trying to reform the caste system, as alleged frequently in scholarly writings. This tradition hardly changed the social structure, and in fact, it gave Brahmins an exalted position as men of knowledge and spiritual wisdom. Without rebelling against the existing social structure, these sects sometimes formed a caste division of their own.

Fárek writes that spiritual equality and social equality are two different notions of equality, and he quotes Dr. Ambedkar, who, interestingly, says that the saints never carried out a campaign against caste and untouchability and preached that men were equal in the eyes of God and not at a social level. The author presents irrefutable evidence to show that Chaitanya Vaishnavas considered the Varna division of people by qualities and qualifications, rather than simply birth, to be the best model for society's growth. Their question also revolved around the qualities of a true Brahmin, criticising both the corrupt priestly practices and the animal slaughter by the Shakta traditions. Thus, in these traditions, there was no rejection of the caste system or Brahmins.

Some caste scholars, through their historical distortions and selective readings, have even gone so far as to propose these Bhakti traditions as the foundational basis for the current Dalit movements. The proposal by one scholar Shyam Singh (2010) that Bhakti movements are 'anti-caste, anti-elite, pro-women, pro-poor, anti-Sanskrit, and affirm a genuine love of God to find solutions to social problems' does not stand scrutiny to evidence. Fárek asks, how can a movement be 'anti-caste' while simultaneously not proceeding to bring about some societal changes? Again, to solve social problems, Bhakti traditions have never discussed "genuine love of God," an imprecise phrase by itself. The anti-Sanskrit narrative is a complete falsity because Ramanuja, Chaitanya, Vallabha, and many Vaishnava and Shaiva groups, produced a vast body of literature in Sanskrit.

### *Endogamy and the Portuguese Roots*

Balu's research programme has shown that a Christian theological understanding of Hindu cultures forms the basis of the current caste explanations. Endogamy as a defining property of caste dates back to the 'purity of blood' ideas and the religious endogamy that the Portuguese and Spanish practiced in dealing with their religious rivals, the Jews, and the Muslims.

Colonials like Blunt (1911), a superintendent of census operations, attempted to define caste as one endogamous group or a collection of groups, which is hereditary in nature. These people of common origin generally claim a common traditional occupation. This tries to ambiguously connect various characteristics of caste, but the most problematic is that a collection of endogamous groups does not constitute a larger endogamous group. Scholars could never decide whether Jati (or sub-caste) or Varna was the endogamous unit. Field data and history provided evidence against both, and the endogamy of sub-castes was flexible, mutable, and varied across time and place. Instead of rejecting the notion due to the many contradictions, colonial scholars and present-day intellectuals have still made endogamy the necessary property of both Varna and Jati. The prohibition of same-*gotra* marriages also complicates Jatis' endogamous nature.

Scholars continue to grapple with the correlation between Varna and Jati, often citing concepts such as endogamy, social hierarchy, ritual purity-pollution, occupation, and Marxist theories as their definitions. However, field evidence of caste mobility, the emergence of new Jatis, changing occupations, and texts inconsistently differentiating between Varnas and Jatis contradict the standard understandings. Varna as 'class' and Jati as 'caste' are also problematic since Jati seems to address many units (tribe, sect, and religious or linguistic minority) depending on the context. According to the author, the problem is not in the definition but rather in the ideas that gave us an understanding of Indian society. Notably, caste and sub-caste emerged in European contexts, whereas Varna and Jati evolved in Indian contexts. It is possible that they refer to the distinct realities of different cultures.

Extensive permissive hypergamous marriages, which involve marriages between different Jatis, provide significant evidence against a fixed endogamy model. The problem is that scholars interpret caste endogamy as religious by nature, established and maintained by the Brahmins. This idea emerged from now secularised Christian discussions, which equated Indian traditions with religions under the control of tyrannical priests and Varna-Jati groups, akin to the castes in the early modern era Portuguese and Spanish empires.

## 'Casta' and Christian Concept of Purity of Blood

The Portuguese referred to social units in sixteenth- and seventeenth-century India as 'casta.' Around the same time that the Portuguese arrived in India, they defeated the Muslim rulers and established a Christian kingdom in the Iberian Peninsula. Many Jews and Muslims, to escape the severe persecution, converted to Christianity. These 'New' Christians were constantly at odds with the 'Old' Christians. Sometimes, the new converts secretly practiced their original religion, a focus of the Inquisition. Old Christians, with their concept of 'purity of blood', differentiated themselves from the new converts who had 'contaminated' blood because their ancestors believed in false religions. Marriages between the two groups were not desirable. This endogamy finally established a distinction between people based on their family origins. Through constant decrees and legislation, the Old Christians rose to the top of the hierarchy, dominating all civil and religious domains. Purity of blood statuses gradually spread through the Portuguese world, especially India, to describe the various groups.

Portuguese, Italian, and Spanish authors in the sixteenth and seventeenth centuries held "caste of the Brahmans" with similar meaning as "caste of the Moors or Christians." Even if some scholars add descriptions of purity and pollution to this understanding, Fárek questions why the Iberian system of descent groups, based on the religious faith of ancestors, should become a true representation of Indian society. As European experience of the Indian social system grew, the various groupings became known as "castes," with endogamy as the underlying characteristic on religious lines. By the nineteenth century, Europeans had written about thousands of castes. Early British Orientalists assumed that the analogy between Christians dealing with religious rivals in Portugal and Spain and castes in India was true.

## *Caste As Part of The Story of Religion in India*

Balu's research says that since Christian theological thinking constrains Western thinking about Indian society, it is not scientific at all. A resolution of contradictions is important in any scientific endeavour. However, serious contradictions in the caste story and many of its ideas, such as endogamy, have not led to a comprehensive reassessment of the entire framework of ideas theorising the caste system. Popper's theory, which holds that the context of the observer's expectations guides all observations in science (theory-ladenness), also applies to the social sciences' approach to the caste system, as it posits that correct interpretations follow accurate observations. Therefore, it is crucial for us to first comprehend the key European frameworks for understanding Indian society.

Early Christians and European intellectuals understood the cultures they encountered in terms of true and false religions. During their exploration of various cultures, there was also an associated attempt to derive a universal history of humankind, based on the descendants of Noah. They assumed the truth of Biblical stories, as well as concepts like God, sin, salvation, the soul, and so on. The search for Indian laws, which the majority followed, was based on the unquestioned truth of the Biblical story about God as the original lawgiver. Thus, all nations had some access to revealed laws or the innate capacity to formulate them. Thus, the dharmashastras of Manu (the "Moses" of India), Apastambha, Gautama, and others became the fundamental laws of the heathens. Of course, these were corrupt versions of the originally pure laws revealed by God.

Manu-dharmashastra may have played a role, but the judgments passed by domestic pandits, friends, family, or the community (panchayats) were beyond the colonial judges' comprehension. These indicate that Indian society developed a different system of problem-solving from the Western legal framework.

As Balu writes:

> What if the dharmashastras played a very different role from that of the European codes of law? Although it seems that Early Orientalists had

developed new theories free from the Christian theological roots, there can be argument for an opposite conclusion. These theological roots, or better to say the whole framework, faded into the background of the discussions during the second half of the nineteenth and in the twentieth centuries. But its questions, problems and whole clusters of ideas still form and constrain the kind of discussions we have today. Many Christian ideas became the "of course" axioms of the secularized Orientalist paradigm.

### The Need for a Better Story

Generations of scholars, starting with the early Orientalists, fixed the story of religion in India. Thus, the Aryans came here more than three thousand years ago. Through machinations, special knowledge, and using the scriptures as an authority, the Brahmins gained supremacy. The original pure *Vedism* degenerated into a *Brahmanism* of mindless rituals and superstitions. Jatis grew in number because strict endogamy within Varnas was difficult, and inter-group marriages happened. The Kshatriya resentment towards Brahmanism gave rise to revolts in Buddhism and Jainism. The later revolts were known as the Bhakti movements. The smart Brahmins adopted some elements of Buddhism and won back their supremacy by the first millennium CE. Brahmanism also adopted Tantric practices. The modern form of Hinduism is the result of this new transformation. This standard textbook today tells the story of Vedism, Brahmanism, and Hinduism in sequence.

The textbook story was structured around theological ideas, with the corrupt priest at the centre of the degeneration of an original, pure religion. The crafty Brahmins exploiting the gullible masses became the focus of the Indian story. Up to this point, the sociological speculations about caste share the same framework. However, textual, and historical evidence renders Buddhist and Bhakti traditions as Protestant type anti-caste movements and the forerunners of Dalit activism untenable. Buddha, Buddhists, and Vaishnava Bhakts emphasised Varna-dharma as the best form of society, even as they sought the qualities of a true Brahmana.

Only in the context of original Christian thought and European experience does the story of caste, sanctioned by scriptures, and based on religious endogamy (like in the Iberian world) with priests as the main villains, make sense. The dominant colonial explanation of the caste system as sanctioned by religious (Hindu) law is a severely limiting framework for understanding Indian culture, says Fárek.

As Balu reiterates, the Western cultural experience of India has assumed the status of a scientific framework for describing Indian culture and society through a colonial consciousness. Fárek ends the Chapter with some possible routes in the future for a better understanding of Indian society. We need to discard the old frameworks which suffer from contradictions and inconsistencies. The priority would be to develop a new theory of the Indian terms *Varna, Jati, and biradari* based on traditional understandings. The Indian ideas such as *guna* (mode of nature), *adhikara* (eligibility or qualification), and *svabhava* (natural inclination) should guide us in this understanding.

## A NATION OF TRIBES AND PRIESTS: THE JEWS AND THE IMMORALITY OF THE CASTE SYSTEM

The moral judgments that arose from the factual dimensions of caste discourse (like a hierarchical social organization, Brahmins at the top, endogamy, and so on) highlighted certain discriminatory practices as an inherent principle of the system. The moral dimension makes the caste system a social organisation that almost turns immorality into a moral obligation. The textbook story makes the Indians who follow the caste system almost blind to its immoral nature, hence their unwavering commitment to following the rules. However, the immorality is plainly obvious to everyone else.

Three major European frameworks formulated the Indian caste system: i) the Christian issues in the Iberian Peninsula; ii) the Protestant problems with the Jews and Catholics; and iii) the Aryan-Dravidian theories. In this important chapter, Jakob De Roover discusses the second framework. Ancient Israel had a social hierarchical model of clans, with the priestly

Levites at the top. De Roover shows how this became a model for Indian society, too.

## India: A Heathen Nation Resembling Ancient Israel

European travel accounts and missionary reports of the seventeenth century crystallised the notion of one heathen nation of India divided into four general tribes or lineages held together in a hierarchical order based on nobility and purity by a caste organisation. These descriptions were not based on any empirical data, but on the concepts available to the describer. Many authors, like Rogerius (1651), started drawing parallels between the Old Testament Jews and the 'Gentiles' of India, transforming India into a variant of ancient Israel. The isomorphism equated the Vedas with the Old Testament, divided people into tribes similarly, and positioned the Brahmins at the top, akin to the priestly Levites. Once this isomorphism was in place, the many similarities began to make their way into descriptions.

The Old Testament made one of the tribes, the *Levites,* hold the office of priesthood as an exclusive hereditary office passed across generations. The Levite priests had a powerful role in assessing society's practices. The Brahmins were the equivalent of the Levites. De Roover says, "This Christian understanding of the ancient nation of Israel described in the Old Testament functioned as the framework for making sense of the people of India and provided terms of description that would remain central to future European accounts of India, its religion, and its social structure." Repeated assertions established the truth in a Goebbelsian manner.

In the Biblical account of Israel, Moses was the lawgiver. The Old Testament and the Mosaic law played a key role in the political thinking of the seventeenth-century Protestant world. This morphed into the general theory that every civilised nation had its origin in a first lawgiver pretending to have a divine revelation of the laws people should follow. The merging of civil law with a divine injunction builds a successful nation, as the authors repeatedly suggested. Manu was the Indian counterpart to Moses. This became a common-sense view by the eighteenth century.

Similarly, the Christian understanding of the Jewish practice of herem (excommunication) paved the way for describing a separate class of people among Hindus outside of caste laws. Rogerius described them as the 'Perreaes', unworthy people who lived outside the main towns and villages. Over the next few centuries, hundreds of similar descriptions of the 'outcasts', the 'casteless', or the 'untouchables' were produced.

According to De Roover, the caste system's basic factual structure is dependent on understanding India as a variant of ancient Israel. Thus, Europeans characterised India as a nation with a hierarchical order of tribes founded by a lawgiver and dominated by a privileged community of priests. Today's textbook discourse still presents the Hindus as a people divided into a hierarchy of castes, with the Brahmins as the privileged priestly caste. It also distinguishes descendants of some originally excommunicated people as a punishment for violation of caste laws.

### The Power of The Brahmins and the Initial Moral Ambiguity of Colonials and Missionaries

The Brahmins, with their binding rituals, were at the receiving end of much moral diatribe by the European authors from the seventeenth century itself. The criticism was based on two sources: first, the Christian critique of Judaism as a bondage to law and rituals, and second, the Protestant attack on the clergy of the Catholic Church. Both Catholicism and Judaism were transformed into negations of the norms of Protestant Christianity. This idea later morphed into conceptualising all 'false religions' (or 'organised religions' in secular terms) into a priestly tyranny of laws. By the eighteenth century, through reiterations in popular journals, books, and dictionaries, the idea of completely dominating Brahmins holding the Hindu nation to ransom firmly fixed into the European minds.

Initially, the missionaries did not regard caste distinctions and practices as parts of an immoral and idolatrous system. Some churches allowed converts from different castes to sit in separate divisions. Reginald Heber, the second Bishop of the Anglican Diocese of Calcutta, for example, said that social distinctions are a part of society, and caste (inclusive of pariahs), is one such distinction that exists naturally in all societies.

### The Evil of Caste: Secularization of Theological Ideas

However, in the first decades of the nineteenth century, the immorality of the caste system became a recurring theme. Caste was considered to be the main framework of a false religion, an oppressive tyranny binding people to unjust laws and practices. Evangelicals and missionary-driven colonials advocated for the dismantling of the caste system, despite a minority of scholars ineffectively challenging the missionary narratives. Today's secular narratives continue the same ideas of the old and new missionaries: that the caste system is an immoral social structure at the core of Hindu religion.

The 'Malabar Rites Controversy', inspired by Roberto de Nobili's works, raised the question of whether customs such as the cotton thread around the torso were religious or civil in nature. This concern about the 'religious' and 'civil' distinctions in social practices dates back to early Christianity. Christians, when they finally gained dominance in the pagan world of the Roman Empire, divided social life into three spheres: *obligatory* (worship of true God); *forbidden* (worship of false gods or idolatry); and *permitted* (neutral to God). This was the same framework for missionaries judging the pagan practices in the colonised worlds. By the 1850s, Protestant missionaries started arguing that caste was a sacred institution and an integral part of the entire system of idolatry. Converts now had to renounce all caste customs. Missionaries also started considering caste as the main obstacle to conversion. As a result, Protestant consensus transferred caste from the 'permitted' to the 'forbidden.'

### Caste Becomes a Religious Institution

Jakob De Roover writes:

> This shift allowed for the birth of the conceptual entity that we call the caste system by bringing together several clusters of ideas into one integral whole: the claims about the nation of the Hindus as a variant of that of the Jews; the conception of the brahmin priesthood and its practices as an instance of false religion similar to the institutions of Catholicism and Judaism; the idea that such institutions deceived the believers into following a set of human fabrications as though these

were divine commandments; and the claim that the Hindu religion revolved around external ceremonies and concerns about purity and pollution.

A coherent understanding of the caste system finally crystallised. This system merged civil law and religion into one by claiming a divine origin for itself. The Madras Missionary Conference (1850) stated it clearly and finally in its declaration that caste, "founded upon supposed birth-purity and impurity, is in its nature essentially a religious institution and not a mere civil distinction."

Westerners found it impossible to grasp the nature of Hinduism with its incoherent mix of doctrines, traditions, practices, texts, myths, groups, and no apparent religious authority. Instead of questioning their own frameworks, they found Hinduism itself a faulty religion with its chaotic structure. However, the firm belief remained that the caste system had certainly held this religion together for centuries. As a result, the European scholars saw caste as the sacred core of the Hindu religion, bringing internal order to their understanding of India. Thus, the caste system held both the nation and the Hindu religion together.

From a Christian perspective, a religious institution is of divine origin, and a civil institution is merely a human creation. Protestant Reformers claimed that the clerical laws of the Catholic Church or Judaism were also human fabrications falsely claiming a divine origin. They claimed that caste was an institution of false religion that deceptively merges civil laws with religious obligations, presenting similar ideas to Hinduism. It misleads Hindus into adopting immoral principles as moral requirements. According to De Roover, the structure of today's conception of the caste system derives precisely from this Protestant account.

The nineteenth-century missionary descriptions of Hinduism and caste correspond closely to contemporary moral discourse on the caste system. Thus, in the present secularised discourses, the caste system gives privileges to only a few born in a particular caste, including the right to discriminate against and humiliate others belonging to 'lower' castes, especially the untouchables or the Dalits. The system allegedly draws on scriptural authority to justify its immoral practices.

De Roover concludes this essay by asking: "How could it make sense to see an alien people discovered on the Indian subcontinent as a variant of the Jews who had lived in the Middle East more than 1,500 years before?" Surprisingly, Indian intellectuals assume that an immoral social organization disguised as moral constantly deceives Hindus, who appear blind to its actual dimensions. Despite their lack of knowledge about Christianity and its internal debates, the present scholars' conceptual vocabulary closely aligns with Protestant descriptions of Hinduism. It is important for us to give better descriptions of the caste system.

## THE ARYANS AND THE ANCIENT SYSTEM OF CASTE

Among the various theories explaining the caste system, Aryans and Dravidians are important. This Chapter by Marianne Keppens aims to understand the flawed discourses mapping these racial theories onto the Indian caste system. According to the standard Aryan story, the Aryans invaded India around 1500 BC, conquered the indigenous Dravidians, and imposed their culture, language, and religion on the latter. The Aryans' Vedic religion later evolved into Hinduism with its religiously founded caste system. Surprisingly, this account of the Aryans and caste system has persisted since its first descriptions in the nineteenth century, in the absence of any concrete evidence.

### *The Aryans: Flights of Fancy by Indologists*

Stanley Wolpert's book, *India*, is a typical example of scholarship linking Aryans and the caste system. According to Wolpert, ancient India had three groups of people: 1) the conquering Aryan tribes, who were the ancestors of the first three Varnas; 2) the conquered indigenous pre-Aryan Dasas, who were the ancestors of the 'inferior' Shudras; and 3) even more primitive peoples, who became the outcastes. Wolpert reads the Ramayana as an allegory depicting the clash between Dasas and the Aryan sadhus and kings. The Vedas, with their few references to the 'dark' Dasas residing in fortified cities ('pur'), serve as the basis for Wolpert's speculations.

Wendy Doniger, an influential American Indologist, talks in her book, *The Hindus*, about the "Vedic people" who conquered the indigenous Dasas and relegated the lowest social position to them. She writes that the early Vedas expressed envy of the Arya for the Dasa because of the latter's wealth. Later, the Dasas became subordinates and slaves. She confusingly depicts the Dasas as both inside of society and yet an "outside class." She makes an extraordinary claim that the word 'vis', the origin of the word for the third class, Vaishyas, means 'everyone.' This does not give scope for adding Shudras below them, except as an afterthought!

The Purushasukta hymn, the all-time favourite for Indologists, is a creation hymn discussing the entire cosmos—man, animal, and nature—as parts of the Primaeval Man or Being. It describes the Brahmins coming from the head, the Kshatriyas from the arms, the Vaishyas from the thighs, and the Shudras from the feet. This has become the single most important source for criticisms of the caste system. Doniger interprets "the lowest and dirtiest part of the body" as representing the Shudras and the outcastes. Feet are not necessarily dirty; they are not the lowest part during a sacrifice when the body is horizontal; and a study of the whole hymn would make such interpretations pervasive with ignorance and bias. For Doniger, the term 'Vaishya', which means 'everyone', is peculiar because it implies a lack of space, even 'above', thereby making the Brahmins and Kshatriyas appear as afterthoughts too. The Brahmins are allegedly the originators of the caste system, not the Vaishyas.

Doniger speculates that the Dasas, or forerunners of the Shudras, entered the Vedic system, leaving their own behind if they had one. Doniger gives no explanation, including the use of force, for the Dasas to do this, except a weak interpretation of the word 'Vaishya'. In this case, either the Dasas were too weak to resist, or the Vedic system had a strong dynamic or attractiveness that automatically drew people in, relegating them to inferior positions without question or rebellion until today. This effectively renders the Dasas and Shudras as permanently foolish individuals.

### *Dealing with the Problem of the Non-Occurrence of an Invasion*

The *Aryan Migration Theory* (AMT) claims that the Aryans came to India and did the same things as in the Aryan Invasion Theory (AIT), but through peaceful immigration. The second alternative is the not-so-dominant *Out of India Theory*, which claims that the Aryans originated in India itself and moved to other parts of the world. This does not speculate on the indigenous population's caste or subjugation. Keppen's Chapter focuses on the AIT/AMT. Hermann Kulke and Dietmar Rothermund (*A History of India*) describe the Aryan conquest as two waves rather than a single invasion. The authors base these speculations on the Vedic hymns themselves, as well as terms like Arya and Dasa. As it does for other scholars, the Purushasukta facilitates the authors' understanding of the caste hierarchy.

A famous scholar, Frits Staal, explains that the smaller migrating Aryans gained domination because of the disintegration of the Indus Valley, leaving a "gap into which anything could fall and disappear" and the "power of mantra" of the Vedas. This fails to explain why the Vedas themselves did not fall into the "large gap"—if "anything" was capable of doing so. Staal does not explain what made the mantras powerful, except through circular reasoning. Keppens says that without attributing magical powers, only a shared culture where the Vedas were already in place could explain their impact on society. The Vedas are not like agriculture, where a large group of people would easily accept a handful of migrants' traditions. The Vedas cannot represent the culture of a separate people, says Keppens.

Keppens discusses scholar Koenraad Elst, who has researched extensively on the Aryan issue and firmly rejects the AMT/AIT theory. Elst says that the Aryans could not have imposed their culture, language, religion, and social structure on the indigenous population without a forcible conquest. A time-tested military force is the only way a numerically small, illiterate, cowherd Aryans can gain dominance over a large, literate civilization. Archaeology fails to demonstrate this, so according to Elst, inconsistency is sufficient to reject both the AIT and the AMT.

The Indological speculations largely do not explain why the Shudras of today owe their unchangeable inferior position in society to their ancestors, who accepted this a few thousand years ago from a people that brought them a civilisation in return. It is far more likely that the Vedic tradition came into being as part of, or within, a culture that was taking shape in India among and across many different peoples. Indological literature, linguistics, archaeology, and genetics in recent times have never shown evidence of how the Aryans reduced the indigenous population of India to a lower position. All studies focus only on where they came from. Aryans are an a priori assumption. Most importantly, archaeological records to date have shown absolutely no evidence of large-scale invasions or migrations into the Indian subcontinent.

### *Aryans and Dravidians: Conclusions from Biblical Themes*

Several scholars, including Thomas Trautmann, have suggested that Biblical chronology was the conceptual framework for the Aryans' postulation as a people. They argue that the idea of an Aryan people goes back to the Biblical notion that each language links to a nation or a people's past. William Jones linked Sanskrit, Latin, and Greek in 1786 and also postulated a connection between these languages and a lineage of nations. He speculated that there was a common descent for Indians and Europeans from Ham, one of Noah's three sons. However, these theories do not explain the indigenous Indians or their subjugation by the invading Aryans.

Strangely, scholars in the early eighteenth century conceived of the Hindu, Vedic, or Brahminical people, but the Dravidians, their languages, and the AIT came in the first half of the nineteenth century. The hypothesis of an Aryan conquest finally originated in the early nineteenth century at the Société Asiatique de Paris and the College of Fort St. George in Madras. Later, scholars from Germany took over the idea. Scholars like Max Müller, Mark Wilks, Langlès, Rémusat, Burnouf, and so on repeatedly told the story of Indians being foreigners in their own land. The Aryans were now the invaders, and the subjugated people became either the southward-driven Dravidians, the Shudras, who took up positions as slaves and servants, or the outcastes.

Towards the middle of the nineteenth century, most European scholars of Indian religion had accepted the hypothesis of the Aryan invasion despite a lack of evidence. Mountstuart Elphinstone, the Governor of Bombay, felt compelled to acknowledge in his influential *The History of India (1841)* that the idea of an invasion was a plausible explanation for the caste system despite the lack of evidence.

All these citations spoke of the caste system with Brahmins, Kshatriyas, Vaishyas, and Shudras in a descending social hierarchy. The outcastes were the lowest and outside the system. They also conceptualised a higher level of division into two main groups. The first group consists of the first three "twice-born" castes. The second group consists of the inferior Shudras and the outcastes, who faced extreme deprivation. According to Elphinstone, the first group formed the community around religious and civil institutions. The Shudras and the outcastes had no rights to perform Vedic rituals as per European interpretations of the Laws of Manu.

Keppens writes that nineteenth-century European scholars wanted an explanation for the social inequalities between the first and second groups specifically and not of society in general. The social inequality between the first and second groups is of a different kind than the inequalities between the three castes in the first group. The final explanation was that these two groups represent two different races, and the first group had conquered the second one. The aboriginal population's descendants do not have a civilisation.

By the middle of the nineteenth century, the conjecture, through repetition, about the invasion of an aboriginal people had acquired the status of fact. Max Müller goes on to suggest that the Rigveda, Ramayana, Manu, and Mahabharata were accounts of Brahminical tribes conquering India step by step. When the idea of two races crystallised, other differences came into focus: language, religion, appearance, and skin colour. Today, scholars continue to affirm the caste system as an Aryan system of racial discrimination, finding it plausible despite the absence of concrete evidence. Keppens concludes by stating that Aryan theory and caste linkages ultimately derive their intelligibility from a set of Christian theological ideas, where each nation uses its own language to transmit its religion through a sacred text.

## INDIAN ISSUES

## CASTE-BASED RESERVATION AND SOCIAL JUSTICE IN INDIA

There is a repeated claim that the Constitution used 'social justice' as a moral normative ideal to justify caste-based reservations. Thus, reservations were the moral means to address the wrongs done to oppressed groups in the past. In this thought-provoking and incisive chapter, Balu looks deeply at the Constitution debates and firmly concludes that purely pragmatic considerations were the basis for implementing caste-based reservations in the country. In their debates, the term social justice never meant a normative ideal.

Social justice, as the parliamentarians, including Dr. Ambedkar, understood it, was instituting certain policy measures by the government that would ensure equality on a social, economic, and political basis. Thus, as Balu says, "caste-based reservation is either an expression of political expediency or a psychological tool to allay suspicions in some communities, or both." Social justice simply means a prudent approach to implementing social security measures.

The only place where social justice has a normative connotation is in Christian theology. Balu writes that, in fact, Taparelli, a politically conservative Italian Jesuit priest, introduced the normative notion of social justice in his 1840s publication, *A Theoretical Essay on Natural Rights from an Historical Standpoint*. This notion later became widespread. Taparelli's students included Pope Leo XIII, who authored the famous encyclical *'Rerum Novarum'* (On the condition of the working classes), hailed as the first official Catholic statement on the social question.

Balu cites Leo Shields, who, in *The History and Meaning of the Term Social Justice* (2015), quoted a Catholic catechism to provide a precise meaning of social justice:

> Society ensures social justice when it provides the conditions that allow associations or individuals to obtain what is their due, according to their nature and their vocation. Social justice is linked to the common good and the exercise of authority. [Catechism of the Catholic Church 1993, Chap. 2, Art. 3]

Unless one absurdly assumes that most parliamentarians debating on the reservations were secret Christians, which makes them immoral and dishonest, it is clear that the underlying idea of the term social justice was not a normative moral ideal but a pragmatic decision to ensure equality in society.

## ARE THERE CASTE ATROCITIES IN INDIA?

Intellectuals, academics, non-governmental organisations, and human rights activists in India and around the world consistently claim that caste atrocity in India is not only high but is constantly on the rise. Regrettably, the international spotlight primarily focuses on caste atrocities in India. However, is this claim supported by the data? In their significant essay, '*Are There Caste Atrocities in India? —What the Data Can and Cannot Tell Us*', Dunkin Jalki and Sufiya Pathan firmly refute this claim. There are two types of data that come into play when describing caste violence in Indian society: the hard data and the soft data.

The hard data is the collection of all well-defined crimes like rape, murder, arson, physical violence, and abduction committed against the Scheduled Castes (SC) and Scheduled Tribes (ST) communities. The National Crime Records Bureau (NCRB) is a government agency that publishes annual reports on crime, and these have separate chapters on caste atrocities. There are also special laws like the Protection of Civil Rights Act (PCR) and the Prevention of Atrocities Act (PoA), which caste scholars include in their studies to record the total number of crimes against the SC and ST populations. One significant issue is that the NCRB data only records the victim's caste, not the alleged perpetrator's caste. It might be as well that the perpetrator of the crime belongs to other lower-caste groups. Only special acts show the perpetrator's caste.

Activists, academics, and the media make sensational claims by quoting absolute numbers of crimes against the SC and ST communities instead of proportions. It is crucial to record crimes against other individual castes as well, in order to support the claim that lower castes experience disproportionately higher rates of crime. Such data does not exist. Therefore, the only way to substantiate the claim of rising violence against the SC and ST communities is to compare the data with crimes against the rest of society. In fact, a comparison with crimes against the rest of society reveals significantly less violence (thirty times less) against the SC and ST populations.

For example, the NCRB (2011) states that the total number of incidences against Scheduled Castes [SCs] in India was 33,719. The sensationalism is in the form of statements like "Every 18 minutes, a crime is committed against SCs; or, every day, twenty-seven atrocities are committed against them," and so on. The authors say that to get a proper perspective it is also important to consider that there were 6,252,729 cognizable total crimes in India in 2011. Thus, the total number of crimes against the SCs was 0.53% of the total reported crimes (33719 divided by 6252729).

In 2011, the SCs accounted for approximately 16.6% of India's total population. If 16.6% of the population faces 0.53% of the total criminal incidents in India, the remaining 83.4% faces 99.47% of the rest of the criminal incidents. *Hence, on average, every percentage of the non-SC population faces roughly 1.19% of the incidence of crime, while every percentage of the SC population faces about 0.04% (30 times less) of the crime.* The authors raise a pertinent question that caste scholars seem to gloss over: "If measuring crime against a group is a reliable measure for atrocities against the group, then can we not conclude that SCs face fewer atrocities than the rest of the population?"

Underreporting of crime is a popular caveat, suggesting that the actual number of crimes is significantly higher than the reported ones. Even assuming as true the claim of some scholars that unreported crimes are one to one and a half times more than reported crimes, it is still nowhere close to what the rest of the population faces. To bring the 0.04% (percentage of crime per percentage of SC population) closer to the figure of 1.19% (percentage of crime per percentage of non-SC population), we would need to increase it by about *thirty* times. One should also assume that underreporting does not occur with crimes against the non-SC population, as it does with the SC population.

Absolute numbers, rather than proportions, also present an inaccurate picture. Jalki and Pathan, citing clear statistics from the NCRB, demonstrate that the percentage of crimes against SCs has not shown any significant rise in the last decade. The *rate of crime* against SCs (i.e., the number of incidences per one lakh of SC population) has, in fact, decreased over the years. For example, in 2013, there were 39,408 cognizable crimes committed against SCs (a crime rate of 19.57 per lakh). Though the total number of crimes shows an increase from 32,996 (1995) to 33,501 (2001) to 39,408 (2013), the crime rate has substantially declined—from 23.24 (1995) to 20.14 (2001) to 19.57 (2013).

Scholars manipulate, cherry pick, and selectively interpret the hard data to present this alarming picture of increasing caste atrocities in India. While this approach would be unacceptable in any other domain, it has gained respect in the field of caste studies. However, the prevalent trend in scholarly articles regarding the use of soft data appears to be more expansive, all-encompassing, and even more severe. Using wide data on 'untouchability' practices or 'caste disabilities' (denial of livelihood rights, high school dropouts, land and labour rights violations, denial of access to public places, delayed law and police help, and so on), the caste atrocity phenomenon seems to be all-pervasive in the country, which ranges from "from mundane acts of limiting social interaction to economic patterns of land ownership to actual acts of violence." Anecdotal incidents make up much of this documentation, and this becomes the basis for making abstract theoretical claims about the age-old exploitative caste system. As Jalki and Pathan say, no study even makes a perfunctory attempt to prove that it is the so-called caste system that causes these social disabilities. This is simply an a priori assumption, even before they undertake their studies. Such studies hardly demonstrate the existence of a "system" that practically mandates immoral behaviour among individuals and communities, as Balu asserts.

The authors Jalki and Pathan analyse caste violence-related writings published in the *Economic and Political Weekly (EPW)* from 1949 to 2000, aiming to identify specific trends in these scholarly writings. They detect that the 'caste atrocities' idea is largely a late-1960s development that caught on in the 1970s. In sixty relevant articles on 'caste atrocities' in 2,283 issues of the EPW journal over 50 years, Brahmins do not feature anywhere as perpetrators of violence except in one. Yet the explanations persistently involve terms like *'Brahmanical caste system,' 'Brahmanical social setup', 'Brahmanism'* and *'Brahmanical model'.*

Similarly, the term 'upper castes' is freely used without providing specific information about their identities. It appears that Brahmins hold such huge, disembodied power in Indian society that they cause caste violence without even getting formally involved. The authors ask: What is 'Brahminical' about violence perpetrated by non-Brahmins? In fact, much of this violence comes from the category of 'other backward classes' (OBC). Thus, scholars explain the violence perpetrated by 'lower-caste' groups by attributing the source to an 'upper-caste' group without any evidence to connect the two. In their enthusiasm to fit data to preconceived theories, caste scholars sometimes refer to the same Jati group as both upper-caste (when a perpetrator) and lower caste (when a victim) for convenience. SC, ST, and OBC roughly constitute 65% of Indian population. Irrespective of the Varna or Jati of the alleged perpetrator, any violence within this group becomes an instance of "caste violence" in scholarly writings.

Between 2005 and 2015, the expenditure related to the PoA increased fourfold, even as the government spent vast amounts of money on various schemes to prevent and compensate for caste violence. This also includes many educational programs. Despite this, we remain uncertain about the definition of caste violence, its etiology, and its prevalence. Yet the legislation and compensations continue to increase. Jalki and Pathan end the essay by saying, "Further research on the source of current assumptions guiding caste studies is required, alongside the generation of new models for understanding Indian reality." The current caste studies are flawed and are doing untold damage to India's reputation.

## ISSUES ABROAD RELATED TO THE CASTE SYSTEM

## DISSIMULATING ON CASTE IN BRITISH LAW

Despite a lack of clarity in the definition of caste, the absence of lists identifying the Dalits in the UK context, and the absence of evidence of any mass discrimination, volumes of literature and opinions build up across continents. There is a regular negative projection of the caste system in Western settings where Indians have settled in recent times. In an important chapter, Prakash Shah examines one such invocation of the caste system in the context of the enactment of the Equality Act 2010 in the United Kingdom, the first provision on caste discrimination in the anti-discrimination legislation of any country. This Chapter demonstrates the indefensible handling of the caste discrimination question in UK law, as well as supporting one of the central claims of this book: that the normative conception of the caste system is a presupposition acting as an explanation of Indian culture and society.

The United Kingdom's Equality Act 2010 opened the way to legal claims for damages for caste discrimination. Caste Indian legal provisions either provide protection under the caste atrocities legislation or provide preferential reservations in various domains. Proponents of the legislation in the United Kingdom have an inadequate understanding of caste and the legal situation in India. For example, Shah writes of ex-Labour leader Jeremy Corbyn, trustee of the Dalit Solidarity Network and co-chair of the All-Party Parliamentary Group for Dalits, who has been very vociferous on the issue of Dalit discrimination in the UK. He praises the Indian Constitution for both outlawing discrimination and providing protected employment for Dalits. However, he overlooks the fact that protected employment discriminates against those who are not eligible for it. The fudging of differences between Indian and UK legislation raises an important question. Why should the UK equality law, based on the imposition of civil law liabilities extending to damages, serve as the suitable model for addressing potential social ills caused by caste?

One way to substantiate the claims about the discrimination problem is to cite the number of Dalits in Britain. Self-evidently, Dalits must face discrimination. However, estimates of the Dalit population have been extremely variable: 50,000 to 200,000 (Lord Avebury), 500,000 (Lord Harries), and one million (James Corbyn). Apart from the constant ambiguity about who exactly a Dalit is, there is no official information or reliable research for these numbers. Legislation requires careful consideration and supporting evidence, as the quoted numbers imply a deliberate attempt to create a discriminatory problem.

### *Presuppositions of an Immoral System and the Push for Legislation on Low Evidence*

'Dalit' refers to those on the Indian government's list of Scheduled Castes, but no such lists exist in the United Kingdom. Jeremy Corbyn's use of the term 'Dalit' in the UK context does not refer to these Jatis, but rather to the exploitative caste system, where the upper castes inevitably discriminate against the lower castes. The term 'Dalit' lacks clarity, referring solely to those who are 'oppressed' due to their caste membership. A simple presupposition holds that an immoral and discriminatory caste system exists a priori. Any dialogue would be only between those supporting or fighting the discriminatory caste system. The supporters are delusional, of course. Prakash Shah writes, "In this 'dialogue,' there is a compelling argument for the students of Indian descent to accept the implicit attribution of the caste system as the explanation for their discriminatory attitudes."

Remarkably, the parliamentary discussions on caste discrimination have been desperate to push for legislation based on isolated, alleged instances of discrimination. The stories do not even consider alternative explanations for an individual's behaviour while dealing with another, apart from caste discrimination, as Shah illustrates in an example where a Brahmin customer allegedly refused to accept change from a shopkeeper.

While waiting for legislation, the UK Case Law has, however, incorporated caste discrimination as a factor to consider in individual claims. This is unusual because there is no single sociological or legal definition of caste, as even Annapurna Waughray, a strong proponent of caste legislation, acknowledges. This lack of definition does not prevent a claim of caste discrimination if some definition links to 'ethnic origins.' Yet, there is a presumption of an inherently immoral caste system where high-caste Indians obligatorily discriminate against low-caste ones. As seen earlier, this is a secularised version of Protestant assessments of Indian culture. Similarly, UK scholars place the tribals (who have a separate category in India) outside the caste order, yet they include them anomalously in claims of caste-based discrimination.

### *Secularising a Christian Theme and Generalising the Account*

Many organisations and individuals, like Lord Harries (Anglican), Lord Alton (Catholic), and Lord Griffiths (Methodist), strongly propagating for caste legislation, have a strong Christian background. In the House of Commons, there are strong connections between MPs who have interns paid by CARE (Christian Action, Research, and Education) and the Dalit lobby. Many Dalit organisations, such as the Copenhagen-based International Dalit Solidarity Network (IDSN), which seeks anti-discrimination legislation to cover caste, have extensive funding from various churches or governments in different European countries.

The drive for caste legislation is part of a wider project of proselytism across the world. In colonial times, missionaries looked at caste as a big obstacle to conversion, and now, in India, converts to Christianity lose access to many reservations, which is an equal obstacle. Legislation in Britain aims to finally boost an international campaign within UN organs to have caste discrimination recognised in some form.

Surprisingly, many secular Westerners who do not necessarily subscribe to Christianity, along with organisations such as the National Secular Society, are actively advocating for the inclusion of the caste clause in the Equality Act. Paradoxically, they are standing on the same side as the Christian organisations, despite being in opposition to them.

Post-Reformation Christendom and liberal secularism viewed Hinduism and caste as a denial of Christian freedom and equality. Hinduism was simply an embodiment of tyranny and a caste-based hierarchy. The social sciences and Indian political thought embraced the normative framing of Indian culture and society as "facts." Shah says that, since a social-scientific description of Indian society was in the framework of secularised Christian theology, both advocates of Christian proselytism and secularism could accept these accounts.

Unfortunately, Indian academics sharing the same assumptions make outrageous claims that reflect only the absorption of stereotypes. Shah gives the example of one such scholar, Sameena Dalwai, who demonstrates this perfectly by using caste as a qualifier for a wide variety of issues. Thus, she refers to the 'caste system', 'caste oppression', 'caste relations', 'caste practices', 'caste pyramid', 'caste discourse', 'caste positionality', 'caste economics', 'caste hierarchy', 'caste situation', 'caste lens', 'caste norms', 'caste subjectivity', 'caste privilege', 'caste violence', and 'caste discrimination'. Finally, caste is a moral degeneracy that the upper castes in India have embraced and are now spreading abroad. The immoral caste system seeps into every aspect of Indian life. Thus, scholars, activists, and institutions finally presuppose a thoroughly immoral Indian caste system, and the only ideal legal thing to do is its eradication.

## AFTERWORD

In the concluding chapter, the editors state that, despite so much scholarship, there is no clear understanding of the Jatis, the nature of the conflicts dubbed 'caste violence', or the term 'social system.' Social scientists, intellectuals, activists, organisations, and courts are clear that there exists an immoral and corrupt caste system. However, these refer to a variety of discrete phenomena in Indian culture: rituals, people assuming different roles in the rituals, festivals, dresses, food habits, marriage practices, land and economic issues, social interactions between groups of people, and even the stories of discrimination and exploitation. The Ghent School's main thesis is that the West, having experienced all of these facets of Indian culture, bound them together in a grand explanation—the caste system.

All the 'facts' of Indian culture they described were true. However, to bind them all in a single explanation of a caste system is false. They write, "There is no unity in the sets of phenomena clubbed together and described as either component parts, causes, or effects of the Indian 'caste system.' More starkly put, the caste system does not exist." The Westerners did not intentionally or mischievously create this caste system; rather, the unity of the diverse aspects of Indian culture was a unity for them, not for the Indians themselves. Conceptualising a system lent stability to their understanding of Indian society.

The claim that a caste system does not exist does not imply any denial of the stories of discrimination and exploitation, as the Ghent scholars make it very clear. These issues need further investigation.

The authors write:

> But strong is the claim that the dominant Western story about the caste system is false, if taken as an explanation of Indian society. The caste system, the entity constructed by the West, is an experiential entity only to the West and not to Indians. In this sense, the caste system is not a part of Indian culture. It has no existence outside of the Western experience of India.

Western travellers, missionaries, and administrators created a caste system because they understood India in terms of the categories they had inherited. We have given scientific status to the colonial explanations of the Indian social systems, and the research should focus on providing alternative explanations to replace the previous ones. Unfortunately, Indians, like the West, accept the 'caste system' as a unit of their own experience. Balu says that this is because of the pervasive 'colonial consciousness' in the country, which is an alteration of the intellectual frameworks of the colonised even after the colonials have left.

The cultural and civilizational superiority of Western culture becomes the driving assumption of Indians when setting forth to understand their own culture. Thus, the centuries-long education of lay Indians, researchers, and academics makes it challenging for them to disassociate themselves from colonial discourses. Regarding the caste system, there is a lack of clarity regarding its actual meaning, despite a persistent insistence on its opposition. The authors finally say that much of the influential work in the social sciences is ideological. There is ample evidence that studies on the caste system and governmental policies (such as reservation) are based on political ideology rather than on scientific evidence.

Our faulty theories of the caste system tend to increase unrest in society. Sound social sciences, which work in an Indian context, are yet to come. A society cannot find solutions based on faulty understandings or by asking the wrong kinds of questions. Constructive criticisms of the existing social science theories should be able to bring forth a better science of caste. The authors sign off by writing, "The main hypothesis is that the dominant descriptions we have today are results of originally Christian themes and questions; they reflect European historical experiences and European thinking about society much more than the real state of society and its domestic understanding in India."

## Chapter 5

# CASTE: SOME ALTERNATIVE NARRATIVES

*Dunkin Jalki, Martin Fárek, Prakash Shah,*

*Garima Raghuvanshy, and Nihar Sashittal*

## Introduction

The classical conception of the so-called 'caste system' evolved and consolidated in colonial-missionary writings and has remained unchanged for two centuries. The present social sciences largely reproduce the classic rendering of 'caste'. Jalki and Pathan (2015) quote the Social Science NCERT textbook (Democratic Politics) for Class 10 (Chapter 4 Gender, Religion and Caste):

Caste division is special to India. All societies have some kind of social inequality and some form of division of labour. In most societies, occupations are passed on from one generation to another. Caste system is an extreme form of this. What makes it different from other societies is that in this system, hereditary occupational division was sanctioned by rituals. Members of the same caste group were supposed to form a social community that practiced the same or similar occupation, married within the caste group and did not eat with members from other caste groups. Caste system was based on exclusion of and discrimination against the 'outcaste' groups. They were subjected to the inhuman practice of untouchability.

Summarily, the caste system rests on four principles:

- Occupational division, sanctioned by Hinduism

- Hereditary membership

- Endogamy

- Exclusion of and discrimination against the 'outcaste' groups (which includes commensality and 'untouchability')

Field studies and societal practices have contradicted each of the properties theorised for the caste system. Strangely, caste scholarship presents the disjunction as a unique feature of the caste system. Caste scholarship holds on to the theory while rejecting the uncomfortable data. Is there an alternative story?

The post-independent academic narrative dominated by leftist/ Marxist thinking did not much change the narrative, as the oppressor-oppressed paradigm was found to be an easy fit for the narrative of the ruled and the rulers. Some post-colonial critique was more vehement, but implausibly argued that the classificatory scheme proposed by the colonials *created* the Indian social order. A small voice at present, but representing decades of serious scholarship mainly led by the Ghent School (initiated by Balagangadhara), takes an entirely different approach to tackle the caste system and to understand its many phenomena, like *jatis*. The present scholarship hardly takes the *jatis* into account, which perhaps is the only reality of our social systems. The Ghent School takes the position that the 'caste system' as such does not exist, but is the construct of the experience of colonials in an alien culture. In trying to understand a culture they were trying to rule, they constructed a meta-narrative to explain the many phenomena under the umbrella of a 'caste system.'

The Oñati International Institute for the Sociology of Law, established in Spain in 1988, supports a global network of scholars working in the fields of law and social sciences. It publishes a peer-reviewed, online open-access journal called *Oñati Socio-Legal Series*. In its 2022 series (2022: OSLS First Online), there are five brilliant articles that capture the work of scholars trying to give an alternative to the standard caste story. It is hoped that this summary of those articles will inspire the reader to explore the work in greater detail. This alternative narrative does not deny the discriminatory practices in society, an oft-repeated criticism, but it has more potential than the standard story to create harmony and assuage the hurt and anger among people.

### Early Muslim Writers on Brahmins

Dunkin Jalki (2022), in an important article, 'Evolution of the figure of the Brahmin in early Muslim writings', shows how the present central role of the "crafty and ostentatious" Brahmins in the caste system originated from early Muslim writings (eighth to eleventh centuries). The earliest Muslim and Jewish scholars spoke about an enigmatic Indian group of intellectuals called *al-Barahima*. Despite some disagreements, scholarly consensus identifies them as the Brahmins of India.

*Al-Barahima*, first appearing in the works of late-eighth century Muslim scholars, is a group of heretical but scholarly people holding human reason as self-sufficient and denying the necessity of prophethood. Through an impressive analysis of the texts and writings of various scholars on these groups, Jalki shows that *al-Barahima* gradually came to represent a set of ideas blatantly antithetical to Islamic ideals as early as the mid-ninth century. This was both a continuation of and a small departure from even earlier references to this group. Islamic scholars had classified the world into four divisions: 1) *Muslims*; 2) *believers* in a revealed book as mentioned in the Qur'an; 3) people who claim to believe a divine *Book* not mentioned in the Qur'an; and 4) *infidels*. There was some initial uncertainty, but a Muslim theologian finally placed *al-Barahima* in the last category as idol-worshippers.

An important aspect of the late-ninth and early-tenth centuries is the development of Islamic universal history, says Jalki. Scholars accorded a place to a region called *Hind* and *Barahima* with its various modifications in their writings. Gradually, the word 'Hindu' came to denote everything black. From the eleventh century onward, Hindus appear as highway robbers, thieves, and moneylenders. In general, the word became a synonym for 'slave'.

The author then traces the most significant period, the late 10th century, coinciding with the period of the prolific traveller and writer Al-Biruni, who consolidated the popular discourse. Using Indian scriptures, the historical precedents, and sociological facts of India around him, Al-Biruni linked *Barahima* and *Brahmana* to build a hybrid entity: flesh-and-blood human beings (real and imaginary), a conceptual idea of the wise person (Brahmana as a way of referring to a jnani), a sociological idea of a social class (Kshatriya or Brahmana varna), and so on. At the end of Al-Biruni's (973–1048) career, Muslim scholars began to talk about *al-Barahima* as boastful, ignorant, crafty, and even cruel people, much like the immoral and corrupt Brahmin priests that Indologists would describe a millennium later.

Al-Biruni offered the fourfold division of Indian society with some outcaste groups. He described the spiritual and social hierarchy as a prominent aspect of Indian society. Brahmins and Kshatriyas were at the top of both hierarchies due to their access to the scriptures. The Shudras, as the menial servants, and the *Antyaja* group, as the lowest doing the "dirty work", had no such access. His interpretation of the Gita finally leads him to conclude a divine sanction of the hierarchy.

The *Barahima* thus transformed into failed elites-cum-priests. This was the period when the Delhi Sultanate (1206–1526) had first emerged. The Muslim scholars of the post-thirteenth century concerned themselves with the fate of Muslim communities in the subcontinent rather than the nature of Indian religions. Yet, as the author says, in the Muslim writings of the thirteenth century, Brahmins were neither the informed rationalists nor the "perverse and wicked a set as can anywhere be found"— as Saint Francis Xavier would call them some three centuries later. The author speculates, as a matter for future research, whether the Muslim image of Brahmins had any bearing on the later Christian one.

Though the author says he does not focus on the contemporary Indian texts in the article, his own research into Shaiva texts (fifth to eleventh century CE) or the Kannada Lingayat texts (post-eleventh century) neither portrays a Brahmin nor speaks about 'caste' the way Muslim scholars like Al-Biruni do. The contention is that, irrespective of what was happening in India, the Brahmin figure that Al-Biruni is talking about is absent in Indian literature, and we must look elsewhere for its origin and development. Strikingly, the contemporary story of the caste system does not seem to diverge much from its Muslim version. Jalki asks, "Why did this story not progress further? If this story never grows, shouldn't one ask if it indeed refers to an actual phenomenon or not? If it never gets old, it can't be real."

## Race and Caste

Martin Fárek—in an illuminating article 'Caste, race, and slavery' (2022)—discusses the evolution of the present scholarship conflating race and caste and how there is pressure on legislative bodies and courts in the US and UK to use caste as a cudgel to inconvenience Indians and Hindus. Fárek offers three main characteristics for comparison: *endogamy*, which preserves the purity of the blood of the groups; *colour consciousness*, or the skin colour of people as the discriminatory mark of both caste and race; and the *hierarchy* of the groups in question.

Fárek demonstrates how the characterisation of endogamy, which guides the complex relationship between thousands of groups (*jatis*) in India, suffers from fallacies, assumptions, and contradictions. Similarly, colour consciousness, where 'fair' becomes superior or preferable, suffers from the vagueness and subjectiveness of the impressions without any backing from either the societal practices or the Indian texts. Considering hierarchy, scholars are yet to explain —if the races and castes are similar social organisations—the existence of thousands of *jati* groupings in India, as against only two basic racial groups in the United States? How could a dual system of race where the inferior can never hope to reach the level of the superior transpose itself to a society with thousands of mobile jatis with no fixed hierarchy and variable group status across time and space?

The most curious is the numerical puzzle. In 1921, the census in India showed that the three upper castes accounted for about 21 million people, as opposed to more than 300 million members of the lower castes, the alleged progeny of the conquered aboriginals. In comparison, the census of 1860 in the fifteen slaveholding states of the US before the Civil War showed 8,039,000 "whites", 3,950,000 slaves, and 251,000 "free colored persons." Thus, while in American slavery, the ruling race numbered more than double the number of enslaved people, in India, the alleged ruling castes comprised only about seven percent of the population. It is problematic to consider that the conquering Aryan race came in sufficient numbers, established their caste system, and despite all that, became a minority (Fárek does not mention it, but on a side note, the Aryan 'migration' theorising of 'trickles' of 'Aryans' migrating to India is an *ad hoc* adjustment to these criticisms of the 'Aryan invasion' scenario.)

But what was the background of the sharp division of two groups in Indian society? Jakob De Roover's work demonstrates the legacy of colonial caste law, which brought a sharp division between 'Caste Hindus' (or touchables) and 'Depressed Classes' (or untouchables) in the current Indian legal system. This twofold basic division in Indian society, typically ascribed to Hinduism, justifies legal and political action today.

Two main steps emerged in the development of Western explanations concerning Indian society. The first was the development of older ideas about an ancient Aryan conquest and enslavement of the supposed aborigines by these Aryan 'foreigners'. This is a purely hypothetical exercise, derived from two different sources: first, Enlightenment thinking about the general development of all human societies, in which slavery was a "natural state" in ancient societies, and guided inquiries into the *Manava-dharmashastra* and other texts available to British lawyers and Orientalists in the 18th century. These texts appeared to confirm these hypothetical divisions. Second was the development of thinking about race during the 19th century. Comparative linguistics, playing its role, discovered the difference between Indo-European and Dravidian languages, and this became proof of the ancient conquest by 'white' Aryans of 'black' Dravidians. This racial caste explanation turned assumptions about Indian society into facts.

Enlightenment theories established the link between caste in India and slavery, prior to the link between caste and race. Castes in India turned into the development of the old division between free people (Brahmanas, Kshatriyas, and Vysyas) and slaves (Shudras). In different ways, the comparisons of slavery and caste continue to be a crucial part of scholarly and political debates today. Dr. Ambedkar not only compared the situation of low-caste people in India with slavery but also thought that the former was worse than the latter.

### The Brushing of Jatis Under the Carpet: The British Example

Prakash Shah—in his essay 'Caste in a new light: Jati in British multiculturalism' (2022)—shows how 'multiculturalism' (supporting the rights of cultural minorities and fostering nationhood) and anti-discrimination laws in Britain paradoxically pose a threat to Indian culture. They create antagonism between groups on the basis of illegitimate criteria and penalise those falsely alleged to be upholders or proponents of the 'caste system'. The UK Equality Act 2010 pulls in 'caste' as a factor for discrimination and targets the *jati* phenomenon, a ubiquitous, ever-proliferating, and non-understood component of Indian society.

Scholars ignore the important social reality of *jatis* (about 4,000 of them today) in their discussions on caste. The Europeans used caste first for *varna*, then for both *varna* and *jati*, and even included terms like *biradari* or *kula*. It is therefore unclear what the term 'caste' specifically picks out in the conceptual language of caste studies. The classical conception of the caste system presupposes that *jatis* are oppressive hierarchical systems that are birth-based, endogamous with exclusionary purity rules, and occupationally restricted. The source of caste is Hinduism; Hindus are its carriers, and its perpetrators are Brahmins. These ideas, clearest in the writings of Christian missionaries, are present in secularised form through the social sciences. However, regarding the 'caste system', two centuries of research have failed to determine its rules, properties, consequences, relation to social conflict, and differences from other social organisations. Prakash Shah demonstrates how most social science theories attempting to pull *jati* into the caste system inevitably fail to describe Indian culture.

The Ghent School, initiated by Prof. Balagangadhara, gives the clearest explanation of *jatis* in its theory of cultural differences. It states that *performative* or *practical learning* dominates in Indian culture in contrast to the *theoretical* or *doctrinal dominance* of Western culture. The *jati* phenomenon clearly fits into the framework of the dominance of performative learning in Indian culture. Locating the theoretical or doctrinal foundations regarding the origin and proliferation of *jatis* is difficult. Though doctrinal criticisms of alleged anti-caste movements do exist, *jatis* constantly evolve as a result of criticisms and not as a result of contestations about doctrinal beliefs.

Scholars, activists, and institutions in Britain have supported legal mechanisms to attack the caste system. Shah demonstrates how both liberal and non-liberal accounts of multiculturalism in the framework of the classical conception of the caste system, as an agency to destroy caste, become intensely inimical to *jatis*. They all suffer from a poor conceptualisation of culture and, where theories of culture do exist, they sustain ideas of cultural differences within Western culture—as differences in the beliefs or doctrines of groups. The *jati* phenomenon is rarely mentioned. Scholars sometimes demand institutionalisation with rules and centralised authorities to define a cultural status of a group. Such a defined cultural status would then require protection. Such institutionalisation does not exist for the *jatis*, except for some structures for charity and legal purposes. This also becomes problematic for the *jatis*, as the author demonstrates when such structures come under the purview of discrimination.

Protection against caste discrimination is an extension of the policy against race discrimination based on colour implemented in the post-war years. The anti-discrimination legislation (the Equality Act 2010) proposed the addition of caste as "an aspect of race" alongside the other elements that had made up the idea of racial groups (colour, nationality, and ethnic and national origins). After intense debates, successive British governments refrained from implementing this constitutionally. The government accepted that there is "no universally accepted functional definition of caste" that can be relied on. However, in 2014, an individual case involving the Employment Appeal Tribunal (EAT) established a legal precedent on the issue. The decision, though acknowledging the lack of a sociological or legal definition of caste, held that this was not a hurdle to recognising caste as part of the provision on ethnic origin discrimination. Reliance on the case law allowed the UK government to avoid implementing the legislative provision on caste.

The campaign for legislation and case law against caste discrimination is aimed at stigmatising Indians as presumptive caste oppressors, says the author. The model failed Indians in Britain, whose public profile had moved to a relatively positive one in terms of employment, educational performance, family stability, and less crime involvement. The author explains how, in Britain, elusive attempts at the definition of caste only highlight our ignorance. For example, under what conditions can a *jati* be a caste and a sub-caste at the same time? The confusion on the meaning of the most basic of terms in almost all caste studies has remained glaring over the last two centuries.

### Modern Narratives of India: Hindutva as a Brahmanical Movement

Following the wins of the Bharatiya Janata Party (BJP) in 2014 and 2019, commentators have painted India as turning towards Hindutva—a hyper-nationalistic, fascist, autocratic, Hindu-supremacist, and a Brahmanical force causing great injustice to the minorities. Garima Raghuvanshy—in her essay 'On the explanatory adequacy of the Hindutva-as-Brahmanical model' (2022)—tackles the most significant anomaly facing scholars on the Hindutva movement's popularity amongst Dalit and "Other Backward Caste" (OBC) voters. How can a Brahmanical movement be the choice of those it seeks to oppress?

There are three central arguments to claim Hindutva as Brahmanical:

- The movement's leaders and ideologues have been and are Brahmins.

- The movement opposes caste-based reservation.

- It opposes proselytization.

This argument rests on the premise that a predominance of Brahmins within an organisation makes it Brahmanical. The author then demonstrates the fallacy of such arguments: the RSS does not maintain caste data of its members; scholars talk about "Dalit Brahmanism" and "OBC Brahmanism" too, following that 'Brahmanism' can exist without Brahmins. Being a description for a vast variety of individuals and organisations—even the 'upper-caste' leaders supporting the 'lower castes'—the term 'Brahmanical' loses its descriptive power. All three major political parties—Congress, CPI (M), and BJP—have been accused of being Brahmanical, but their different political outcomes compels us to conclude that the BJP's differentiating factor is not its Brahmanism.

Regarding opposing caste-based reservations as "casteist", Raghuvanshy says the fundamental problem is that it is almost impossible to find a consistent stance on caste-based reservations amongst the many organisations and individuals foundational to the Rashtriya Swayamsevak Sangh (RSS) and its many affiliates (Sangh Parivar). The BJP appears as determined as every other political party in India to increase reservations, legal protection, social welfare benefits, and political representation for Dalits and OBC communities. However, it is impossible to test the criticism that the BJP does all this in bad faith.

The anti-proselytization stance is another proof of its Brahmanism since conversion allegedly involves freeing oneself from the shackles of the caste system. This is an old idea perpetuated by Christian denominations across centuries and even by Dr. Ambedkar. However, this link is tenuous. Caste is apparently a part of Indian Islam and Indian Christianity too. Pro-reservationists want to extend caste-based reservations to the 'low-caste' converts on precisely this claim that discrimination against them does not seem to dissolve after conversion to Islam or Christianity. Thus, the views of both parties converge on the idea that the majority of religious conversions in India are not for religious belief but for economic and other reasons. The difference is only in the ethics and modus operandi of conversions.

Even if we accept that the Hindutva movement is Brahmanical, what accounts for the movement's significant popularity amongst Dalit and OBC communities? There are, again, three explanations:

- A crisis in Dalit politics

- Economic uplift has created a Dalit middle-class amenable to the Hindutva movement

- The movement aggressively woos Dalits and OBCs to gain popularity

The author highlights problems and contradictions in these explanations. Particularly striking is one claim that says Dalit is not a viable identity with no "shared experience" to unite the many communities considered Dalit. All of them seek hierarchy (as sub-castes and sub-sub-castes) at their respective levels once the "exogenous pressure" that forges an artificial unity goes away. If so, what do we make of the received view on the caste system, which tells us that Indians have five categories—of Brahmin, Kshatriya, Vaishya, Shudra, and Panchama—but with huge internal heterogeneity in each of the groups?

If economic betterment leads to Dalit communities supporting the Sangh Parivar, this implies that it is their economic condition or aspirations that play a decisive role in their political-ideological preferences, not their caste disadvantages or caste consciousness. This puts into question another important tenet of the received view on the caste system—namely, that economic betterment does not remove caste disadvantages because these operate according to an arbitrary birth-based caste hierarchy. Finally, the criticism that aggressive wooing of the Dalits by helping "marginalized people to develop themselves" should not count as criticism but democracy fulfilling its purpose.

As a logical end to the arguments, the author shows that caste systems and the resultant discrimination are not intrinsically or culturally Indian, but they have become a universal global phenomenon. The description of the Hindutva movement as Brahmanism itself and explanations of success amongst Dalit and OBC communities lead to multiple fundamental questions to the received view on the caste system, which in turn is the foundation of everything from terms such as 'Brahmanical', 'Brahmanism', 'upper-caste' and 'lower-caste', and even 'Hindutva'.

### *Atrocity Literature: A Major Blow to India Not Sufficiently Countered*

Nihar Sashittal does not strictly belong to the Ghent School, but his work is relevant to this book and takes forward the work of Sufiya Pathan and Dunkin Jalki. There has been a serious failure to understand and present claims based on empirical evidence for caste violence or atrocities. In an important paper—'The enigma of caste atrocities: Do Scheduled Castes and Scheduled Tribes face excessive violence in India?' (2022)—Nihar Sashittal disproves the almost "given" conclusion about "widespread and disproportionate violence" against the Scheduled Castes (SC) and Scheduled Tribes (ST) people. This widespread notion permeating all academic-political-legal-media discussions and international monitoring agencies, Sashittal points out, is due to serious conceptual fallacies and distorted statistics—cherry-picking, data illiteracy, floating numerators, and intuitive statistics.

As per the UN criteria, atrocity refers to three legally defined international crimes:

- Genocide

- Crimes against humanity

- War crimes

Strangely, in the present Indian legal language, atrocity has undergone "semantic expansion" and refers not only to heinous crimes but all offences like coercion, intimidation, trespass, harassment, cheating, forgery, insult or humiliation, disrespect to icons, and so on. "Concept creep," both "horizontally" capturing *qualitatively new phenomena* and "vertically" capturing *quantitatively lesser phenomena,* increases the scope of atrocity crimes. The semantic expansion gives it a split character: a dilated definition that includes all crimes, irrespective of the motives or severity, for collecting statistics on crimes; and a constricted definition for interpretation, giving the sense that these crimes refer to the most heinous and necessarily motivated by caste.

The use of the term 'atrocity' was rare through the decades of the 1950s and 1960s but caught on in the 1970s. As the author notes, mentions of 'atrocity' began to increase in these yearly reports, from barely any mentions in the report for 1969–70 to over three hundred times a decade later in the report for 1979–80. In 1974, the Ministry of Home Affairs (MHA) started collecting statistics on crimes against SCs or STs, beginning with the four most important violent crimes—murder, grievous hurt, arson, and rape—but would soon encompass all offences under the Indian Penal Code

(IPC). By the late 1970s and early 1980s, therefore, the term 'atrocity' had become an "omnibus identifier" for caste violence where the victims were specifically from a SC or a ST.

Statistics of only crimes against SCs and STs by non-SCs and non-STs, respectively, and not of any other populations, created the impression that these crimes exist only against SCs and STs, or that they exist against them in excessive proportions. As *ad hoc* adjustments in defining crime, since 2016 the records have started excluding crimes against SCs where STs are perpetrators and against STs where SCs are perpetrators. The Prevention of Atrocities Act, 1989 (PoA Act) defined a range of new offences that did not require establishing caste as a motive. The NCRB (National Crime Records Bureau) started publishing these records in 1994. Gradually, 'atrocity' became arbitrarily conflated with 'hate crimes'. As Nihar Sashittal writes in 'The enigma of caste atrocities: Do Scheduled castes and Scheduled Tribes face excessive violence in India':

> Many papers that analyze these crimes also nest their thesis within the literature on the caste system, as a result implying that these crimes are motivated by caste (see e.g. Bros and Couttenier, 2010; Sharma, 2012, 2015). That is despite the fact that the official and legal definitions of atrocity used in the collection of these statistics repeatedly confirm that the offenses are not necessarily based on caste considerations...... However, the non-SCs and non-STs who are the said offenders of these crimes, by definition, include people of all religious affiliations in India, including Hindus, Muslims, Christians, Sikhs, etc. The religious identity of the perpetrator is not recorded or published in the official statistics. Hence there is no systematic data on the religion of alleged offenders in the official statistics.

The author shows that less than 40% of the total cases of IPC crimes against SCs and STs and less than 30% of the total cases of crimes against them under all three laws combined (IPC, PoA of 1989, and Protection of Civil Liberties, 1995) are violent as listed by the NCRB. A significant proportion of lesser offences are not necessarily violent but are more susceptible to variations in reporting levels. This makes using them as proxies for the levels of violence fraught with inaccuracies. Apart from these, the misrepresentation of the data due to laxity and politicisation, mostly driven by advocacy groups, raises serious questions about the ethical use of crime statistics. Though underreporting has been a criticism of many studies, there is an equal possibility of overreporting, as the author demonstrates from the actual conviction rates.

The author draws on the statistical data of six major crimes (murder, rape, arson, kidnapping and abduction, dacoity, and robbery) and "hurt" as the seventh for the period between the mid-1970s and 2019 for crimes against SCs and STs. Strangely, 'hurt' was not included in the NCRB's list of violent crimes until 2016. Sashittal says that this was perhaps because the definition of this crime until 2014 did not differentiate between cases of "simple hurt", which did not necessarily involve injury and constituted the majority of these cases, from "grievous hurt" which involved aggravated form of hurt leading to significant bodily injuries. For each of the violent crimes, the rates for crimes against SCs and STs are significantly lower than the average rates of these crimes in the overall population in India. Significantly, the pendency times in courts have been lower for major crimes where the SCs and STs are victims.

'Atrocity' is a strong word that raises a sense of outrage and has deep implications for the fabric of society. Without denying the existence of discrimination and crimes in society, it is thus important to rigorously examine the claims about atrocities for rational policy implementation.

## Conclusion

Three phenomena have intertwined in the present understanding of the caste system. First is the continuing colonial story of the caste system, which made it almost morally obligatory for Indians to become immoral; the institutionalised hierarchy (forward castes, backward castes, scheduled castes, and so on) created by successive governments in their desire to achieve social justice without trying to understand what *varnas* and *jatis* actually mean; and, finally, the lived experiences and actual societal practices where *jati* makes the most sense and yet is least focused upon by caste scholarship. There are a lot of contradictions, fallacies, ambiguities, and confusion when the three mix to generate newer narratives with mainly conflict as their essence.

SN Balagangadhara (2012) says that the caste system is an example of "solid knowledge" that the West has about India. It is the origin of all evil. But looking from another perspective, it is an antique system that survived Buddhism, Bhakti movements, colonisation, Indian independence, world capitalism, and even globalisation. Thus, it must be a stable social organisation. In the absence of a centralised authority for enforcing the caste system, it appears to be an autonomous and decentralised organisation. The proliferating *jatis* show that it is a dynamic, self-reproducing social structure. Since it exists in all religions in India, it adapts itself to any new environment it finds itself in. Since it has survived under all political regimes, it must be neutral to political ideologies too.

Balagangadhara asks and says,

> Would not such an autonomous, decentralized, stable, adaptive, dynamic, self-reproducing social organization, also neutral to all political, economic, and religious doctrines and environments, be the most ideal system if one really existed as such? This most ideal caste system derives only from the present descriptions of the caste system and does not require any additional theories or assumptions. Hence, European narratives about the evil caste system may not amount to much.

The only lived reality of people in the Indian social system are the *jatis*. Thousands of these exist based on occupation, language, ethnicity, customs, traditions, and even gender, with their own rules of marriage, food, clothing, belief in gods, and so on. They have proliferated, dissolved, merged, split, and migrated up and down across time and geography on the social-political-economic scale. On the other hand, *varnas*, always four in number, have remained constant across centuries. Varna categories have been based on ideas like *guna* (nature), *swadharma* (duty), and *karma* (quality of work). Our huge body of scriptures, focusing more on duties than rights, has been inconsistent in placing them in the hierarchical order, but none deny any Varna or jati member the attainment of *moksha*—the ultimate purpose of human life. One of the most complicated, dubious, and confusing discourses on social structuring in India has been to correlate the *jatis* to the *varnas*.

As the Ghent School shows (*"Western Foundations of the Caste System"*), three important colonial ideas played an important role in consolidating the narrative of a 'caste system' in India: the Portuguese origin of the word *'casta'*; the Protestant criticism of Jewish and Catholic priesthood as the background of the colonial criticism of the Brahmanical priests; and the Aryan theory with its racial connotations. The word 'caste', most surprisingly, does not have an equivalent in any of the Indian scriptures. It was a Portuguese import applicable to their world when they landed on the shores of Goa. In the Iberian Peninsula, with the dominance of the Christian rulers, Jews and Muslims either converted or emigrated. 'Casta', based on the purity of blood ideas, divided the population into the New Christians—the recent converts —and the Old Christians—the older ones with pure blood. Caste grew in the Western context; *varna* and *jati* grew in the Indian context. It is a possibility that they might refer to different phenomena, and one culture studied another using its own framework.

Thus, as these scholars claim, there is no unity in the sets of phenomena clubbed together and described as either component parts, causes, or effects of the Indian caste system. The dominant Western story about the caste system is false if taken as an explanation of Indian society. The only hope for understanding our culture and reclaiming our harmony has to be found in the ideas of the Ghent School. Everything else only adds to the confusion and the increasing creation of fissures in society.

Chapter 6

# ON THE IMPOSSIBILITY OF REFUTING OR CONFIRMING THE ARGUMENTS ABOUT THE CASTE SYSTEM

*Sufiya Pathan and Dunkin Jalki*

## Introduction

Dr. Dunkin Jalki and Dr. Sufiya Pathan, two formidable scholars, are at the forefront of establishing new narratives in caste studies. They belong to the Ghent School initiated by SN Balagangadhara and have done a tremendous amount of work that calls the current understanding of the so-called caste system into question. The current discourses are not only tearing apart India's social fabric, but they are also giving India a bad reputation worldwide. Today, India is most closely associated with its pervasive and 'evil' caste system. The Ghent School critically contests this narrative, and the result is an important book titled *Western Foundations of the Caste System*, edited by Dunkin Jalki, Sufiya Pathan, Martin Fárek, and Prakash Shah (Palgrave, 2017). This chapter, however, is a summary of an important article written by Dunkin Jalki and Sufiya Pathan, titled "The Impossibility of Refuting or Confirming the Arguments about the Caste System" (2015), in which the authors elegantly demonstrate how every single criterion that forms the theoretical foundation of the caste system encounters serious problems when confronted with actual data from societal practices. Based on the insights of SN Balagangadhara, the article shows that the nature of the entity called 'the caste system' is such that we can neither confirm its existence nor deny it. And this has led to an unending proliferation of writings on this elusive topic. This is an incredible claim to make. Let us find out what it means.

### The Disjunction Between the Idea of the Caste System and the Ethnographic Data

Orientalist translations of Hindu texts—such as the *Institutes of Hindu Law: Or, the Ordinances of Manu* by William Jones (1798), describing a divinely ordained rigid system of hierarchy with Brahmins at the top and Shudras at the bottom—inaugurated the academic or social-scientific study of caste. Until the mid-nineteenth century, this 'textual' approach to the study of caste held sway. There was a stable consensus on many aspects of this "monstrous" system among scholars sympathetic and unsympathetic to India.

In the middle of the nineteenth century, caste studies took an important empirical turn, subsequently becoming the cornerstone for the sociological study of castes in India. The inauguration of the census in India in 1871 became an important starting point for the gathering of field data. A little later in the twentieth century, this led to the proliferation of sociological village studies in India and the unending collection of empirical facts from the ground, which was supposed to have proved the existence of the caste system. However, huge problems soon arose in the interpretation of the data. The complex data collected from the field gave a varied and unsatisfactory picture of the caste groups. The authors quote Henry Waterfield, who, in his *Memorandum on the Census of British India of 1871–1872*, writes, "Great pains have been taken by the writers of the several reports in the classification of the population according to caste. The result, however, is not satisfactory, owing partly to the intrinsic difficulties of the subject, and partly to the absence of a uniform plan of classification, each writer adopting that which seemed to him best suited for the purpose."

The troublesome disjunction between theoretical assertions about the caste system and empirical field evidence regarding caste persists to this day. In addition to the classical *varna* model, colonial officials gathering data in

1871 utilized a range of alternative classifications based on employment, nationality, and race. Because the fourfold *varna* system of the textual sources could not yield empirically valid results, numerous classifications were required. A British physician and an officer, William Robert Cornish, who supervised operations in the Madras Presidency, thought it was exceedingly doubtful that the Hindus were ever composed of four classes. Similarly, C. F. Magrath, the officer entrusted with the compilation of castes from Bihar, advocated for the rejection of Manu's now meaningless division into four castes. The struggle of colonial scholars to codify the caste system produced one of the most enduring axioms, which scholars have repeated for over a century—namely, *the caste system is extremely complex*. BR Ambedkar thought that the mysteries of the castes remain in the domain of the 'unexplained,' not to say of the 'ununderstood'.

He notes in *Castes in India: Their Mechanism Genesis and Development*:

> I need hardly remind you of the complexity of the Subject [of the caste system] [...] Subtler minds and abler pens than mine have been brought to the task of unravelling the mysteries of Castes; unfortunately it still remains in the domain of the 'unexplained,' not to say of the 'ununderstood'...I am not so pessimistic as to relegate it to the region of the unknowable, for I believe it can be known.

While missionaries at the beginning of the nineteenth century had some consensus about the four-*varna* model of the caste system, colonial officials and scholars did not share that consensus once empirical studies began. After 150 years of continuous scholarship, there is still no consensus on any of the fundamental aspects or properties of the caste system. The article presents the questions that SN Balagangadhara has raised elsewhere: Is endogamy (marrying within the same group) a characteristic of caste groups? Is it a hierarchy? Is violence a necessary consequence of the caste system or merely a historical occurrence? The empirical records of diverse Indian caste practices have, in fact, become a burden to caste studies rather than a source of strength. As more practices are recorded, more cracks have appeared in the theories of the caste system as more facts remain unexplained. Scholars do no more than develop more *ad hoc* hypotheses to account for the exceptions. Still, they never do one thing: question the validity of the classical theory of the caste system.

### The Classical Conception of the Caste System

Despite all the problems we have noted so far—the lack of consensus among caste scholars on the fundamentals of the caste system, for instance—there is some agreement on a textbook version of the system, allowing scholars to continue their studies without questioning its existence. Here is a version of that entity. As exemplified by various Social Science NCERT textbooks, the caste system comprises four fundamental properties: (a) occupational division sanctioned by rituals (Hinduism); (b) hereditary membership; (c) endogamy; and (d) exclusion of and discrimination against the 'outcaste' groups (which includes commensality and 'untouchability'). This is the Classical Conception of the Caste System (CCC).

However, as noted earlier, the article shows that two hundred years of field data have failed to establish the CCC. Not just that, as the article further shows, caste scholars of the past 100 years have frequently acknowledged this disjunction. In some sense, this shows the intellectual acuity or integrity of the past scholars. In the past five to six decades, caste scholars have stopped recognizing this as an issue, or when they do recognize it, they declare this disjunction as a unique feature of the system.

The article presents two examples—a micro and a macro—to demonstrate these developments. Let us begin with the micro example first.

### Endogamy: A Test Case

Consider the 'caste endogamy' as a test case to understand the arguments made so far. As the scholarly consensus goes, endogamy (marriage within one's own community) is an important feature of the caste system. As many scholars argue, it is the only characteristic that can be called the essence of the caste system, and which is peculiar to caste. However, a discussion of endogamy requires clarification on what constitutes an adequate unit of caste for marrying within one's own caste group. When caste scholars realize that castes (either the larger units like Shudra or the specific Shudra castes, like Kurubas of Karnataka) are not primarily in-marrying groupings, they are inevitably confronted with this difficulty. The article cites an interesting example from the field in Karnataka. Castes such as Kurubas and Nayakas have numerous 'sub-castes', like Haalu Kuruba, Jenu Kuruba, Sanna Kuruba, Dodda Kuruba, Kaadu Kuruba, among the Kurubas, and Myasa Nayaka, Valmiki Nayaka, Beda Nayaka, Uru Nayaka, and others among the Nayaka caste. Even to this day, these sub-castes prefer to marry only among themselves. If a caste is defined as an in-marrying group, what is the caste's primary unit: a caste, a sub-caste or a sub-sub-caste? Nayaka or Myasa Nayaka; Kuruba or Kadu Kuruba? Caste scholars provide an *ad hoc* answer by now recognizing sub-castes as real castes. If sub-castes are 'real castes', what about larger groups like Kuruba and Nayaka? What is 'Shudra' then? What unites multiple sub-castes into a unified whole, known as a caste?

One prominent scholar, Louis Dumont, admits that endogamy as a principal basis for caste would have to admit many exceptions. Thus, he considers endogamy to be "a corollary of hierarchy rather than a primary principle". That is, Dumont moves in the direction of saying that 'the caste system' (read, hierarchy) gives birth to 'endogamy', and not the other way round. Does this help us understand 'endogamy' or 'the caste system' any better? Readers are encouraged to delve deeper into this issue. What would help in their exploration, for sure, are some of the subsequent writings of Dunkin Jalki, Sufiya Pathan, and other students of SN Balagangadhara.

Let us continue with endogamy and the idea of an appropriate 'unit of caste' necessary to understand endogamy as a property of the caste system. Some castes in India follow an additional line of classification called *Gotra*, roughly translated as a lineage. Castes do not prefer to marry within the same *gotra*. A Vadakalai Iyengar Tamil Brahmin, for example, seeks someone who is (a) Brahmin (caste), (b) Iyengar (sub-caste), (c) Vadakalai (sub-sub-caste), and (d) not from the same *gotra*. (And we will not mention here the language and regional preferences when one is choosing a partner.) Is the Vadakalai sub-caste (and the caste system thereof), then, exogamous, endogamous, both, or neither? If you are not confused enough at this juncture, consider this: as per Dumont's logic, if endogamy is a corollary of caste hierarchy, so should exogamy be. We would leave it to the experts in the field to explain it to you. An acclaimed writer like BR Ambedkar would say that the essence of endogamy requires a "right understanding" and goes on to provide one, too. The so-called "right understanding" is that, in an originally exogamous (that is, marrying only outside the limits of a caste) Indian culture, artificial divisions created endogamous units. These endogamous units were further divided into smaller exogamous sub-units. If you are trying to figure out what this 'exogamous-within-endogamous-within-exogamous' caste system is, let us point out, as the article does, that this, we are told, belongs to the remote pre-historical past of India. What do we have today, then? 'Castes are endogamous units', plain and simple. If you feel we have aimlessly circled between square one and one hundred only to find ourselves back at square one, welcome to the field of caste studies. At least the reader will appreciate the popular adage now: 'The caste system is complex'. But where does this complexity lie? Is it in the field data or its explanations? Whatever the answer is, recall what the article had said earlier: the problems created by the anomalous observations on the field have now been dubbed characteristic of the caste system and, thereby, of Indian society itself. Do you wonder how this incredible situation came about? The answer is simple and seemingly very convincing. Because of Brahmins, of course. What else.

BR Ambedkar, in *The Triumph of Brahmanism: Regicide or the Birth of Counter-Revolution*, writes that "This isolation among the classes is the work of Brahmanism. The principal steps taken by it were to abrogate the system of intermarriage and interdining that was prevalent among the four *Varnas* in olden times." When scholars have failed to explain the 'complex caste system', it looks like they simply blame it on the Brahmins. And once this process is placed in some remote past, its alleged antiquity precludes it from any further historical or empirical examination. Suppose this is not sufficient to safeguard your arguments against any criticisms. In that case, scholars soon resort to another line of contention: they declare that the rationale and the enforcement of endogamy have shifted through time and context. Give these claims a little more moral shielding (*to question the idea of the caste system is to defend immorality in*

*India*), and the arguments about the caste system and its properties not only become indisputable but also everyone's responsibility to embrace and spread.

Endogamy has the 'property' of changing in such a way that it is both a property of the caste system and yet not describable as such. In short, the so-called caste system exists in India at times, in certain regions, in certain contexts, and for reasons other than caste. This is how one must speak about Indian culture if we are to hold on to the notion of CCC, despite noting obvious flaws in it.

### Are Arguments About Caste a Theory?

From a micro example, the article moves on to a macro example. It analyses Declan Quigley, a popular name in the field, who is supposed to have provided one of the sharpest critiques of research on caste, including the much-acclaimed work of Louis Dumont. Quigley notes that historical and ethnographic investigations have repeatedly demonstrated that our "theory [of the caste system] is at best inadequate, at worst wholly misleading. And yet it has remained remarkably resistant to attempts to modify it." In his essay 'Is a Theory of Caste Still Possible?' (1993), he notes that most of the so-called "defining characteristics of caste" are not, after all, unique to the "Hindu communities or to the ideology of Brahmanism," as caste scholars would have us believe.

Quigley identifies the issues that result from how empirical data is handled, since most caste theories appear to involve an unjustifiably arbitrary selection of facts. According to Quigley, caste scholars, as exemplified by Dumont, chose empirical facts that supported their beliefs and dismissed those that contradicted them. His solution begins by talking about the institutions of caste and accepting the usual aspects attributed to caste in CCC accounts. He arranges the empirical facts in such a way that none of the CCC's characteristics are diminished or ignored. He agrees that the institutions associated with caste are also present in varying degrees in other civilizations at different periods in history. All of these institutions, however, come together in a way that is unique to the Indian caste system.

How do they all come together? Quigley proposes a model of Indian society where the king is the central figure. According to him, the caste system is a product of a certain degree of centralization, which involves the organization of rituals and other services around the king and dominant lineages. A beehive-like structure, in which the king sits at the centre and "attaches other castes" and their services to himself, leads to the caste system. Thus, all kinds of inter- and intra-caste activities, competitions, and fights will continue as long as we notice them on the field.

In the ritual-based hierarchy, the castes that supply the king's priests will undoubtedly have a higher status than the castes that supply the farmers' priests. Untouchables who are subjected to oppression are excluded from the community entirely since their primary function is to act as scapegoats and to take out pollution (i.e., whatever threatens social order) beyond the community's boundaries. Similarly, some people in the area (renouncers, independent sects, and members of different ethnic groups) do not fit within the local caste system. Quigley thus explains all of the fundamental elements of the caste system.

In this arrangement, the closer a caste is to the king, the higher its standing (whether religious, economic, intellectual, or other social status). In today's post-monarchical Indian society, the crucial question is who the king is and who concentrates "ritual and other services" around him. The answer is that when Hindu kingship collapsed in the face of colonialism, well-to-do members of dominant castes became the new kings. What exactly is a "dominant caste", and how does one determine which caste is dominant? Quigley uses a beehive-shaped model to explain this phenomenon. In this model of social structure, it is not the Brahmins who are at the centre, but the elites or dominant castes who link with other castes "by using their resources to employ members of other castes to perform various services for them."

How does this model account for the whole caste system, which includes several 'upper' and 'lower' castes? Quigley answers that it is not only the dominant caste households that would strive to reproduce this pattern by employing members of other castes to perform various jobs for them. Obviously, the greater one's wealth, the greater one's ability to accomplish this. With an ingenious move, Quigley claims that no household is so destitute that it cannot afford to hire others to perform specialized ritual functions (funerals, marriages, or caste initiation rites). Thus, unlike other intellectuals, Quigley contends that the Brahmin caste does not occupy the top of the hierarchy but that all castes play this role. That is, any caste can serve as "ritual specialists"—i.e. priests—to another caste. The caste system, thus, is explained here as a collection of many little beehive-like assemblages involving many different caste households. There is a king-like dominant caste in the midst of each beehive-like arrangement, as well as a priest, various service providers, and a scapegoat (for taking out pollution or whatever threatens social order).

Since the caste system is an arrangement of priestly services and all other services around a dominant caste, in practical terms, the caste system comes into existence by virtue of anything and everything that Indians do in their day-to-day lives. Thus, caste is not a product of Hinduism; in fact, Hinduism is a product of caste organization. "This is a breathtaking argument", say the authors, Dunkin Jalki and Sufiya Pathan. For, what Quigley achieves here is worth at least a Padma Vibhushan, if not a Bharat Ratna. Why blame the Brahmins alone? In Quigley, immorality is now "made characteristic of every single Indian. That is, every single Indian now is responsible for bringing the caste system into existence."

Quigley is not saying anything new. Entire nineteenth-century writings on India and its culture are replete with such claims. For instance, here is an excerpt from Alexander Duff (in *India and India Missions: Including Sketches of the Gigantic System of Hinduism, Both in Theory and Practice*), who quotes a nineteenth-century missionary: "Idolatry and superstition are like the stones and brick of a huge fabric, and caste is the cement which pervades and closely binds the whole. Let us, then, undermine the common foundation, and both tumble at once, and form a common ruin." The story is replicated in twenty-first-century scholarship while proposing a radical break. This has been the story of the last 150 years: first, an exercise in critiquing the writings on caste only ends up attempting to bolster the CCC; and, second, the entire contemporary scholarship on caste is a rehash of the CCC ornamented with more empirical data and sophisticated language.

Instead of viewing the flaws as grounds for questioning the very foundations of the 'theories' of the caste system, scholars have either explained them away by developing a plethora of *ad hoc* hypotheses or just ignored them. What kind of conceptual entity must the CCC be in order to withstand 150 years of empirical (and conceptual) refutation? It is not unquestionably the poor faith or stupidity of generations of brilliant scholars trying to understand Indian society. SN Balagangadhara's hypothesis provides a better understanding, says the article.

### The Caste System as a Western Experience of India

As we have seen so far, scholars of the last 200 years have failed to prove the existence of the caste system. But can we at least refute its existence? This brings us to the claim that makes up the title of the article: such is the nature of the entity called the caste system that we can neither prove nor refute any claims about it. Why? According to SN Balagangadhara, the so-called caste system exists only in Western experience. When early European travellers and visitors arrived in India, they faced a culturally unfamiliar world. They had to transform this alien world into a familiar habitat gradually. During the adaptation process, they developed a variety of new signs, heuristics, shortcuts and maps (both cultural and geographical), which assisted them in making a home in India. The 'caste system' is a pattern in the imaginary lines they drew to connect the diverse entities they encountered in India— both real and those they imagined. No wonder, then, when scholars begin to provide empirical evidence to prove this entity, they generate more problems.

Let us understand some of the ingredients that have gone into the creation of the caste system. (Remember that, as Indians, we will never understand all the ingredients or the connecting lines here, as we do not share the European experience of India.) In its early stages, the caste system was portrayed as a tale of wicked Brahmins, their sinful acts, and oppressed people. This narrative, as SN Balagangadhara has shown, is about the Protestant Reformation's anti-clerical attitudes and how the Catholic Counter-Reformation reacted to them. Starting with Martin Luther, theologians across Europe were lambasting the Catholic Church and the role that priests played at the time. In analysing Indian society, Francis Xavier, a Catholic priest and a saint, appears to be reproducing Luther's criticism of Catholic clergy as early as 1543. Xavier portrays Parava and other local populations in his letter to Ignatius as illiterate, confused, destitute, and exploited, but intelligent people anxious to receive Christ. On the contrary, Xavier portrays Brahmins as unscrupulous priests who constantly exploit "the ignorant people whose blind superstitions have made them their [Brahmins'] slaves" in the name of religion. He ends his diatribe by declaring, "If it were not for the opposition of the Brahmins, we should have them all embracing the religion of Jesus Christ."

Multiple European writings about India were merely Europe's attempt to understand Indian society through the lens of their own culture: a church, a people, a "false" but nevertheless a religion, a class of exploitative priests, and so on. European writers have encountered such clever priests and superstitious masses all over India. The concept and the experience of the caste system arose out of these attempts. Since it is a line drawn to connect a new dot on the cultural map that the West created for its own use in navigating India, there was and is, no end to what gets counted as part of the caste system. Anything that can be connected to a previous dot with a new imaginary line, from texts to practices, irrespective of where or when it is found, will qualify as part of the caste system: whether it be an ISRO event or a temple inauguration, a cricket team composition or an election speech, a minor incident in an obscure novel of a boring writer or a real act of cruelty.

Balagangadhara says:

> The notion of such a system [the caste system] unified the British experience of India; they implemented certain political and economic policies based on their experience... In fact, this experience was of no particular object but constituted the basis of their going-about with the Indians. By creating such a 'system', the British lent stability, coherence,

and unity to their cultural experience. Both the caste system and the Indian religions are constructs in this specific sense. It is not as though colonialism brought 'Hinduism' and 'the caste system' into existence. The Europeans spoke about these entities as though they existed....

### Concluding Remarks of Jalki and Pathan

The underlying concept of the caste system has permeated not only our most basic observational accounts of Indian culture but also the way Indian institutions and the state function. Today, a critique of the 'caste system' and the subsequent reconceptualization of caste studies have many significant and profound ramifications. Despite being fundamentally faulty, the so-called theories of the caste system have been very effective. Whether professional or popular, the literature produced over the decades has largely been political rather than scientific. These erroneous perceptions of India have a tremendous impact on both India's internal policies and its international relations.

On the one hand, most of India's development activities from its 'Poverty Alleviation Programme' to its education reforms, are based on perceived caste inequalities. The question is not whether India has serious social issues (like economic inequality and growing social unrest) that require urgent and compelling attention. The point is, why should we presume that the caste system is to blame for these issues? What if, as Balagangadhara claims, the caste system is a Western experiential entity? On the other hand, unscientific social theories about India, particularly the caste system, have a significant impact on how the West sees and treats India. As a result, the dominant frameworks through which the world community addresses issues concerning India are centuries-old, unscientific, and overtly racist, albeit disguised as humanitarian. Even a scientific feat, such as a Mars mission, generates headlines in the British press, such as "How can poor countries afford space programmes?"

Balagangadhara cautions that, in a rapidly globalizing world, if what the West knows about India resembles what it claims to know about the caste system, it will result in a massive calamity. India will not fare much better if it accepts European perspectives on itself as scientific theories about its society and culture. It is high time to acknowledge the flaws in the concept of the caste system and the literature on it. The writers of this incredibly thought-provoking essay conclude by stating that we must now acknowledge the nature and dire repercussions of the wider Western project of portraying its experience in India as social-scientific knowledge about Indian culture.

## Chapter 7

# CONTINUOUS DISTORTIONS IN DISCOURSES OF INDIAN SOCIAL SYSTEMS

*Jakob De Roover and Marianne Keppens*

## PART 1
### The Caste System

Dr. SN Balagangadhara, in his book *Reconceptualizing India Studies*, says:

The 'caste system', the origin of all evils and an obstacle to all progress, is an example of the firm and solid knowledge which Europe and our social sciences have about India. But no one in the world has so far shown how and in what fashion 'the caste system' is a coherent system. It is only an assumption. As a system arising from antiquity, it survived Buddhism, Bhakti movements, colonization, Indian independence, world capitalism, and even globalization rather strongly. Hence, it must be a very *stable* social organization. It is an *autonomous and decentralized* organization, and no social-political regulation could eradicate the system. Hence, it must be a self-reproducing social structure. It exists in one form or another in all religious denominations and in different environments. Hence, it *adapts* itself to any new environment it finds itself in. New castes have come and gone, and hence, this system is also *dynamic*. Since it has survived under all political regimes, it must be neutral to political ideologies too. Would not such an autonomous, decentralized, stable, adaptive, dynamic, self-reproducing social organization, also neutral to all political, economic, and religious doctrines and environments, be the most ideal system if one really existed as such?

He continues:

> The British—like the current social sciences—put across meta-theoretical claims about the *jatis* in the form of a coherent structure called the 'caste system'. The evidence we routinely produce: the horror stories of 'caste discrimination'; the social humiliation of groups; the phenomenon of 'untouchability'; the presence of poverty, and such like. This phenomenon of discrimination is neither unitary nor monolithic. If its presence is evidence of the existence of 'the caste system', then the latter is present everywhere in the world. Discrimination, poverty, and social humiliation of groups are in slavery, in the feudal societies of Europe, in the capitalist societies of today, and so on. These phenomena are compatible with multiple social structures. On their own, these phenomena are not evidence of one specific social structure.

Sensationalism is the answer to the claim of a specific ideology. Some lines from Manu and some anecdotes from a few people constitute the evidence. Not one person has laid this alleged ideology bare; not one person knows what the components of this ideology are. By creating the 'caste system', the British did not describe what existed in Indian culture per se but constructed a pattern and a structure lending coherence to their cultural experiences. It is false because it falsely assumed that the experiential entity was a real entity in the world, and it is imaginary in that it does not have an existence outside the experience of Western culture. The present social sciences, a parrot-like reproduction of Western theories, whether Marxist, feminist, or post-modern, simply continue these discourses on the caste system.

What is the story behind the creation of the Brahmin myth and the idea of untouchability for social classification? After an initial background of ideas regarding reservations and portrayal of Brahmins as villains, this Chapter is primarily a summary of two extremely important papers from the University of Ghent faculty in Belgium: 'Scheduled Castes Vs.

Caste Hindus: About A Colonial Distinction And Its Legal Impact' by Jakob De Roover (2017); and the second, 'The Brahmin, the Aryan, and the Powers of the Priestly Class: Puzzles in the Study of Indian Religion' (2020) by Marianne Keppens and Jakob De Roover. These papers should be compulsory reading for any citizen interested in seeing a better portrait of the country. They show how false and imaginary narratives are creating deep fissures in the country, which tragically have no basis in social reality but are simply a continuation of the colonial legacy.

## Reservations

India is the only country in the world with a constitutionally extensive programme of positive discrimination in favour of such deprived groups as the ex-Untouchables and the tribals. There are seats reserved for them in parliament, state assemblies, public institutional jobs, and admissions in professional faculties. This was done to integrate deprived groups into the mainstream of political life, to remove the handicaps resulting from their centuries of neglect and oppression, and to break down the social barriers imposed by caste-conscious Hindus.

An initial fifteen-year programme now continues unabated and has almost become a permanent government policy. Dr. Bhikhu Parekh says that the policy of positive discrimination raises important questions about the nature of justice, the trade-off between justice and such other equally desirable values as efficiency, social harmony, and collective welfare, and the propriety of making social groups bearers of rights and obligations. It also raises questions about the nature and basis of inter-generational obligations, the redistributive role of the state, the nature and extent of the present generation's responsibility for the misdeeds of its predecessors, and the meaning and nature of social oppression.

Justice is generally an individualist concept, defined in terms of what is due to an individual based on his qualifications and efforts. If social groups are subjects of justice-based rights and obligations, the concept of justice must obviously be redefined in non-individualist terms. The conceptualisation of agency and responsibility must be in social and historical terms, so that we can demonstrate continuity between the past and present oppressors and oppressed. We must also analyse the nature of current deprivation and show that it is a product of past oppression and confers moral claims on the oppressed. These questions become particularly important in India, where the idea of positive discrimination has no roots in the indigenous cultural tradition and is much resented, says Dr. Bhikhu Parekh, a British academic of Indian origin, a Labour Party member of the House of Lords, and a retired Professor of Political Philosophy.

Parallels can be found with the positive discrimination of blacks in the US, but much work exists in these areas, unlike in India. There are few studies on the subject either challenging or articulating the theory of justice lying at the basis of reservations. Some work, however, relies on American literature without appreciating that the historical relations between caste Hindus and the 'Untouchables' and tribals bear little resemblance to those between American whites and blacks.

### Brahmins As Villains

The Brahmins have been responsible for creating a decadent society, said our colonial masters. The social sciences of today start their theories assuming the truth of the previous assumptions. Our textbooks describe the Brahmins as oppressors, exploiters, and creators of the caste system. Our academics and intellectuals keep repeating the story till it becomes a firmly established truth. The left-influenced academia with their favourite theories of exploiter and exploited, the missionaries, and the brainwashed intellectuals, continued the British story post-independence. Brahmins were neither rich nor powerful at any point in history. There were very few, if any, Brahmin rulers in India. The present social sciences just build up data to show the validity of previous truths; rarely do they turn back to ask whether these narratives might be false. What is the actual status of Brahmins in society?

Brahmins denying education is another myth. *The Beautiful Tree* by Dharampal is a revelatory book that shows the British themselves documenting that there was no truth in the story of denying education to anyone. In many feudalistic excesses, many non-Brahmin communities, as landowners, were responsible for oppressing the deprived. Somehow, our social sciences ensured that Brahmins became the prime villains in society. Many thousands of Brahmins lost their lives in the Islamic invasions and the Goan Inquisitions, as they were the primary target of the ire of the invaders. Francis Xavier made his position clear when he wrote to the king of Portugal, his patron, "If there were no Brahmins, all pagans would be converted to our faith," calling them the "most perverse people". The plight of thousands of Konkani Brahmins was no different from the Pandits of today's Kashmir. Modern Brahmins suffer from an unjustified guilt complex as it becomes almost impossible to counter the propaganda. So deep is the narrative that, in fact, some of the harshest critics turn out to be Brahmin-born.

Meenakshi Jain in *The Plight of Brahmins* writes that the Mandal Commission report marked the culmination of the attempt at social engineering that began with the Christian missionary (followed by British government) campaigns against the Brahmin community in the early part of the nineteenth century. The British distrusted educated Brahmins, whom they saw as a potential threat to their supremacy. Brahmins were prominent in the freedom movement, confirming the worst British suspicions of the community. Jain quotes an observer as saying that "seventy per cent of those felled by British bullets were Brahmins." Even though, for centuries, Brahmins and non-Brahmins had been active political and social partners, the fissures grew with the machinations of the British. The British, rewriting Indian history, started portraying Brahmins as oppressors and tyrants, keeping down the rest of the populace.

Some British observers concede that there was little difference in the condition of the Brahmin and the rest of the native population. H.T. Colebrooke wrote, "Daily observation shows even the Brahmin exercising the menial profession of a Sudra... it may be received as a general maxim, that the occupation, appointed for each tribe, is entitled merely to a preference. Every profession, with few exceptions, is open to every description of persons; and the discouragement, arising from religious prejudices, is not greater than what exists in Great Britain from the effects of Municipal and Corporation laws." The British census operations, especially those of Risley (1901), were determined to show race as the basis for the caste system. They destroyed the flexible *jati-varna* system and raised caste consciousness to a feverish pitch, inciting animosities and a general hardening of the system. Caste consequently became a tool in political, religious, and cultural battles.

Post-independence, many studies have shown Brahmins to be in a continuous downward spiral. Land holdings have decreased. Traditional occupations like family and temple priesthood, recitation of the Vedas, and practice of Ayurvedic medicine no longer prove remunerative nor command respect. A few decades ago (1978), the Karnataka state finance minister stated the per capita income of various communities: Christians: 1,562; Vokkaligas: 914; Muslims: 794; Scheduled Castes: 680; Scheduled Tribes: 577; and Brahmins: 537. Such is the deep antipathy to the Brahmin community that, despite consisting of hundreds of *jatis,* with no uniform rules of living and social interaction, success is a result of 'privilege' and individual faults are projected onto the whole community across the length and breadth of the country.

Meenakshi Jain quotes one study in the previous united Andhra Pradesh—*Brahmins of India* by J. Radhakrishna—which showed 55% of them living below the poverty line, 10% higher than other groups. This study also showed that the largest percentage of Brahmins were domestic servants. The unemployment rate among them was as high as 75%. The rest of the country is no different, perhaps. The British attacked our Brahmins for many reasons, but it is sad that the dominant leftist theories trapped in the exploiter-exploited paradigm failed to look beyond what the colonials said.

### *Defining the Dalit in Modern India: A Political and Legal Reality Only*

Jakob De Roover says in his paper that the colonials divided the society into 'Caste Hindus' and 'Depressed Classes'. The Indians simply continued with the narrative. In 1950, the Constitution passed a Scheduled Castes Order to include a set of groups for special benefits and provisions. The Supreme Court insists on guidelines for intelligible differentiae distinguishing the persons inside and outside the groupings. However, there seems to be no such clear criteria, even as the notion of untouchability does not really help.

This, paradoxically, applies to a wide set of practices that are prevalent in both groups.

The Constitution gives equal rights to all citizens and prohibits discrimination on grounds of caste, religion, race, sex, or place of birth. Particularly, special provisions appear to discriminate (*positive discrimination*) precisely on such grounds. Jobs in the public sector, lowering of qualifying marks in competitive exams, promotions in jobs, and protection by laws against any form of speech, deed, writing, or action under the PoA (Prevention of Atrocities) Act are forms of positive discrimination. Hence, the legal system of contemporary India gives a decisive role to the membership of a specific set of caste groups. It thus becomes crucial to identify which groups in Indian society belong to this set of castes. One must also presume that a deep exercise has taken place to identify these groups with reservations and exceptional legal provisions.

Lelah Dushkin, in 'Scheduled Caste Policy in India: History, Problems, Prospects (1967) says,

> The concept 'Scheduled Castes' is relevant only in a context of statutory provisions, government programs and politics. Outside this context, 'scheduled' castes do not exist. Rather, there is a diverse population, numbering 64.5 million at the last census, born into numerous communities, each with its own identity, traditions, and problems. While the communities may face similar problems, they are often deeply at odds with each other. They were 'scheduled' by the government and can be legitimately treated as a single category only when dealing with aspects of this relationship with the government.

The difficult question is: on what empirical grounds has the government transformed more than one thousand two hundred communities into a single category of Scheduled Castes?

SCs should encompass the formerly Untouchable Castes who suffered from severe social disabilities. In other words, the feature that distinguishes these castes and supports their special status is that of untouchability and the ill-treatment and backwardness related to it. This also functions as the official government criterion. In 1965, the Lokur Committee, established by the government to revise the SC lists, adopted "the test of extreme social, educational and economic backwardness of castes, arising out of traditional practice of untouchability." The decisive factors are not social or economic backwardness, age, income, or disability but a single characteristic of 'untouchability'. The Constituent Assembly, largely reproducing British legislation, never clearly defined 'untouchability' despite its decisive role in formulating caste legislation. In today's India, it is common to speak of 'Dalits' and 'Caste Hindus' as two distinct sections of the population. The criterion is clear: to count as a Dalit, one should be a member of one of the more than one thousand two hundred groups listed in the updated version of the Constitution (Scheduled Castes) Order. What was the rationale behind this Schedule's classification of castes?

### *The Beginning*

Let us begin in the beginning. In the Government of India Scheduled Castes Order of 1936, the King's Excellent Majesty ordered that "the castes, races or tribes specified in Parts I to IX of the Schedule to this Order shall, be deemed to be scheduled castes..." The schedules attached to this order provided lists of groups for every province of British India, which would from then onwards count as Scheduled Castes.

Broadly, there are two ways in which the order concerning the scheduled castes could have come into being: either it reflected the existing structure of Indian society or this order simply stipulated a division and classified groups of people accordingly. If the first was the case, then the Scheduled Castes Order should be the result of existing research in Indian society. If the second is true, then the caste legislation of contemporary India enforces a colonial decree that commands that the Indian population needs division along certain lines. Hence, it becomes crucial to find out how British officials drafted the list of SCs.

The Committee took what they called two "generally accepted tests of untouchability" from the previous 1911 Census Superintendents. These tests said that people who met the following criteria should count as Untouchables: "those who are denied access to the interior of ordinary Hindu temples" and "cause pollution, (a) by touch, (b) within a certain distance". This was confused, filled with circular logic, and begging questions right from the start. Many of the 'exterior' castes considered polluting by 'interior Hindus' also had strong caste organisations and included numerous individuals of substance and education. Many *jatis* in both the 'interior' and 'exterior' groups practised many forms of untouchability internally amongst themselves too. Two things remained clear throughout all this confusion: (a) the British were convinced that there must be a distinct class of Untouchable Castes external to the caste system; (b) they faced major obstacles in identifying this class and saying who was in or out.

It became clear that the term 'untouchability' did not refer to any recognisable characteristic(s) of some distinct set of groups and their members. Untouchability was to refer to a variegated series of practices and situations. Sometimes, it was banning entry into temples, sometimes it was refusing to take water from some groups, sometimes it was related to the custom of providing separate cups for different groups, sometimes it was taking a bath after physical contact, and sometimes it was cleaning the house after some member of a group entered there. It could also indicate the fact that a group lived in separate quarters at the borders of a village. The list was never exhaustive, and other practices were added to it. During the censuses and in the committee reports, it turned out that some such practices existed in certain parts of India but not in other parts. 'Untouchability' covered a set of actions or practices but remained unclear which common trait those practices shared.

### *Parliament Debates*

The Parliament debates after independence had severe difficulties in classifying these depressed classes, who were at the receiving end of untouchability. Dr. Banerjee of Bengal, for example, asked for clarification on the word 'untouchability'. For him, in the last 25 years, the word had had different connotations, leading to confusion: sometimes it means merely taking a glass of water; sometimes it is in the sense of admission of 'Harijans' into temples; sometimes it means inter-caste dinner; sometimes it means inter-caste marriage. Mahatma Gandhi, the main exponent of 'untouchability', used it in various ways and on different occasions with different meanings. What is the real implication of this word? This was a vexing issue.

The situation became even more complicated once one considered the fact that practices labelled as 'untouchability' are also visible in the interaction among so-called 'high-caste Hindus'. Within the Depressed Classes too, the different practices that came under the term 'untouchability' were also among and between these castes. Inevitably, this would also count as 'untouchability' on the ground of religion or caste. But how could this characteristic then distinguish the 'Untouchables' from the 'Caste Hindus'? Basically, the claim is that if one human being refrains from touching or approaching another human being, this becomes caste-based untouchability when the former belongs to the Caste Hindus while the latter belongs to the Untouchable Castes. And how can one recognise these Untouchable Castes? Well, they are the ones that are subject to caste-based untouchability. This route leads us into a vicious circle.

In May 1949, in the end phases of the Assembly's work, Mahavir Tyagi sharply said that the term 'Scheduled Castes' is fiction. There is a variety of castes with different problem situations collected from various provinces and put into one category. He questioned how Dr. Ambedkar, with his education and standing, belonged to the Scheduled Castes. He said there were plenty of Brahmins and Kshatriyas who were worse off than some belonging to the Scheduled Castes. It is the individual or the family that gets the benefit, not the whole caste, Tyagi said emphatically. Another member, Mullick, conceded that it was impossible to give a cut-and-dry definition of untouchability.

### Internal Feelings of Odium

This evolved into a common indication of 'an internal feeling of odium' expressed in a variety of practices, different in different parts of India, which show that these castes have their political rights refused. 'An internal feeling of odium' that expresses itself externally opens another set of problems due to its vague nature. How could one ever assess which internal feelings lie at the root of external behaviour? BR Ambedkar himself had difficulties identifying the Depressed Classes. He agreed to confine this term to

Untouchables only, but intended to be even stricter. He wanted to exclude those for whom the same kind of consciousness of social discrimination does not exist. These were likely to take advantage, he said.

Dr. Ambedkar classified all practices as 'untouchability', sharing the common characteristic of being outward registers of the same inward feeling of defilement, odium, aversion, and contempt. Now, inward feelings of odium, aversion, and contempt exist among all kinds of people towards all kinds of other people. Therefore, merely being the object of such inward feelings or 'suffering from social odium' cannot, by itself, characterise the condition of the Untouchables. These inward feelings of odium among 'the Touchables' expressed outwardly in their behaviour towards 'the Untouchables' are decisive. How then could he already know who the Touchables and the Untouchables are?

Dr. Ambedkar made the distinction between applying the test of 'causing pollution by touch' in its *literal sense* and in its *notional sense*. In the *literal sense*, untouchables are only those persons whose touch causes pollution and hence is avoided; if touch is unavoidable, then a purification process ensues. In the *notional sense*, an untouchable is a person who belongs to a class commonly held to cause pollution by touch, although contact with such a person may, in local circumstances, not be avoided or may not necessitate ceremonial purification. Thus, Ambedkar's comments on 'ascertaining the Untouchables' reflected an entire story about Hinduism and the caste system. He knew that 'untouchability' would be present wherever there were Hindus; he knew that there were Touchable and Untouchable Hindus all over India; the question simply was how to count the Untouchables. Here, no uniform test of 'untouchability' is applicable, since all the practices labelled as 'untouchability' were expressions of the same odium and contempt. All of this shows how obscure the notion of untouchability was.

### *Was It an Age-Old Division?*

In the 1930s, the division of the Hindus into 'Touchables' and 'Untouchables' was presented as though it were an age-old social division sanctioned by the Hindu religion and reinforced by its orthodox followers. Both Gandhi and Ambedkar, ironically on two sides of the fence, perpetrated this notion of depressed classes. Was the distinction between Caste Hindus and Untouchables really an age-old division within Hindu society? No, it was not. Simon Charsley has shown that the notions of 'the Untouchables' and 'Untouchability' were created by the British administration in the early twentieth century. When Sir Herbert Risley became Commissioner for the 1901 Census in India, he sent to every Census Commissioner, as a part of his standard scheme, four Sanskrit-named 'Shudra' categories, of which the last was 'Asprishya Shudra', explained as "castes whose touch is so impure as to pollute even Ganges water". This system failed, and the category of 'not-to-be-touched Shudra' did not prove to be useful. His major criterion of the Brahmins' willingness to take water was irrelevant in many regions.

The decision to classify certain people in Indian society as 'Untouchables' cannot have been a matter of administrative convenience; in fact, the census project showed that it brought inconvenience to the administrators. Over the years, the same problems have come up repeatedly. That is, some framework made the bifurcation between Caste Hindus and Untouchables appear self-evident despite its inadequacy. As some administrators admitted, the caste census merely mirrored the classificatory scheme they had decided to use and not the structure of the society that was its object. Basically, the census research revealed that the structure of Indian society did not correspond to the conception of the caste hierarchy it had started out with. In the process, officials and scholars stumbled upon the problems that have dogged the study of caste to this day. They could neither provide a coherent hierarchical classification of castes nor identify the Untouchables or 'exterior' castes in any consistent way. They drew upon the classical account of the caste system as a conceptual framework for their studies, policies, and laws in India, but the results constituted a massive exercise in falsifying this account.

### Modern Indian Understanding

Nevertheless, the post-Independence Government of India continued to rely upon these results to decide which groups should be Scheduled Castes. The 1965 Lokur Committee drew extensively from what it called "the standard works of reference on castes and tribes by recognized authorities." It was referring to the works of British officials and old colonial census publications. As recently as 2012, the Standing Committee on Social Justice and Empowerment was unhappy to note that the Registrar-General of India "is referring to old literature of the pre-independence era in determining the socio-economic status of castes for clearing proposals for inclusion/exclusion of castes and there is no new literature on the demographic and economic status of castes." It points out that there are basic cognitive problems confronting the currently dominant account about Indian society and the so-called 'caste system' and its division of the Hindus into 'Touchables' and 'Untouchables'.

Today, commentators frequently react with indignation when one points out the problems confronting the classical account of the caste system. Worse, questioning this orthodoxy and its hackneyed claims about 'the plight of the Dalits' is often denying the existence of injustice in Indian society. Injustice, inhumanity, and other oppressions do occur, but to consider an overarching framework to explain these is an intellectual misunderstanding bordering on dishonesty. These situations and events cannot be coherently conceptualised in terms of the 'caste system' and its oppression of the 'Untouchables' or 'Dalits'. There appear to be no intelligible differentiae that distinguish all the persons grouped together as SCs from others excluded from that group. Indeed, the class of Scheduled Castes exists, but only in the Indian legal and political system. 'The King's Excellent Majesty' ordered how the people of India should have a division into Scheduled Castes and others, and we continue to follow the legacy by caste legislation to this day.

## PART 2
## THE POWER OF THE BRAHMINS IN INDIAN SOCIETY: UNINTERRUPTED NARRATIVE

The leaders and intellectuals of post-colonial India not only succumbed to the colonial account of the 'caste system', but also accepted the social divisions among the people created by British legislation. It is as though they felt compelled to transform the tenuous distinctions inherent in the colonial account into existing social divisions in India. Marianne Keppens and Jakob De Roover, in their recent powerful article 'The Brahmin, the Aryan, and the Powers of the Priestly Class: Puzzles in the Study of Indian Religion', show how the classical account of the Brahmin priestly class and its role in Indian religion has seen remarkable continuity during the past two centuries. *Christian-theological* ideas concerning heathen priesthood and idolatry; *racial notions* of biological and cultural superiority and inferiority; and *anthropological speculations* about 'primitive man' and his 'magical thinking' explained the role of Brahmins in Indian society. Twentieth and twenty-first century scholarship rejected the explanations, but the core claims about Brahmanical power continue as facts.

The past centuries saw many shifts in the frameworks for the study of humanity. Most of our theories about human physiology, psychology, society, and politics have changed substantially. Hinduism now refers to a body of culturally related traditions rather than one religion; the Aryan Invasion Theory has severe deficiencies; Christian theology and Biblical chronology no longer dominate the social sciences like archaeology, linguistics, or history; racial theories of superiority and inferiority stand rejected, as do evolutionary accounts tracing the development of religion from the primitive to the civilised. Yet the account of the Brahmin and his role in Indian religion stays unchanged.

### The Basic Account of The Brahmins

What is this basic account which has stood like a rock across centuries? As a priesthood, the Brahmins claim to mediate between the devotees and their deities by means of sacrificial rituals. They are the creators of a four-tiered hierarchy of classes, which assigns the highest position and status to their own priestly class and the lowest to the Shudra, or servant class. Traditionally, the learned Brahmin is the recipient of many privileges; in fact, he was a higher being for lesser humans to revere. As a minority lacking military prowess and political and economic power, the Brahmins drew on their ritual status to seek a special alliance with the warrior-ruler class. They reduced the lower castes to a state of subjugation by imposing all kinds of restrictions, such as denying their members access to the Vedas and treating them as impure or untouchable, and generally sought to prevent upward mobility between castes.

Consistently over the last few centuries up to the present day, these claims, commonplace in Europe and India, continue prominently in introductory works, encyclopaedia entries, and other sources as elementary facts about the history of Indian culture and religion. What accounts for this? Does it originate in the West's inclination to represent 'Eastern' cultures as superstitious counterparts to its rational self; or in the colonial power leading to hegemony in the knowledge production of Orientalist scholarship; or in the theological and ideological framework of European scholars? There could be some other reasons too.

## Dominant Explanation for Two Centuries

Since colonial times, several interrelated elements came together to explain '*The Mystery of Brahmanical Power*' in this field of study: the *Aryan Invasion; ritual homology; and the varna system.* However, in the last three decades, scholars have increasingly challenged this thesis. The classical account traces the power of the Brahmins to their ritual status and expertise, which gave them apparent control over invisible forces in the natural and social world; made them indispensable to tribal leaders and warriors seeking wealth, prestige, and success in warfare; and sustained their supremacy in a *varna* system that expanded as the Indo-Aryan invaders subjugated the indigenous population starting in 1500 BCE.

The Brahmin priest derived his authority from his access to a network of rituals and the capacity to control invisible powers, attributed to him by superstitious 'magical-thinking men' who believed his rites and spells could cause events in the natural and social world. In the late Vedic era, this system evolved into a four-tiered hierarchy of *Brahmins* (priests), *Kshatriyas* (warriors-rulers), *Vaishyas* (traders, artisans, and landowners), and *Shudras* (servants). The conquest of the local tribes living in India relegated them to the lowest rungs. To garner legitimacy for this social order, the Brahmins claimed it was divinely ordained and rooted in a primordial sacrificial ritual.

## *Challenges to The Model*

Each of these elements has been severely challenged by recent changes in the study of Indian culture. There is no longer an invasion model. Either it is migration or even a reverse migration out of India based on archaeological, textual (Rig Veda), and linguistic records. How could peaceful migration and prolonged contact between groups account for the growing dominance of the Vedic religious and social order? How did the Brahmanical elite keep its social ideology in place for hundreds or even thousands of years and spread it among substantial populations without building an institutional apparatus for sustaining, disseminating, and implementing this social ideal?

Scholars have now drawn upon the notion of *'homology'*. The priestly class spread its social ideology by encoding it into creation myths and sacred texts, thus providing the mystifications and legitimations that supported an extremely rigid, hierarchic, and exploitative social system. In this way, their normative hierarchy had an inscription into the natural order and was presented as stable, self-evident, and beyond dispute. Such explanations are variations on a general 'theory', where a priestly elite promotes a social order under the guise of religion and instils false consciousness into the populace. One author, Brian Smith (1994), says that priests who wielded magical knowledge could, by means of the substitutes the *varna* system provided, control the natural, supernatural, and social worlds from within the confines of their ritual world. Another expert on ancient India, Johannes Bronkhorst (2016), claims Brahmins had supernatural powers by collecting powerful formulae in the Atharva Veda.

Authors repeatedly appear to attribute extraordinary powers to the Brahmin priestly class. These magical powers protected kings and had them accede to Brahmanical supremacy, and when the Brahmins lost the support of the ruling classes, they could always fall back on their supernatural powers. Extraordinarily, this priesthood succeeded in having other groups endorse its exceptional status—even though several had far more military, political, and economic power. The status of the Brahmins was thus derived from their power-giving knowledge of rites and spells.

The authors also suggest that the Brahmin class was able to show that it possessed forms of power-providing knowledge. In summary, either the people living in India could not see the obvious, or the Brahmins had the capacity to deceive people into seeing and believing what was not there, or a combination of both. Contemporary scholars cannot possibly mean to ascribe supernatural powers to the Brahmin class, yet this is what their sentences do. The classical account *presupposes* that Brahmins must have possessed extraordinary powers.

### Classical European Accounts of the 16<sup>th</sup> and 18<sup>th</sup> Centuries

With new travel reports in the sixteenth and seventeenth centuries, the Brahmins were transformed into representatives of false religion and idolatry. Like in other pagan nations, they were responsible for the sacrifices to the idols and prone to all the sins of a corrupted clergy. The influential sixteenth-century humanist Justus Lipsius, for instance, included the Brahmin priest in a work intended for the teaching of princes to show how the maintenance of superstition would be an irremediable error for any Christian prince. In the following centuries, more details would add to this descriptive scheme, but its core remained invariant. The classical account of the Brahmin has remained stable during the past two centuries.

A popular Dutch periodical, Weekblad voor kinderen, was published on a weekly basis from 1798 to 1800 by Johannes Van Der Hey in Amsterdam targeting children between six and twelve years old. In 1799, it devoted one of its issues to the inhabitants of the Indian Subcontinent (*De Indiaanen*). It says, in summary:

> …The Hindus divide into tribes, which are the 'castes'. Of the four main castes, that of Brahmins is the noblest and most distinguished and enjoys the highest of privileges. In the religion of the Hindus, people consider the 'idle Brahmin' holy, while 'the useful servant' is 'scandalously impure'. There is also a fifth caste of Parias', which consists of the refuse of all the others; they cannot touch others, cannot enter temples and markets, and cannot even walk the streets where Brahmins live. These two tribes or castes of the Hindus, namely that of the Brahmins and that of the warriors, are supposedly pure descendants of the Caucasian lineage of the

human species. The two lower castes have a Mongolian origin or originate from the intermingling of both these main lineages of humankind…

Firstly, this was presented as facts about the world. In the arrangement of its material, the magazine attributed the same cognitive status to its account of 'the Indians' as it did to its descriptions of metals, geographical regions, plants, and snakes. It was transmitting *elementary information* about the world to children aged between six and twelve. Secondly, the publication of such an account compels us to look for the sources of such knowledge. There were hardly any texts translated from Sanskrit into European languages; the information about India came from classical Greek sources, travel accounts, and reports by Christian missionaries, merchants, and officials. In this case, the author's claims were from a handful of works published in French and English in the decades before: second-hand descriptions and reflections by two French philosophers, a controversial work compiled by a former Jesuit, Nathaniel Halhed's *Introduction to A Code of Gentoo Laws (1776)*, and observations of a few European travellers.

Thirdly, the magazine clearly placed its themes within a larger framework. The editors explicitly wrote that they aimed to educate the children into "good people, citizens, and righteous Christians." The doctrines of the Brahmins "clearly show some traces of the great truths concerning the eternal and immutable existence of God, the creation of the world, and the fall of humanity from its original state of innocence and happiness." Such observations relied upon the Christian idea that all of humanity had once upon a time been aware of the Biblical God and his relation to humanity, while the more civilised nations retained fragments of this knowledge. Fourthly, the same religious framework gave shape to the author's moral assessment of the Hindus. He asked his readers: "Should one not be astonished and filled with sadness, esteemed pupils, when one sees that people who know of such elevated truths as God's unity, eternity, immutability, and omnipresence can also believe in ridiculous stories?" Finally, in his explanation of the origin of the four castes, the author reveals racial notions of the superiority and inferiority of nations. The northern part of the globe, the author argued, is suitable for inhabitation by people created by their Creator to exercise their own powers towards becoming more perfect and more susceptible to rational and moral greatness and true happiness.

More than two centuries later, we possess far more empirical information about Indian culture than the eighteenth century had access to, and yet the core elements of his description of the Brahmins continue as facts about Indian culture in our times.

### Demons and Idolatry

In the early Middle Ages, the 'Brachmanes' were the legendary wise men. That the Brahmins traditionally constituted a priesthood or priestly class is one of the central claims of the classical account, which appears to be as self-evidently true as it was two centuries ago. How did this transition from wise men to evil priests happen? By the nineteenth century, the Brahmin was the local Indian incarnation of a larger category: that of 'the heathen priest'.

Along with references to the ancient Brachmanes of lore, similar claims about the modern Brahmins populated the philosophical dictionaries, universal histories, encyclopaedias, and other popular texts of the eighteenth century: these priests not only claimed to be masters of magic, augury, and rites, but also posed as mediators between the people and God; they kept the secrets of religion to themselves and deceived the other pagans; the elevated status attributed to them resulted in their excessive ambition and pride. Bringing together notions of magic, sacrifice, superstition, and idolatry into a coherent whole, this account was easily digestible for educated Europeans. In brief, the theologians argued that the worship of false gods and idols consists of *trafficking with demons*. That is, when the 'magi' or pagan priests sacrificed to idols, they were addressing demons, evil spirits, and fallen angels who had several kinds of powers and acted upon the world. These ritual experts learnt to invoke the demons by rites and incantations and thus to have them serve the desired ends.

This was the standard Christian explanation of the worship of false gods: so many attempts to invoke demons and have them effectuate desired events in the world. It explained how heathen religion could sustain and reproduce itself on an everyday basis. Why would people keep worshipping deities and revering the priests who performed the rites if the idols were merely dead objects and the priests were only impostors? The account answered this question: idolatry had the capacity to reproduce false religion and keep it in place because its magic invoked demons who could either cause the desired effects or instil this illusion in the idolaters.

This account of idolatry was not some fanciful speculation by a handful of church fathers. For more than a millennium, it served as a standard explanation for the everyday reproduction of heathen religion in pagan societies and for the seductive power held by similar practices even in Christian societies. Along with the variations, its basics kept recurring in Western thinking well into the modern era. They became commonplaces about idol worship, the power of sorcery, and the agency of demons, which were central to several debates and practices in European history. The long-lasting concerns about witchcraft and the accompanying practices of persecution drew upon these commonplaces, as did the early modern descriptions of the Brahmin class as the priesthood of Indian heathendom.

### *Moving Across the Centuries: Demons Dissolve and Aryans Appear*

In early modern scholarship, however, the demons gradually ceased to play the role of existing agents whose actions had effects on the world. Consequently, the causal forces became a variable or placeholder that needed some other explanation. The invisible spirits no longer counted as a genuine connection between rites and events in the world. Rather, pre-modern 'primitive pagan' humans lived under the *delusion* that such causal forces operate in the world because of their magical and pre-scientific thinking. During the nineteenth century, this explanatory scheme also entered scholarship about ancient India and its Brahmanical religion.

The idea that the performance of rituals provided this class with exceptional powers was closely related to the growth of the Aryan Invasion Theory during the nineteenth century. Today, it is widely known that Biblical ethnology fed this 'theory' and attempted to trace the descent of human nations and languages from the sons of Noah. Author after author, Max Mueller included, built detailed discourses based on speculations and minimal evidence on the invading Aryans subduing an indigenous dark population and driving them south. Shudras were the original inhabitants of India, whom the superior Aryans enslaved, making them an inferior or external caste.

In this context, the Brahmin priesthood acquired its prominent position by monopolising the knowledge needed for performing rituals, pleasing the military powers, and keeping the original inhabitants as Shudras. The story about the Brahmins' arrogation of a supreme, or even divine, status soon spread across Europe. While some details differed, the core elements remained the same. One presented the Aryans as a civilised family of tribes, possessing the expansive vitality of the Japhetic races (descendants of Japhet, one of the three sons of Noah), who had encountered the black aboriginal peoples of India, probably Chamites (descendants of Cham). Even the early *Encyclopaedia Britannica* subscribed to the story of Brahminical sacrificial power, laying claim to supreme authority in regulating and controlling the religious and social lives of the people.

In these nineteenth-century accounts, the Christian belief that the heathen priesthood manipulated invisible forces through its rites and incantations transformed into a 'meta-level' explanation: the Brahmins *claimed* that they possessed this power, and the superstitious people believed in this *delusion*. The earlier religious account of the functioning of idolatry took on a new form in these 'scientific' studies; it was now the belief system of the ancient Indians.

### *Protestant and Enlightenment Themes*

This was generally a reflection and repetition of the anticlericalism that pervaded the eighteenth- and nineteenth-century intellectual world in Europe, especially its Protestant and philosophical circles. This was a general critique of the priesthood, which ascribed a similar degenerated status to the Roman Catholic clergy and the ritual experts of non-Western religions. Hence, the Brahmins were cunning priests, posing as privileged mediators between man and god, who had used their monopoly on ritual knowledge to arrogate a position of supreme authority over the people's religious and social lives. The second conceptual scheme at the heart of the nineteenth-century accounts was the discourse about the biological and cultural superiority and inferiority of races, which was so popular in this era. The conquering of an 'inferior', 'dark-skinned' race by another 'superior' one with a lighter skin; the vitality of the Japhetic races; the low cultural level of the indigenous population and its subjugation as the lowest rung of the caste hierarchy; the attempt of one race to avoid contact with another out of fear of the corruption of its faith—each of these explanatory factors derived from this framework and would fail to make sense in its absence.

Both conceptual schemes—the theological and the racial—were crucial to the speculations about the Vedic people and the rise of its Brahmin priesthood. If we were to remove them, little would remain but a handful of just-so stories about the ancient history and tribal warfare of India. There were scholars who disbelieved the story completely, like Lieutenant-Colonel Low (1849). The story was quite implausible to them. As Colonel Low says, "…if indeed that even would be sufficient, that the then occupants of India were a savage, unlettered, and unreligionized race or races, ready to view the strangers as demigods, and to bend their necks to their civil and spiritual domination—and to yield up their native freedom to the unmitigated thraldom of caste…"

The idea of Brahmanical ritual power travelled from the nineteenth to the twentieth centuries, transmitted by key authors such as Hermann Oldenberg. His account of ancient India was a familiar story about the evolution of religion through different stages, starting with the savage stage, where magicians manipulate the many spirits that populate the world and animate its objects. Later, the spirits give way to divinities, personifications of natural forces, from whom favours materialise by means of sacrifice and prayer. Vedic religion is still a barbaric one, Oldenberg wrote, since it has not yet taken the step of incomparable importance in the evolution of religion—the association of the ideas of God and good. The art of properly performing these sacrifices and prayers is the main theme around which the whole spiritual life of the poets of the Rig Veda revolves, according to Oldenberg.

Within this larger framework emerged the idea that the Brahmins had created a "pre-scientific science" of correlations or homologies (Oldenberg 1919). That is, these priests postulated a web of hidden interrelations connecting the ritual realm to the cosmic and human realms; drawing on their privileged access to this esoteric system, they claimed the power to perform rituals that obtained the desired effects. This ritual science, according to Michael Witzel (2003), based itself upon the strictly logical application of the rule of cause and effect, even though its initial propositions (e.g., 'the sun is gold') are something that is unacceptable. This idea is reproduced in more recent accounts of ancient Indian religion and ritual homology.

### *Background Cognitive Cluster of Ideas*

The above helps identify the background cognitive conditions under which Brahmanical power could appear sensible and plausible. The cluster of ideas was: the Aryan conquest of racially and culturally inferior people and the latter's subordination as the lower class(es); the priest's capacity to manipulate deities and spirits by means of sacrifice and prayer; his arrogation of social supremacy through a monopoly on ritual knowledge; the evolution of religion from a primitive belief in invisible forces to a more elevated spiritual faith in God; and so on. Christian doctrine, Biblical ethnology, and racial theories today have no place in the scientific study of religion, yet the classical account of the Brahmin largely survives, even though it originally depended on concepts drawn from these frameworks.

The mystery of Brahmanical power seems to emerge from the discarding of these concepts: neither 'heathen priesthood' and 'superstition' nor 'Aryan conquest' and 'magical thinking' can account for the Brahmins' extraordinary status, since both sets of notions have been rejected by twentieth- and twenty-first-century scholarship. To fill in the missing link, scholars have a compelling need to introduce an alternative force that accounts for the connection between the priesthood's ritual role and the success of its social ideology. This is where 'ritual power' and 'homological thought' arrive. The scholars are in a double bind: the explanatory structure of their accounts requires attributing supernatural powers to the Brahmin class but, in our day and age, they cannot do so in explicit terms; hence, there is ambiguity in explaining Brahmanical power and status.

## Some Explanations for this Continuity

How can we explain their remarkable continuity and stability, given the collapse of the cognitive conditions under which they survived and flourished from the seventeenth to the twentieth centuries? One type of explanation would be that continuity at the level of factual observation (first-order facts) goes together with discontinuity at the level of theory formation (second-order explanations). This route, however, clashes with the consensus that emerged from philosophical and historical studies of science during the past 75 years. Today, we know that scientific research does not produce a collection of theory-independent facts, which competing theories then explain; instead, our observations take the form of descriptions already structured by theoretical schemes. Words such as 'religion', 'priest', 'mediators', 'sacred', 'worshipper', 'caste', and 'ideology' are not theory-neutral observational terms, but theoretical terms embedded in larger clusters. Hence, the resulting descriptions of 'facts' concerning Indian culture must be structured by such larger theoretical schemes.

In this direction, the work of Imre Lakatos, a major twentieth-century philosopher of science, could help us find an alternative theory for this remarkable continuation of the Brahmanical supremacy idea. Lakatos characterised scientific progress in terms of competition between research programmes: larger frameworks forming the basic units of science, within which a succession of theories come about. Every research programme consists of three elements: a *hard core* of basic theses and assumptions; a *protective belt* of auxiliary hypotheses that surrounds this core; and a *heuristic* or problem-solving machinery consisting of sophisticated techniques.

Scientists regularly encounter observations that conflict with a theory's predictions and other types of problems. However, there is no discarding of a research programme simply because it faces some set of anomalies; instead, its protective belt allows the scientists to cope with these problems by *immunising its hard core* against falsification and generating new auxiliary hypotheses. Giving up this core of fundamental assumptions would result in the disintegration of the entire research programme, which has generated or promises to generate a succession of theories. There is a revision of the more flexible set of ideas forming the protective belt.

We can begin to make sense of its peculiar combination of continuities and discontinuities. The basic assumptions about the religion of the Brahmin are part of this programme's hard core, whereas the claims concerning the Aryan invasion, racial superiority, magical thinking, and the *Varna* ideology are part of its protective belt. The latter ideas form a more flexible set of auxiliary hypotheses, which scholars can modify and revise in the face of anomalies to protect the research programme from refutation. Indeed, this has happened regularly, not only during the past decades but also in the centuries before. Between the seventeenth and twenty-first centuries, in the face of empirical and conceptual problems, the auxiliary hypotheses moved from theological notions of heathen idolatry to anthropological concepts of magical thinking and to the current claims about homology and ideology; or they could shift from the idea of an Aryan invasion and conquest to peaceful migration and contact. But the hard core of assumptions concerning the religion and priesthood of ancient India needed immunity against falsification; if scholars failed to do so, their entire research programme would break down (and this in the absence of any promising alternative).

This, of course, generates new questions for further research. How did its hard core come into being, and from where did it derive its basic assumptions about Indian religion and the Brahmin class? Are we dealing with two (or more) competing research programmes or with a succession of theories sharing the same hard core? Do the internal problems that plague recent scholarship show that the programme's protective belt has exhausted its heuristic potential and is losing its capacity to generate new hypotheses in the face of accumulating anomalies?

### Personal Concluding Thoughts

Whenever our intellectuals, today or past, accept Europe's conceptualisations, they are just repeating Christianity's critique of the pagan 'priests' without Christianity being fundamental to the construction of Indian culture. They keep repeating the West's endless mantras of anti-

Brahmanism, which is tragic and puzzling. This 'colonial consciousness'—continuing intellectual violence after colonials have left—makes them assess Indian culture through Western lenses.

Where have we gone wrong in dealing with Indian society? The colonials had a purpose: to break our society, but why did our own humanities or political and social sciences fail us after independence? The colonials inflicted far more damage on our consciousness, which Dr. SN Balagangadhara calls 'colonial consciousness'. This is the continuing violence of colonisation at an intellectual level, but in a different timeframe, by permanently altering even the way we think. The stories of Brahmin supremacy, the creation of untouchability and Dalit caste, and many such are continuing colonial stories. They reflect more legal and political realities than any social reality. Hugely false semantics and descriptions trap India, and we have internalised these falsities as true pictures of ourselves.

It is sad that, despite reservations and protectionism, Dalit anger is on the rise. The so-called forward castes and the Brahmins are still the brunt of deep anger from the Dalit side, which is simply a creation of political-legal systems. The Brahmins are the object of ridicule and hate, with a special virulence. Ironically, corrective measures have increased anger considerably on both sides over the decades following independence. By creating categories like Forward castes, Backward castes (with further sub-categories like A, B, C, and D), and scheduled castes, successive governments have happily promoted the racial categories we detest so much. The inherent feelings of superiority and inferiority are the necessary outcomes of such a hierarchical division of the different categories. The fault lines in the country run deep because of these divisions created by politicians and encouraged by academics with a dominant Marxist ideology running in their veins. Our natural sciences declare boldly that all humans share 99.99% of genes; any slightest notions of race or inherent superiority or inferiority of a group of people are completely wrong. Yet, our political and legal machinery has been precisely doing that for so long and so emphatically. They are instilling false notions of superiority, inferiority, guilt, anger, and shame in various proportions in society while paradoxically wanting to create an equal society.

The caste system does not exist. Let it dissolve—the sooner, the better. There are only the constant four *varnas* and thousands of *jatis*. The only reality of Indian social systems are the *jatis*, the thousands of them arising, gaining prominence, falling, dissolving, or evolving continuously into newer forms by admixture. Let the *jatis* have their own social rules, flexible or otherwise, concerning profession, marriage, food, eating, customs, *pujas, devas, devis,* and so on. Each *jati* has independence and confirms the basic philosophy of the Indian system—an *indifference to the differences. Varnas* happen to be a larger meta-structure, perhaps a normative ideal, which is difficult to correlate with the *jatis*. In the classical *Varna* scheme, where does one fit jatis or communities like the 'Reddys', the 'Kapus', the 'Patels', or the 'Kammas'? It is an incontestable fact that they are generally the most well-to-do in the social, political, academic, and economic spheres. They may be the Sudras, since they are intuitively unlikely to be the other three: Brahmins, Kshatriyas, or Vysyas. It is unfortunate that the negative connotation of the word "Sudra" has become deeply embedded in the collective Indian psyche. Problematically, neither intellectuals nor caste scholars are interested in correcting such ideas, which could potentially lead to more fusion than fissure in Indian society. One struggles with the understandings of the caste system, but these inconsistencies have never bothered our academics, scholars, intellectuals, or politicians.

It is an amazing aspect of Indic civilisation that even religions like Christianity, Islam, and Judaism took the form of traditions and evolved richly by interacting with others —until the colonials came with their theories and baggage of solutions meant specifically to deal with the internal problems of Christianity in Europe. The post-independent Indian political leaders looked at the material prosperity of the West and firmly decided that all solutions in India must come from Europe. There was a strong heritage of the past that told a different story about *Varna, Jatis,* religion, and so on. The strong left-influenced academia firmly rejected our past too, while superficially appearing to counter the colonial narratives. The result is that, over the past seven decades, our systems have managed to anger just about everyone.

Dr. Martin Fárek, a scholar at the University of Pardubice in the Czech Republic and associated with Dr. SN Balagangadhara's Ghent School, says that we should aim to develop a new theory of the phenomena described by the Indian terms *varna* and *jati*. It is extremely important to gain insight into the traditional Indian understanding of these concepts. Only then can we consider in what sense this traditional thinking is relevant to theorising society in India. If we really want to take the traditional Indian understanding seriously, a new approach to its research is necessary. It will focus on theorising the domestic Indian framework within which ideas such as 'guna' (mode of nature), 'adhikara' (eligibility or qualification), and 'svabhava' (natural inclination) make sense. This kind of research will create new hypotheses, which should enable us to answer important questions such as: What is the Indian framework of understanding of *varna, jati,* and *biradari*? How do Indians decide about the status of different people? Our ancient scriptures and dharma were always about duties and not rights. Modern societies with a focus on rights might just be misinterpreting the notions of *varna* and *jati* in our social systems.

Perhaps, society and its political, legal, academic, and intellectual machinery should be batting for equality of opportunity. That should be our top priority in the decades to come. Group reservations cause group injustice and social fissure. Reservations and other forms of positive discrimination have their place in a concerned society but arguably, should be at the individual level. The criterion could be anything, like economic backwardness, for example. Anything except poorly defined 'social backwardness' or the 'ex-untouchability' (untouchability practices are officially illegal today) status of an entire group. Despite tolerance and acceptance being our biggest strengths, absorbing and assimilating every culture across thousands of years, it is ironic that the country stands in the dock, allowing a rhetoric of Brahminical supremacy and Dalit exploitation. We need a great revival and great unity. It is time for us to dissipate the anger and start fresher narratives. Will our humanities take the challenge?

Part IV

# CULTURE

"An ingrained and dominant spirituality, an inexhaustible vital creativeness and a powerful, scrupulous intelligence created the harmony of ancient Indian culture."

**– Sri Aurobindo**

## Chapter 8

# RECONCEPTUALIZING INDIA STUDIES

## *SN Balagangadhara*

Balagangadhara's *Reconceptualizing India Studies* is an important book that looks at the present-day socio-cultural narratives of India with regard to its many aspects, such as caste, religious fundamentalism, corruption, and so on. Balu strives to show that most of these narratives are only a continuation of the colonial descriptions of India. The colonials, in trying to understand the alien land they were ruling, experienced a different culture. In this attempt, they constructed some meta-narratives that could bind many of the experiences into a single, overarching explanation. In the colonial period, Indians believed that most progress came from the Western world and, apart from perhaps a few isolated instances, like Buddha, we did not have much to show. The theme of the book primarily rests on the question: What if these colonial descriptions are false? Today, a 'colonial consciousness' prevents us from setting up better narratives about India. We stand today as equals to the West after centuries of subjugation, and thus, says Balu, it would be an important exercise to reevaluate India studies.

The caste system story is a prime example. What if the dominant description of the caste system as a prime obstacle to progress and a source of all evil in Indian society is unscientific? The present descriptions also make the caste system autonomous, decentralised, stable (since it is resistant to all reform across time), adaptive (to all religious, political, and economic environments), and dynamic (since it is always evolving). Would not such a description denote, contrarily, an ideal social system and not certainly an evil one?

Based on its theories, studies, and assumptions, Europe generated knowledge about other cultures. India, too, generates knowledge about the world, just as it did in the past. However, in gross ignorance, why is it that Indian intellectuals use predominantly European frameworks as the benchmark to study themselves and the West too? Balu asks, "Indian and European cultures differ from each other on views about human beings, but what made one the standard?" This book thematically deals with the idea that as India evolves and faces the West as equals, learning should happen across cultures rather than always being a one-way street.

## 'Culture' and 'Cultural Differences'

The word 'culture' has so many definitions that some want to discard it altogether, begins Balu in the section of the book on cultural differences. The problem, however, Balu says, is that there is no clarity on what a definition is and what it should do. It cannot function to explain all the ancillary claims of the word defined. Balu concludes that the so-called defects of the term 'culture' are based on a casual application of language and philosophy. These are the properties of any and every word in natural or artificial language.

As with the natural world, humans also need to cope with society in order to survive. Various mechanisms—like child-rearing practices, schooling, family life, rituals, ceremonies, religious functions, and other group interactions—transmit the resources (customs, traditions, and institutions) available to humans for coping with the social world. A culture is the specific way in which society learns to use the resources available for socialization.

There are dominant and subordinate learning processes in any culture that determine its output. A specific combination of dominant and subordinate learning processes constitutes the culture's learning configuration. Here is Balu's strongest thesis: religion forms the dominant learning configuration in Western culture, where the "why" question is important. The output of this culture consists of theories, speculations, and finally, atheism. Rituals form the dominant learning configuration of Indian culture, where the "how" question is vital. Such a culture focuses more on performative ability and builds societies and groups. Thus, cultural difference between individuals is a truly valid concept as it entails a specific way of using the resources of socialisation, says Balu. Cultural differences are thus not social, biological, or psychological in nature.

### Comparative Science of Cultures: Why Is It Extremely Relevant?

Balagangadhara initiated an important field of study, the Comparative Science of Cultures, at the University of Ghent in Belgium. Balu explains why such an enterprise is important. The existing social sciences have a deep symbiotic relationship with Orientalism. Borrowing and reinforcing each other, they make uniform claims about non-Western cultures. To understand themselves and other worlds, Western intellectuals developed the social sciences.

Problematically, other cultures ended up adopting the same methodologies to study both themselves and the West. The deeply colonised social sciences rarely present an indigenous point of view. Balu writes that when Indian anthropologists, psychologists, or sociologists do their work in their respective fields, it is really the West talking to itself. Therefore, we urgently need to decolonise the social sciences, which should be a comparative exercise that builds upon the previously hard-won insights of social science studies without blindly rejecting them. Finally, studying the coloniser's description can lead to an understanding of the coloniser's culture in return.

Analysing the European 'discovery' of Indian religions or exploitative caste systems through a stepwise comparative exercise will help us decide whether their claims are true or not. Similarly, with regards to ethics, the West developed its ethical theories (virtues, vices, universal norms, and moral life) based strongly on its theological vocabulary. Other cultures, like India, developed their ethical domain in a different manner and it is entirely possible that the norms of one culture may not hold true for all of humanity. According to Balu, peculiarly native Indian traditions have produced little about other cultures, ethics, or the caste system, but modern intellectuals are eagerly reproducing what the West says about these issues.

Colonialism, power, and violence established a clear asymmetry in the narratives, where the Western narrative became the norm. Indigenous understanding, if there was any, faded into the background. The present Orientalist and social sciences, the only frameworks available today, are simply adding to the Western descriptions. Comparative sciences aim to restore narrative symmetry, particularly by rejecting the developmental ordering of history, which places Western culture at its peak. Scientifically and objectively, comparative studies aim to show that diverse cultures have different but alternative forms of life. For example, if earlier scholars thought of Indians as immoral, it may not be because they were all racists. A better answer would come from comparing the nature of ethical thought in both cultures. Such an answer may lead to a better alternative theory of ethics.

### Rethinking The Post-Colonial Project: Orientalism and Social Sciences

Edward Said's *Orientalism* (1978) emphasised that the Orient, as a place and an idea, is a reality *in and for* the West. For the Oriental people themselves, Orientalism has no meaning. Critics felt that Said was unable to say what the falsity in the Orientalist image meant. However, for Balu, Said's work makes sense within the framework of cultural differences. If one views Orientalism as expressing the differences between the Orient and the Occident, then clearly, while describing the Orient, the Occident is describing itself. Orientalism then becomes a route to studying the Occident or Western culture.

The reports by merchants, missionaries, or bureaucrats, and their later analysis, became descriptions of the 'Orient' and the Orientalist discourse, respectively. However, Balu says that Orientalism was not a true description, though it appeared neutral, but simply *an experience*. The problem arises when post-colonial thinkers also believe these to be true descriptions because of colonial consciousness. The West built up the social sciences, based on the concepts and truisms available in its culture, to study the world and itself. Thus, the social sciences can be a self-image of the West. Problematically, social sciences and Orientalist discourse constrain each other with the same set of questions and frameworks to answer them. Hence, when post-colonial academia debates Indian social issues, the conceptual language is no different from Orientalism.

Balu says, for example, that both Oriental descriptions and a modern cultural psychologist like Richard Shweder, using the same conceptual language, conclude that Indians are immoral people. Similarly, Hinduism (or other religions) and caste systems are descriptions of India shared by Orientalists and the present-day social sciences. Balu says that the colonials experienced many practices in an alien land. The widespread phenomenon of practices, rituals, texts, philosophies, and social practices was all real, but they needed a coherent meta-structure for these experiences.

Europeans, informed by their own religious roots and social understandings, thus created religions and a 'caste system' by giving a stable pattern to a multitude of customs in India. Balu says, "Hinduism and the caste system provided Westerners with a coherent and unifying experience… It is false because it falsely assumed that the experiential entity was a real entity in the world, and it is imaginary in that it does not have an existence outside the experience of Western culture."

The facts provided by the Orientalists were the starting point for writing in the social sciences. Hence, the grand project of non-Western intellectuals in critiquing Orientalism is to decolonize the social sciences. This would pave the way for better descriptions of world cultures instead of the one-sided present understandings.

### *Colonialism and Colonial Consciousness*

Colonialism appears to be a self-explanatory phenomenon of evil and immorality, but there is no adequate explanation for it. The perception that colonisers belonged to a superior civilisation was equal for both the coloniser and the colonised. Colonisation was simply an expression of the coloniser's obvious scientific, technological, and military strengths. Therefore, the colonised also bear moral responsibility for the evils of colonialism, as they continue the same process, albeit in a different era. This is precisely the 'colonial consciousness' that traps most Indian intellectual narratives.

An example is the discussion of India's corruption phenomenon. According to popular belief, India's caste system is conducive to corruption. The West characterized the caste system as a symbol of all the evil and regressive aspects inherent in the Indian social structure. Undeniable anecdotes become the basis for making the immoral practices allegedly more than the combined effects of other large-scale phenomena like racism, slavery, apartheid, and even fascism. In the end, all Indians become immoral because caste division cuts across all religions.

Finally, the Indian ethics that produce such survival strategies must be corrupt. Previously, colonials—like Charles Grant, Hastings, and Buchanan—thought of Indians as intellectual imbeciles, some within a few days of landing in India. The contemporary intellectual message stays the same, as the discourse on corruption in India leads to the conclusion of extensively corrupt social, caste, and ethical systems.

The first descriptions of India by travellers and missionaries lie at the root of this narrative, which makes Indians immoral almost as a moral obligation. The early reports described the 'heathen' Indian religions, devil-worshipping people, and exploitative Brahmins. This became a common view over centuries through repeated affirmations. These ethnographic descriptions primed generations of Marxist, liberal, and other Western intellectuals. Western culture's civilizational superiority, rooted in Christian theological ideas, became its empirical truth and premise. The common-sense notions transformed into facts in our political and social sciences.

Colonial consciousness is a belief that serves as both a premise and a logical conclusion to the colonised's descriptions. The most violent aspect of colonialism is that it creates and sustains such a consciousness. Colonialism generates a set of attitudes and beliefs—a feeling of shame about the home country's culture; the conviction of backwardness; and the desire to learn from the colonizer. The post-colonial thinkers of today are simply continuing the colonial narratives about India in a slightly modified language.

Balu says:

> Colonization was not merely a process of occupying lands and extracting revenues. It was not a question of us aping Western people and trying to be like them. It was not even about colonizing the imagination of a people by making them 'dream' that they, too, would become 'modern', developed, and sophisticated. It goes deeper than any of these. It is about denying people and cultures their own experiences, rendering them aliens to themselves, and actively preventing any description of their own experiences except in terms defined by the colonizers. This is the continuous saga of cultures and peoples colonized by Western culture.

### Understanding India and Her Traditions: An Open Letter to Jeffrey Kripal

Jeffrey Kripal, a professor in the US, in his book *Kali's Child: The Mystical and the Erotic in the Life and Teachings of Ramakrishna*, employs Freudian psychoanalysis of Ramakrishna and suggests that the latter's sexual trauma and unconscious homoerotic tendency *somehow* generated his religious life. Kripal also states that there are two different Ramakrishnas: one Vedantic and the other Tantrik. Many Indians expressed outrage, but this became an instance of prejudice and fundamentalism.

Balu writes a letter to Kripal, demonstrating why the Hindu response makes perfect sense. Kripal, by re-describing Ramakrishna's religious life in terms of sexual pathology, trivialises, distorts, and denies the experience of the saint's followers. For Kripal, the only framework from which to view other cultures is his own, even as he denies that Indians too can have an equally valid and legitimate experience. These explanations, by fundamentally denying the experience of another culture, cause violence. A sense of wrongness prompts a few to respond strongly and quickly acquire the label of fundamentalists, while the majority remain silent due to their lack of cognitive response to such trivialisation and distortion.

Kripal describes Ramakrishna's religious life as a transformation of the 'dark natures' of psychic energies into the 'gold of the mystical,' which is fundamentally a reduction rather than an explanation. Balu writes strongly that Kripal's ideas of a 'boring Vedanta' or tantriks as infringement of middle-class morality are sheer ignorance on the part of Kripal and a failure to understand Indian culture and the Vedantic ideas of Brahman, Maya, or Enlightenment. Thus, as Balu writes, "In trivializing the phenomena that Kripal wants to explain, he renders his explanations trivial."

Kripal's use of psychoanalysis to evaluate Ramakrishna is finally mischief and gossip, and so is the use of empty terms like 'somehow' and 'almost alchemically', which are placeholders for any future explanations. Kripal's understanding of the word 'secret' in Indian traditions is flawed. 'Secret' mantras (like the gayatri) in India's guru-shishya traditions make little sense to Kripal. Balu says that using Freud's stories to understand Ramakrishna is similar to using creationism to portray Darwin's theory. Balu sums up his reaction to Jeffrey Kripal's efforts: "I am ashamed and upset by the trivialization; I feel disgust and loathing at the gossip; I react with horror to the violence you inflict."

### Are Dialogues an Antidote to Violence?

A colonial attitude, assuming the superiority of Western narratives, persistently generates literature, both from the West and India, which causes violence to Indian culture and traditions. Is a dialogue possible? The attempts become futile as the dialogues too become skewed in favour of the Western intellectuals. Balu argues, in an important section, that the basic structure of dialogue is such that it paradoxically increases the hostility and violence. Similarly, because of the skew favouring the West, political liberalism, with its notions of fairness and justice, fails to decrease violence in intercultural encounters.

Karl Popper says that reason and dialogue are the only alternatives to violence. Balu disagrees and shows that it is not a poor understanding of the participants, but the requirements of reason as embodied in such dialogues that generate violence. There is historical evidence for the simultaneous violence and dialogue of ancient Christianity and Roman *religio*; the religious wars; the Reformation and Counter-Reformation; and so on.

Balu explains this by looking at two controversial books authored by Paul Courtright and Jeffrey Kripal on Lord Ganesha and Ramakrishna

Paramhansa, respectively, which generated calls for apologies and withdrawals. Balu addressed Kripal previously. The problematic Freudian interpretations in the former transform Ganesha into a symbol for the Indian psyche, which performs rituals for this god. Finally, an *interpretation* of psychoanalysis functions as an *explanation* of the Indian psyche. For example, Indians offer puja to Shiva Linga because... (it is a symbol for fertility, it represents the phallus, and blanks filled in by other suitable psychoanalysis). Such an explanation requires evidence, which the author fails to provide, says Balu.

Western scholars defend psychoanalysis in understanding religions while Hindus disagree. It is unreasonable to believe that Hindutva fundamentalism has brainwashed the emotional Hindu to such an extent that they do not understand academic freedom. However, this is one stand which scholars on a moral high ground take. Balu says an alternative stand could be that Kripal and Courtright might have initiated a dialogue with the Hindus about their religion by making the first move. What would now be the structural results of a rational dialogue?

Western scholars studying Hinduism inflict violence by denying the experiences of people whose religions they talk about. The scholar sways a rational dialogue in his favour by making many unproven assumptions and several cognitive moves that the Hindu cannot question: (1) the scholar attributes implicit premises to the Hindu; (2) these premises explain Hindu practices; (3) these explanations presuppose the truth of Freudian psychology; (4) this theory structures the phenomena requiring elucidation; and (5) the Hindu logically defends the scholar's moves.

Unfortunately, the Hindu cannot refute the premises and offer alternative explanations unless he is an intellectual expert, knowing many facets of Indian culture. Thus, the onus of proof distributes unevenly between the participants in the dialogue. This violence in the experiential world makes Hindus react violently. The Hindutva movement draws well-educated Hindus into its folds because it can attach itself to this sense of violation. The scholar dismisses Hindu interpretations by calling them minority or fundamentalist opinions. The former switches between explanation and interpretation freely.

The Hindu can argue only against the interpretation but to do so he must challenge the psychoanalytical explanation. This would become a fringe opinion. The Hindu ultimately loses the debate and leaves the conversation. Thus, the asymmetric argumentation generates only anger, leading to either silence or violence.

### Intercultural Encounters, Reasonable Dialogues, and Normative Political Theory

'Normative liberal political philosophy' also fails to critically examine the notion of rational dialogue (reasonable, transparent rules of discussion, and participant neutrality). It also fails in inter-cultural dialogues. The actual discussions between different cultures lead to results that undermine the claims of political liberalism, says Balu.

Western scholars (like Montesquieu, Diderot, Hume, Gibbon, and Peter Gay), when they initiate a dialogue with other cultures, end up placing them as inferiors. Cicero, similar to some other Greco-Roman thinkers like Plutarch, Epicurus, and Lucretius, was a priest as well as a scholar and poet. Yet, the arguments against the existence of God and other liberal ideas in his *De Natura Deorum* became the arsenal for Enlightenment thinkers of the eighteenth century against religion. Modern Western scholars, offering many explanations, thought that the ancient scholars were either inauthentic, dishonest, fearful, or simply prudent. Some wrote that the Roman thinkers could write which went against their public persona because most of the citizens were illiterate and didn't know what the priests were doing in private.

Similarly, when the West typically comes across traditional practices— let's say an African rain dance or the Ayudhapuja (worship of instruments) in Indian culture—instead of trying to understand the traditional practices of other cultures, they simply impute superstitious beliefs. Invariably, the structure of the dialogue ends up showing the non-Western culture as inferior or irrational. Balu says, "The process of understanding and exploring how 'reasonable people' could come to different 'reasonable' conceptions compels the modern Western mind to deny an entire culture and its people even an elementary understanding of social and natural events. Even though we have set up a 'reasonable' dialogue, the results of this process are anything but fair."

In intercultural dialogues, a skew occurs when one culture (the West) makes assumptions about the beliefs of another culture (the East, or the Global South). An African believes that the rain dance actually causes rain. Such assumptions render the individuals of the non-Western culture incapable of engaging in dialogue. When the starting point is about the protagonists' beliefs rather than human practices, intercultural dialogues are the cause of misunderstandings, not a solution.

The nature of these dialogues violates the rules of dialogue and compels one to accept a relationship between beliefs and behaviour. Political liberalism assumes independence from specific philosophical and metaphysical doctrines, but it clearly assumes the truth of Western cultural folk psychology, rooted in Christianity. Thus, the burden of proof is uneven between the participants in the dialogue.

A 'reasonable' discussion appears to take place only between people who share implicit common-sense conceptions or the same folk psychology. Political liberalism is tyrannical in demanding that only those members sharing a common Western history are competent to enter a reasonable discussion. Political liberalism is flawed because it implicitly calls its own cultural folk psychology a reasonable 'comprehensive doctrine'. The West assumes this doctrine is true, while other cultural folk psychologies are false and unreasonable. Balu says, "Reasonable pluralism, which assumes the inevitability of reasonable people coming to different reasonable judgements, forcibly bows to the logic of its cognitive mechanisms and denies pluralism... It too affirms the familiar theme of Western superiority." One advocate, Ackerman (*Why Dialogue?*), believes that political liberalism remains humanity's best hope in a culturally diverse world. If true, this is more of a reason to despair than hope, says Balu.

### *The Secular State and Religious Conflict*

Secularism and religious conversions are controversial issues in the Indian context. Historically, for centuries and without secularism, India has dealt with pluralism far more successfully than the West. Secularism, a solution for European Christendom at a specific period of its history, when applied to the Indian context has paradoxically generated religious frictions and the rise of Hindu fundamentalism, Balu writes.

Indian society consists of both pagan traditions and Semitic religions. Secularism, in the Indian context, thus faces difficulties unknown to the original Western cultural background from which it emerged as a separation between the church (a single religion) and the state. In the Indian debate, three parties and two frameworks clash in offering a solution. *Secularists*, in line with Nehruvian thinking, defend the obligation of religious neutrality in a liberal state. The *anti-secularists*, who offer an alternative system based on traditional values, are divided into Hindutva and Gandhian anti-secularists. Despite some differences, both sub-divisions agree that Indian traditions produce more tolerant politics than Western secularism.

Secularists agree for religious conversion; the anti-secularists are averse to it. The difficulty in India is because the Semitic proselytization dynamic clashes with the non-interference aspect of the still alive pagan traditions. Balu writes that a Hindu endorsing that all traditions are part of a human quest for truth, while a Muslim or Christian believing that their religion is the only true revelation while all others are false, involves a deep conflict of values. Which side does the liberal and neutral state take? Balu says that allowing conversion and not interfering with Christianity or Islam actually shows a tilt toward the claim of Semitic religions. The state, in fact, is not so neutral and liberal towards the Hindu side.

Article 25 of the Constitution contains the clause "freedom to propagate" yet, ambiguously, the Indian state legally restricts conversion by persuasion. Balu says that if one takes conversion to be a matter of persuasion, one must presuppose that religion involves the question of doctrinal truth. It accepts one religion's truth as opposed to another's falsity. Not India-specific, this is a general flaw of the liberal secularism model, which takes a critical attitude towards proselytization and yet supports religious freedom to convert.

India transplanted the Western liberal state model into Indian soil, consequently endorsing the notion that religion is a matter of truth. Such a stance makes sense in Western culture, where different Semitic religions compete for truth values. It does not do so in another cultural milieu where the pagan traditions are a living force. The Indian state looks at Indian traditions the way Semitic religions do and, by legislating, forces a rivalry between Semitic religions and Indian traditions when none exist. Simultaneously, an 'agnostic' stance compels it to withdraw completely and let the communities solve this problem on their own.

Unfortunately, the hostile colonial representation of India against Hindu traditions, fundamentally a Protestant description of India, guided Nehruvian secularism. A pagan perspective, in contrast to a Semitic perspective, sees no rivalry between Hindu traditions and Semitic religions. However, the state forces the pagan traditions in India to mould themselves like the Semitic religions. Hindu traditionalists inevitably took a militant defence against this brand of secularism, generating an uncharacteristic 'fundamentalism' and religious violence.

So, what are the solutions? A harmonious cultural diversity, far exceeding that of the West at any time in its history, existed in India. Despite some clashes, not only systematic persecutions were absent, but there was a tendency amongst the traditions to absorb elements from each other. For reasons that are unclear today, even Christianity and Islam took the form of traditions in India. They lost the drive for proselytization, developed an indifference to the 'other', and positively interacted with Indian traditions. Balu says that this picture of traditional Hindu-led pluralism may lead to more harmony than the secularism of today, and this should be an area of future research. The premises of the liberal, neutral, and secular state simply fail to accommodate the pagan traditions forming the majority.

### Indians Going to the West

Non-Resident Indians, as well as Indians getting increasingly Westernised, confront questions regarding traditional practices (like bindi), sati, caste system, cow, phallus worship of the linga, and so on. Indians struggle to answer the questions that appear intrinsically intelligible to them. The answers are neither unitary nor satisfactory to both Indians and Westerners. But by studying why they are even asking these questions we can gain more knowledge about the West through a reversal of gazes.

Instead of answering that these are traditions, which are simply ancestral practices handed down through generations, there is an attempt to give intelligent explanations. There is also an attempt to rigidly codify Hindu practices and observe them strictly to become super-orthodox Hindus. Sometimes, gurus and teachers help with this codification and develop justifications for the many practices. However, in the attempt to codify and justify the practices, rigidity comes to the Hindu traditions, which lose their capacity to absorb other elements. Indian traditions are known for their flexibility yet staying within defined boundaries. Balu writes that we would end up sacrificing the very vitality that characterises Indian traditions and which has allowed them to survive over the millennia and in different environments.

Because Indians have learned not to ask such questions about our traditions, the questions become difficult. Western culture compels us to provide a satisfactory answer but these questions, which appear sensible to Western culture, do not make sense to us. Balu's strongest claim is that when Western culture quizzes us about the nature of Indian traditions, the West is telling us about itself. The past reformers and the present Indians do not understand what Western culture means when it asks whether 'Hindus believe in God,' or why Hindus worship lifeless statues. A rigid and codified Hinduism has little place in addressing the problems our children face. Balu says our basic task lies elsewhere: instructing our children about the West while we pass on our traditions to them.

### Concluding Remarks of Balu

Colonialism, introducing a new framework for experiencing our world, told us that we were primitive and superstitious. The caste system was our social structure, and 'Hinduism' was our main religion. Unfortunately, the colonized post-Independence Indian intellectuals took over their descriptions as incontestable facts. The attack on our social and religious structures continues unabated.

In terms of caste, the British made meta-theoretical claims about a coherent system to explain the different practices of various jatis they encountered. The discriminatory stories became empirical evidence, while sensational cherry-picking from texts like Manusmriti became theoretical support. Problematically, discrimination, humiliation, and poverty are compatible with multiple social structures (like capitalism, European feudalism, and slavery) and not specific to only one social system. The British were incoherent in even classifying the caste divisions, introducing many weird categories (like sub-castes and sub-sub-castes). It is only a presumption that caste constitutes a coherent system.

Regarding Hinduism, contemporary descriptions are the same as the previous Jesuit scholars, content-wise. Only the value judgements are positive for the former and negative for the latter. Counter-narratives also remain in the same framework when looking for a single scripture (Vedas), a single God (Brahman), or a single prophet (Krishna). They transform Indian pagan traditions into pale variants of Semitic religions which, in turn, never understood India's traditions. Balu writes that the only cause of friction in the country is *the attempt to convert traditions into religions.*

The Islamic and Christian rulers set narratives about 'false gods' and the 'false religion' of Hindus based on their understanding of one 'true' God versus many 'false' gods. The corrupt Brahmins allegedly created the immoral caste system, an integral part of false religion. Any despicable social phenomenon (sati, dowry, child marriage) seems to have its roots in the immorality of religion, priests, and the caste system. Balu writes that the framework for these 'discoveries' was not empirical investigations but theological beliefs. The popular narrative across centuries described a pure *Vedic* religion degenerating into *Brahmanism* and later into *Hinduism* as we know it today through the impact of Upanishads, Buddhism, and Jainism. Such nonsense, repeated many times, became common-sense knowledge for our intellectuals.

The Indian 'reformers' of the past (like the Brahmo Samaj), agreeing with the colonial narratives, began constructing a pure 'Hinduism' based on the Vedas and Upanishads. Believing Indians to be superstitious and caste-ridden, they also tried to identify core texts, doctrines, and values, along with a central god (like Brahman), modelling Hinduism as a pale variant of Protestant Christianity. The Hindutva movement was a more extreme reaction. The reformers failed to understand the nature of the religiously inspired criticisms. This standard textbook picture of Indian culture, which Western culture provided, is secularised Christianity. This is because the claims are incomprehensible without presupposing the truth of Christian doctrines, yet they appear comprehensible without knowing anything about Christianity. Finally, Balu says that intellectuals in the West and in India today believe in the truth of Western descriptions of Indian culture, and there is an urgent need to start studying both the West and India from our own lenses and setting a better narrative.

Chapter 9

# WHAT DOES IT MEAN TO BE INDIAN?

*SN Balagangadhara and Sarika Rao*

## *Introduction*

India has a great intellectual heritage and a huge corpus of texts (the broad five groups—Vedas, Upavedas, Vedangas, Puranas, and Darshanas) covering all fields of human activity—*apara* (worldly) and *para* (other-worldly), which is a testimony to the capacity of Indians to create knowledge by reflecting on their own experiences without any foreign influences.

The periods of colonial rule (Islamic and European) severely disrupted this capacity. We turned from creating knowledge to having to protect it from annihilation. In the process of protection, many times Indian intellectuals moulded themselves to Western criticisms against us and formulated their responses. The colonials said we were a corrupt religion with a corrupt priesthood. Our intellectuals, like Raja Ram Mohan Roy, accepted this and tried to create a 'pure' Hinduism based on the Upanishads, ridding themselves of the 'superficial' rituals and the 'tyrannical' priests. The whole so-called Hindutva process was initiated as a response to colonial criticisms. There was never any attempt to look at alien religions and alien cultures from our viewpoint.

Independence should ideally have presented the opportunity for a break when, finally, we could have rejected the colonial discourses and adopted an Indian lens through which to view ourselves and the world.

This was an opportunity to recover our lost tradition of creating knowledge independently. Sadly, it was a lost opportunity. Academia now became filled with a noxious Marxist philosophy intensely inimical to Indian traditions. The view of linear history was clear: a primitive Indian past that needed steering to a golden future (represented by modern Europe). In a few crucial generations, our education system would successfully deracinate most Indians.

Our social sciences, too, remained as colonial in their outlook as possible. Their tools did not change, and their results did not differ significantly from those of the previous colonials. Western social sciences became a form of secularised theology; hence, in a perverse manner, our social sciences too were forming the same conclusions about India as Christian missionaries had made in the nineteenth century. Our social sciences also concluded that Hinduism is a religion constructed by the wily Brahmins with a very immoral caste system.

At no point did they question the older narratives of the colonials about whether religions or the caste system truly existed in India. Was the phenomenon of Hinduism, which the colonials called a 'religion' something else? As for the *varnas* and *jatis* (the latter being the social reality of India)—do they really configure into a caste system? Is anybody aware of these caste rules? Despite the huge contradictions arising from matching theory to social data, why did we persist with the colonial understanding of India?

These are important questions. However, the reason why we glossed over them was mainly the 'colonial consciousness' thesis of Dr. SN Balagangadhara—a persisting violence on the colonised caused by a permanent alteration of their intellectual frameworks. This happens in a different period, much after the colonials have left. In the seven decades of a corrupted narrative foisted on us by a deep nexus of politicians, academia, media, and the bureaucracy, most Indians respond with a numb silence to the question, 'What does it mean to be an Indian?' Balu and Sarika begin the book, 'What does it mean to be Indian?' by emphatically saying that the received view about the answer is either false or fragmentary.

We remain divided, angry, confused, and saddened by the situation in the country today. Everyone has a reason to be angry. One needs to read this book carefully to understand what Indian culture is and why we need to be proud of it. This one can do without hating the West, as do many other narratives in support of India. Dr. Balu shows that both the West and the East stand as equals, and we can both learn from each other. However, Indians need to throw off the yoke of colonial consciousness and view themselves and the West through their own lenses. This is an urgent task for the future.

### Histories, Itihasas, Myths, and Stories

'Secular historians', standing against the 'religiosity' of the masses, taught us that our stories were merely disguised historiographies, poetic exaggerations, or lies told by our ancestors. There is a typical Indian attitude, beyond the comprehension of somebody from the Western traditions, that says, "Rama and Krishna may not have existed, but Ramayana or Mahabharata are always true." What separates this Indian attitude from the West when dealing with stories and legends? In the Western intellectual tradition, the dominant idea is that myths are false, and facts (the basis for scientific historiography) are true.

However, growing up as Indians, we learn that we should treat our stories and epics (*Itihasas*) as different from the claims of our history, geography, and science lessons. As Dr. Balu asks, '*What do we want, a history or a past?*' Converting *Itihasa* into history would destroy our past, as the remembered past of a thriving and rich culture. Importantly, regarding divine stories, the issue is not about the existence of divinities and whether their world also exists, but that such stories are *not* about humans and their world. One can make true or false statements only about the human and the mundane. The huge number of stories unique to Indian culture play a very important role in knowledge transmission. These stories are *exemplars*—entities solving problems or trying to execute original actions in novel situations. As action heuristics (rules of thumb), they are neither true nor false.

The British were the heirs to the traditions of the Church and later Enlightenment philosophers who scrutinised Roman and Greek epic narratives for logic, coherence, and truth value. They failed to understand that these were not true or false doctrines and were not descriptions of the world. These 'mythologies' became simply superstitious expressions of primitive fears and hence were either lies or poetic exaggerations.

British 'liberalism' and the Nehruvian 'secularism' unfortunately brought another reaction into existence (exemplified by some Sangh Parivar elements), which claimed that stories about the past are *literally our histories* and not poetic exaggerations or lies. These ideologues of the Sangh Parivar threaten to destroy Indian culture with a catastrophic cocktail of nationalism and Christian discourses on history, says Balu.

## Culture and Cultural Differences

In an important chapter, Balu discusses his thesis on culture and cultural differences. Any culture builds two rich, complex, and interlinked storehouses of *linguistic* (texts, scriptures, newspapers, and books) and *actionable* items (modelled on family, friends, and society) to flourish in the two basic surrounding environments—the *natural* and the *social*. These storehouses are the resources for socialisation. In the broadest terms, *'culture'* is the available resources for socialisation. Cultural differences reside in *how* the culture utilises resources.

The diverse learning processes (the socialisation resources) coordinate and establish 'a configuration of learning' where one learning process is dominant and other processes are subordinate. Cultures originate, reproduce, and transmit across generations through these configurations of learning, and the differences between such configurations (which are dominant and which are subordinate) determine the cultural differences. Religion creates a configuration that creates Western culture; ritual creates a configuration that produces Indian culture. Thus, cultural differences are not along geographical, linguistic, social, psychological, or biological lines.

Christianity and Islam entered India and adapted to the existing culture. They held their beliefs and practices by adapting to Indian uses of the resources of socialisation. In this process, these religions undergo modifications in how the believers live their daily lives, which do not affect the content of their beliefs or their places of worship. It is exactly this kind of adaptation that many madrassas and evangelicals militate against. A vibrant Indian culture allows for these religions and absorbs their drive to create other configurations of learning within its own multiplicities.

### Experiences, Anubhava, and Denial of Indian Experiences

Indian traditions have made *experience* and its interrogation central to their inquiry and the creation of knowledge. In Indian culture, knowledge is mainly *experiential* in nature (practical knowledge). The goal of the knowledge is to then shape and transform the human experience in turn and give it structure. We slice the raw materials of experiences (events, persons, objects, thoughts, feelings, and perceptions) into manageable fragments and give them structure.

We use the 'resources of socialisation' available in our culture to structure our experiences. These are family life, friends and peer groups, formal and informal education, civil institutions and organisations (schools, trade unions, political parties, media), stories, rituals, lore, legends, poetry, and so on. We thus structure our experiences, and we learn how to do that from our cultures. An unstructured experience becomes a reason for trauma. Anubhava, the Sanskrit equivalent of experience, indicates an appropriate way of being in-the-world with regards to things, events, actions, and people that we encounter. The emphasis of Anubhava is on apt transitions from one state to another *(state change),* which also involve learning.

A significant difference between Western experiences and Indian experiences (or Anubhava) is how we look at truth and falsehood. For Western culture, truth and falsehood divide the world of statements into two exhaustive partitions. Indians, in a different way, privilege knowledge above truth. While knowledge is always true, not everything that is true (like a telephone directory) is also knowledge. Thus, in Indian culture, even truth (a true statement or a 'fact') can surprisingly hinder learning and prevent the emergence of knowledge. It is knowledge (always true) that liberates, but not truth.

When filters interfere with the process of learning, we stop having access to our experience. The factors preventing access to our own experiences and thus impeding knowledge are many: ignorance (Maya), culture, society, and individual psychology are some impediments. To this was added the two periods of colonialism (Islamic and British), which introduced filters causing a crippled state and a crippled experience instead of an apt state. Balu says the crippled experience and the crippled human became the norm and the normal.

One way of preventing access is by adopting an alien way of looking at Indian texts, like 'verifiable' historical facts. Western traditions, even today, end up denying Indian experiences that cause great intellectual violence. The Western explanations of Indian experiences that we routinely reproduce (fertility cults, symbolisms, sexual repressions, hypostatising abstract concepts like 'nation', the 'reification' of experiences into objects, and so on) hint that there is no such thing as 'Indian experiences' unless they are Indian 'hallucinations', says Balu. We sense 'wrongness' when this happens, but there is silence for the response.

In a note of caution, Balu says that ordinary people, philosophers, and scientists often confuse an explanation of experience with 'experience' itself. Consequently, rejecting the explanation does not equate to rejecting the experience itself. If we deny the existence of 'the' Indian caste system or deny its causal role in 'explaining' oppression in India, it does not mean we deny the existence of *jatis* or oppression in Indian society.

### *Reflecting on Experience: Superstructures and Substructures*

Taking the example of anger, Balu shows how Indian culture structures and accesses experiences differently than in the West. We share with our fellow humans a biological 'substratum'—the *sub-structure* of our personality. Resting upon it is a unique *superstructure* expressing our individual psychology. Introspection, depth psychology, and psychoanalysis—typical products of the West—analyse the different layers in the *superstructure*. The higher we go, the more unique we become, which, in fact, becomes the problem.

In contrast, Indian culture would teach that the *superstructure* consists of many idiosyncrasies (like anger) and is almost inconsequential. Indian culture focuses on the foundation or the *sub-structure* leading to self-knowledge. Introspection generates pain (and such allied emotions);

self-knowledge makes one happier and generates a sense of freedom. In one culture, introspection of the unique identity is the route; in another, the 'unique' is incidental and contingent. In the West, one deals with the internal mental life as an expression of the unique 'self' that each human being has; in India, there is neither an inner self unique to each one of us nor is there a privileged knower that cognises the meaning of these unique expressions. This perhaps explains the lack of popularity of psychoanalysis in Indian culture.

### Colonial Experience and Colonial Consciousness

Colonialism has been one of the most significant events for Indian culture. What exactly is immoral about this? 'Colonial consciousness', an important thesis of Balu's research programme, is a framework that denies access to our experience and makes us reproduce some sets of colonial ideas as though they describe our experience. This process continues to the present, long after the colonisers have left. British colonialism introduced the framework about the superiority of Western culture being 'objective' or 'scientific' that was both presupposed and proven. The colonised accepted this.

Islamic rule laid the foundation by impacting our culture in multiple ways. They did not merely rule, collect revenues, convert forcefully, or destroy temples. Islamic colonialism impeded the transmission of the many theories about people, society, and nature that had crystallised in Indian culture. Islamic colonisation damaged the production and capacity of intellectuals to produce our 'equivalents' of Western theories. These intellectuals turned simply to protect the existing traditions. The British colonised us before recuperation was possible.

How does the development of colonial consciousness and acceptance of colonial claims happen? Balu says that it is because of the secularisation of many religious ideas. Religion expanding through the well-known direct conversion of people is almost inconsequential when compared to the second way of expanding, *secularisation*. Christian doctrines spread far beyond the confines of the community of believers when they achieve a 'secular' clothing and become acceptable to other non-Christian cultures.

The secularisation story of Western culture is that the Enlightenment thinkers successfully 'fought' the dominance of Christianity in social, political, and economic life. Humankind now looked at 'reason' and 'scientificity'. As heirs to that period, we are proud citizens of the modern-day world, believing in democracy, reason in social life, human rights, and a private religion away from state intervention. Balu shows that these ideas, however, are simply Christian theological ideas in a secular mantle, as though they are 'neutral' and 'rational'. This is not to suggest a conspiracy, but there has been a secularisation of ideas about Man and Society present in the Bible.

The process of secularisation is evident in many areas of social discourse. For example, according to Christianity, Hinduism was immoral and is the foundation of the immoral Indian 'caste system'. Our present social and political sciences repeat precisely this story. This secularisation is invisible to Indian and Western intellectuals, because the research framework of the social sciences was set up explicitly by Christian theologians using resources of Christian theology. The problems of state and society, the limits of political power, and so on were actual issues confronted by the Church. The so-called social sciences have taken over these questions and answers, but the explicit theology fades in the background.

Western intellectuals are blind to secularised theology because that is all they know. That is why, when one draws upon the resources of the existing social sciences, one is drawing upon Christian theology. Balu reiterates that even if the social sciences openly oppose a straightforward Christian understanding, their conclusions are no different. This is an insidious process of secularising Christian ideas.

The British framework secularising the Christian framework recast Indian traditions in terms of religions; it described Hinduism with a 'tyrannical priesthood' as a variant of Catholic Christianity and Buddhism as a variant of Protestantism. This became the core experience of Indian culture too, as a class of Indian intellectuals accepted their claims.

Colonial consciousness is at work when our thinkers believe that 'Hinduism' also needs 'reform'. The Protestant Reformation in Europe was a rebellion against human additions that the Roman Catholic Church had 'introduced'—like the canon laws, the practice of indulgences, and so on. Thus, religion becomes corrupt when human beings add to God's revelation. The Indian 'reformers', in the name of Protestant Reformation (Brahmo Samaj, for example), want to similarly 'delete' things from the 'original revelation' and 'add' new things.

## Colonial Consciousness and the Example of Law

Internalising many 'axiomatic' ideas of Western culture—such as law being the foundation of a civilised society and a nation—is another example of colonial consciousness. For the British, the practices of different communities, no matter how old and venerated, should have their foundation in law. The British came with the absolute conviction that human beings are set on earth to obey the laws of God. They located the laws that governed the Indian culture in a text (the laws of Manu), which they codified and insisted that the people of India followed. Manu acquires the exalted status of a lawgiver for the 'Hindus', even though it is unclear what exactly his act resulted in regarding religion, social practices, and the creation of a nation.

However, Balu asks, "What if Law is not the foundation of society but *merely a tool* to regulate reasonable interactions and find reasonable solutions to human conflicts in a society? What if Law does not create a nation, but instead groups become cultured people precisely because of the colourful variety of their local practices? What if Law does not dictate but allows old customs and traditions to do their work?" The introduction of such a judicial system forced the Indians to become volunteers in the process of denying their own experience. Laws took on a status and force they had never had in their culture, even if they were their 'own' laws. Indian intellectuals have now started providing a scriptural foundation for cultural practices.

The author says that the way the West arranges its own society is neither an argument for its civilisational superiority nor evidence of the inferiority of other ways of organising social life. If Indian intelligentsia believed this, it is not possible that people seek the intervention of the apparatuses of the state in human practices that carry the stamp of traditions (Sabarimala, Jalikattu, and Pasubali as examples). Balu rues that such an impotent consciousness constitutes the class of Indian intellectuals today who fail to produce any interesting reflections and bring about any regeneration of the Indian culture.

### *Religions and Traditions*

One example of colonial consciousness is the persistent idea that there are religions in India. The West did not provide a false or wrong description of the social and cultural reality in India. But, problematically, the unity they created by tying these 'facts' together is a unity only for them called 'Hinduism'. Balu says that the theory that guided Western culture was Christian theology.

The beliefs and practices that went into constructing this unity do exist. Indeed, the puja, the sandhyavandanam of the Brahmins, the Sahasranamams, the Purushasukta, and our notions of dharma and adharma, all exist, says Balu. Only that these beliefs and practices (even when taken together) do not constitute either a religion or a unified phenomenon termed 'Hinduism'.

In this sense, Hinduism as a 'religion' (a sociological and metaphysical impossibility as he discusses elsewhere in detail) has no existence outside the colonial experiences of India. The colonials could not imagine that cultures could exist without religions and thus constructed Hinduism (with offshoots like Buddhism, Sikhism, and Jainism). Indian traditions had nothing like One Book, One Temple, One Messenger, or even the universal concept of God (there is no concept of God in Jainism or Buddhism). Yet there was an overlooking of all contradictions and inconsistencies.

Balu discusses the varied arguments 'proving' Hinduism and shows that they are simply false and unjustified claims. Amongst the various arguments that he throws down, one is that 'Hindutva' would not be possible without Hinduism. He says this presupposes being true, which requires proving. The burden of proof is the other way: one must show that Hindutva comes into being because of Hinduism. Is there an alternative description of Indian phenomena? Yes, India is a land of traditions.

Problematically, intellectuals are transforming some of the multiple Indian traditions into a single 'religion' called 'Hinduism'. While the term 'Hindu' might be convenient, the danger is in trying to develop 'doctrines', 'theologies', 'catechisms' and our own 'Ten Commandments' so that we could identify people following 'Hinduism'. Being a 'Hindu' is simply a continuation of ancestral traditions. The hallmark of traditions is an 'indifference to differences' that transcends the standard 'tolerances' and 'acceptances' forced on religions through secularism.

Balu says, today, we are not yet able to make sense of the presence of these two properties of traditions (broadly sampradayas and paramparas): (a) the enormous flexibility in belonging to a tradition and the sharpness with which the boundaries are drawn between traditions; (b) the possibility that any element could be absent from a tradition and yet it could maintain identity and distinction. Personal habits and attitudes (including atheism) also do not determine belonging to a tradition. Reason always works as a break for excesses of practices in traditional cultures. Thus, no modification of traditional practices has ever resulted in great ruptures in the social or cultural fabric of India.

Traditions are not religions or philosophies. They are what they are—traditions. To an ill-formed question, 'Why practice a tradition?' (why Bindi; why Linga puja; why bangles), the simple answer is that there is no 'special' reason to continue a traditional practice. For someone rooted in Semitic religions, the claims of religions must be true if they are to remain religions at all. What is the way traditional cultures approach their texts? Rama or Krishna may or may not have existed, but the Ramayana and Mahabharata are always true. The notion of 'truth' to characterise practices is to commit a *category mistake* in traditions.

### Studying Ourselves and the West from Our Background: Problematic Discourses

We relate to our own traditions and our own cultures the way the West has understood them. However, this is not a reason for us to become enemies of the West. We need to 'reinvent' and 'rediscover' the process of transmitting our culture the Indian way. Balu insists that, as a first important step, we should try and describe the West as it appears to us, against the background of our culture, without reproducing the theories and descriptions of the Western intellectuals.

How does the West appear to us? How do we appear to ourselves? Balu says we need to do this because our relationship to ourselves and our past is determined by what the West has said about both. A tremendous amount of intellectual violence ensues when the West, with their own terms of debate, sets the narratives about India and flatly denies our experiences. (Lingam puja is phallus worshipping; Ganesha's trunk is actually a limp phallus; Lingam puja is a fertility cult; and so on.) We need to say that because the traditional description has the form of a definition (Shiva puja=ritual to this form) no sensible discussion or dissection about traditional practice is possible.

Taking the examples of puja, idol worship, polytheism, and God, Balu then shows how we have made European descriptions and translations our own without questioning them. These borrow heavily from Christian theological concepts. Transposing such ideas to understand our traditions and practices leads not only to confusion but, finally, deracination. As Balu puts it, to understand the mother, we needed to understand the mother-in-law. This was the position of intellectuals in trying to understand Indian traditions and cultures within the framework of Western cultures and Western theories.

Similarly, many discourses (Sanskrit, temple entry restrictions for menstruating women, temple practices that offend certain groups, the 'caste system', and Brahmacharya Sadhus avoiding women) attempt to prove the discriminatory nature of Indian traditions. Balu shows that common to these and many such arguments are their 'normative' assumptions and judgements.

### *Colonialism, Colonial Consciousness, and the Impact on Translations*

Translations play an important role in understanding different cultures, but there is violence when there is no understanding of the individual cultures. This routinely happens when Indologists and Sanskritists translate our texts. Both are ignorant of Indian culture, and yet we accept them. This reveals another layer of 'colonial consciousness'. We have taken to English because we do not (intuitively) know what words from our own languages mean.

Colonialism and colonial consciousness work through the use of certain Indic words that stopped making sense to us except as translations in English. We accepted such translations of words like *Manas, raga, iccha, chitta, gyana, buddhi, vikara, Bhavana, Dharma, papa, punya, adharma,* and so on. Their descriptions replaced our reflections about our own experiences, and their translations became our translations. We did not understand the meaning of the words we used in our daily language, and we were unable to challenge their descriptions or their translations. In both periods under colonialism, we continued learning to use the words without being able to identify for ourselves what these units referred to. 'Manas' became 'mind'; 'bhavana' became 'feelings'; Dharma became 'ethics', 'law', and 'religion'; 'Ishwara' named a god; 'Deva' became 'God'; 'puja' became 'worship'; and so on.

Thus, earlier generations of Indians did not object to the translations of the British: we knew neither 'Dharma' nor 'normative ethics'. Our understanding of 'Ishwara' or 'Brahman' is as shallow as our understanding of 'God'. Balu, using 'freedom' as a concept, says that, according to Western culture, moral action is impossible if it is not 'free'; according to us, without strict determinism, moral action is impossible. Yet, 'freedom' is a 'self-explanatory' concept for most of us. We neither understand the technical (or theoretical) terms we use in our daily intercourse nor the English words we translate into native languages.

## Concluding Remarks

To the question, 'What Does It Mean to be Indian?', the book does not provide easy answers. Every single Indian needs to read this book, which is packed with ideas we seem to be only vaguely aware of. Some ideas are easy to grasp; others require intense thinking on the part of the reader to do the unpacking and reach an 'a-ha' moment. The book can be difficult to read in some places, but the author promises right from the beginning that this book is for the intelligent and thinking layperson. There is never a spoon-feeding of ideas.

Almost everything is wrong with the way we understand India. We are full of colonial understandings regarding our 'religions', our 'caste system', our stories and legends, our psychological attitudes, our understanding of texts and scriptures, our understanding of law, and so on. It is an uphill task to first dethrone our present narratives and then understand ourselves fresh. At no point does Balu ask us to hate the West. He only insists that we develop our own social theories, our own lenses through which to view ourselves and the West. We have seen through Western lenses till now and that has caused great damage to Indians and Indian culture.

The book requires slow and repeated reading. It is not possible to understand everything that the author is trying to say in one go. It should stimulate its readers to explore other seminal works of Dr. SN Balagangadhara and his school regarding Indian religions, caste, and many other aspects of Indian culture: *The Heathen in His Blindness*; *Western Foundations of The Caste System*; *Reconceptualizing India Studies*; *Europe, India, and The Limits of Secularism* are some of these. Whatever the final impact of Dr. Balu's ideas, the following is certain: they help one understand how important the humanities and social sciences are in building a country; they provide the foundational basis of a country by providing a correct understanding and a pride in one's own culture and heritage before one can think about the sciences and technologies.

Sadly, we ignored this foundational base, and a selective ideology occupied this vacuum. Most people ran after the sciences in independent India, and a consequence of this is, of course, great achievements, but accompanied by a sense of shame towards our own heritage. Indian culture is not perfect, but it has solutions for its problems too. For too long, we have only listened to what people have said about us. It is time that we start speaking about ourselves from our point of view. As a next step, we can talk about the world from our perspective. We may even have solutions for the world. That is a task for the future, and there is no better place to begin than this powerful book.

Chapter 10

# CULTURES DIFFER DIFFERENTLY

*SN Balagangadhara*
*(Editors: Jakob De Roover and Sarika Rao)*

## Introduction

This book, a collection of eight brilliant essays written at different periods of Balu's research programme starting in the 1980s, explains many of his ideas. For Balu, culture is fundamentally the resources of socialisation available for an individual and the community.

The most amazing aspect of Balu's writings is that there is something to take away for everyone, from the layperson to the highest academic. In straightforward language accessible to all, he puts across the most complex ideas. The same text, intensely illuminating for a layperson, would perhaps set the course for further research in an academic institute. It is a rare gift to be able to compose academic papers and make them as readable as thrillers. The year 2021 is important for India, in my view, for seeing the release of two of Balu's books, *What Does It Mean to Be an Indian?* and *Cultures Differ Differently.* These mutually reinforcing companion books are transformative and necessary reading for everyone, especially Indians, troubled by many narratives.

As Balu explains in his book *Reconceptualizing India Studies*, we need to understand Indian and non-Western cultures better because they now have an important role to play in world affairs for perhaps the first time in 500 years. It becomes a huge challenge since the study of India has emanated mostly from Europe in the last three centuries. In popular conception, Europe seems to be the source of huge intellectual and material achievements in almost all fields, while India's contribution remains one Gandhi, one Buddha, and a little bit of yoga. The sole purpose of Indian thinkers appeared to be to sustain immoral practices like oppression, caste, and sati. It is disturbing that Europe has been studying India for centuries, telling us whatever wrongs we have in our culture and country, and in reverse it does not know what to learn (even if there is anything to learn in the first place) from India.

Modern Europe became the future vision of a stagnant India for all our political thinkers and academics in post-independent India. Balu asks a very important question that forms the bedrock of most of his research programme: *What if all the colonial descriptions of India are false and are solely the result of the knowledge of India generated by colonial rule?* Western intellectuals created specific theories and assumptions for looking at other cultures and these seem to have become the only way of looking at the world. Generations of Indian intellectuals believe that only these European theories of the social sciences and humanities can be true.

Indian traditions like Advaita, Buddhism, Jaina, Saiva, and Vaishnava have also developed their theories of human beings, societies, ethics, morals, ideals, politics, arts, and languages as their contribution to human knowledge, but there is gross ignorance of these. It is one of the greatest peculiarities of the huge corpus of Indian knowledge, based solely on indigenous experiences, to remain indifferent to the study of alien cultures. The contemporary Indian intellectual scene not only continues the trend but also unquestioningly accepts the discourses about India by alien cultures as true. Indian and European cultures differ in many ways in their views about human beings, but what makes one the standard? How did the situation arise that Western culture decided its own method was the correct way to look at all humanity and our ideas receded into the background in the realm of 'specialised studies'?

## Culture and Cultural Differences

The concept of culture is controversial, with countless definitions of the term, some of which deny the concept altogether. Balu says that most of the linguistic and philosophical objections to the term 'culture' arise from conceptual confusions that do not require a rejection of the concept. He says that these so-called defects of the word 'culture', based on a casual application of language and philosophy, are properties of any and every word, whether from a natural or an artificial language. Despite all the negative criticisms of the word 'culture', the term 'cultural differences', however, has a lot of meaning and value. 'Differences between cultures' can be climatological, biological, or psychological in nature— all these are clearly different from the commonly-perceived notion of 'cultural differences'. Hence, what makes a difference, specifically a cultural difference?

Coping with human groups is as important as coping with nature for the survival of our species. Human beings living in the group are socialised within the framework of groups. The reservoir of learning consists in the resources of the group—its customs, traditions, and institutions. Child-rearing, schooling, family life, and group interactions are the mechanisms of transmission of these learning processes. In the process of learning (making a habitat) and 'learning to learn' (using the resources of socialisation), the group builds its culturality. Culturalisation thus becomes the 'how' of both learning and teaching. The variety of mechanisms is wide and immense, ranging from family interactions, friendships, religious ceremonies, rituals, schools, clubs, and associations to name a few. Balu says that a difference between individuals is a cultural difference and not social, biological, or psychological in nature if it entails a specific way of using the resources of socialisation.

Because of the great diversity of environments, human nature, and human achievements, there are different kinds of learning processes in different social groups. One kind of learning process builds societies and groups; one kind creates poetry, music, and dance; and one kind develops theories and speculations. These kinds of learning processes, in different degrees and combinations, lead to a common adaptive strategy in a specific group. In a social group, one dominant kind of learning process subordinates other kinds of learning processes. A specific combination of dominant and subordinate learning processes makes up a configuration of learning, and cultural differences are because of differences in these configurations. This is the strongest thesis of Balu while dealing with cultural differences. The West has a learning configuration rooted in religion where the 'why' question is important, and this dominant kind of learning generates theories and speculations. Indian culture is different; its dominant kind of learning has roots in rituals which, in turn, build societies and groups. The 'how' question is important here.

### Comparing Cultures—Why?

At an individual level, a person cannot be a typical 'Indian' or 'Westerner', but it is perfectly valid to describe cultural differences as they are real, observable, and empirically describable. These cultural differences emanate from differences in configurations of learning in different societies where there is an interplay between dominant and secondary modes of learning. Why do we need to compare cultures? The existing social sciences, primarily Western initiatives, have a deep symbiotic relationship with Orientalism or India studies. They augment each other in their claims about non-Western cultures, the non-Western man, and his society. The present social sciences become deficient as they continue the legacy of Orientalist writings. Thus, in a peculiar manner, Indian intellectuals, using Western methodologies (the social sciences), look at both the West and the East in the same way as Western intellectuals. Balu rues that our social sciences have been so colonised that a question of asking how the world would look from our viewpoint becomes meaningless.

When the West, studying India, problematised many narratives (Hinduism, caste, law, and so on), our social sciences did not question the older narratives but simply built on older theories by providing more 'facts'. With the language tools remaining the same, when Indian anthropologists, psychologists, or sociologists do their work in their respective fields, it is really the West talking to itself. We thus urgently need to decolonise the social sciences, which should be a comparative exercise, taking off from the previous social science studies without rejecting the hard-won previous insights. This task of decolonising should be a transcendence beyond the 'us' versus 'them' binary, emphasises Balu. Modern sociology describes the ills of the Indian cultural systems, presuming the truth of the Orientalist descriptions of non-Western cultures. Hence, to better study the non-West, there is a need for comparative research into cultures. Finally, the Orientalist description is an oblique reflection on Western cultural experience, even though it appears as a description of other cultures. We can thus study the culture of the describer (the West) through the medium of his descriptions (Orientalism) and thus reveal the nature of Western culture through comparison of cultures.

Comparative sciences seek to restore symmetry by rejecting a developmental ordering of history with the benchmark Western culture at the peak of cultural development. Comparative studies want to prove that different cultures are different forms of life, and they confront each other as alternatives to one another. Post-colonial studies lack this kind of objective, non-arbitrary, and scientific comparative research. Comparative studies thus seek to replace *ad hoc* hypotheses with alternate, universally applicable theories, which would be the correct 'critique' of proper understanding. The West and the East finally stand as equals in this exercise.

### Stories in Indian Culture

In Western culture, stories may entertain and form a genre of literature, but they do not instruct. Balu shows how stories constitute a differentiating point of our culture with many consequences. We never realise that the incredible variety and stock of stories for every situation in Indian culture play an important role in the socialising processes of a growing child. They work both as theoretical models representing small parts of the world and as practical exemplars that one can emulate. As theoretical models, stories are continuous with other learning products such as philosophy and scientific theories.

Most importantly, without any explicit morals or methods of practical action, stories teach the specific Indian cultural way of learning: *mimetic* learning. Mimetic learning or practical knowledge through exemplars creates new and original actions from old actions, just as new ideas generate from old ideas. Unlike in Western culture, where moral principles need to be context-free (applicable in all situations), exemplars are always context-bound. However, they are generative of new actions in different contexts.

Mimesis and learning with exemplars are typical of Asian (specifically Indian) culture, where the most important consequence is that instructional authorities need not be coextensive with religious, moral, political, or divine authorities. Balu explains how this mimetic learning by exemplars intriguingly explains many things of Indian culture: the 'strictness' of the family and the teacher in an individual's life; the importance given to the relation between individuals presupposing a moral community; why immigrant Asians turn out to be better in mathematics and engineering than any other ethnic minority; the essentially conservative nature of India where tradition weighs heavily; and the resistance of the Indian 'caste system' to any centralisation of 'political' and 'religious' power.

About the practical action-knowledge unique to Indian culture, Balu says:

Unlike the natural world, which is law-governed, a social world is the creation of human actions; the knowledge of creating it is the practical action-knowledge. Incredibly complex forms of social organisation can exist, continue to adapt themselves, and expand without being governed by any laws. A social organisation becomes an 'accumulated' practical knowledge. To seek to understand a social organisation by looking for its 'laws' might be as absurd as the denial of the law-governed character of the natural world. Spheres such as morality, law, social organisation, and human interaction belong to the realm of practical knowledge. Practical knowledge is cumulative, perhaps to a greater degree than knowledge in the theoretical sphere. The form of social organisation, the so-called 'caste system', is one such cumulative result. That is why no Indian could tell you what its 'principles' or 'rules' are. Yet, it reproduces itself because there is knowledge available (action-knowledge) to reproduce it. Its ability to 'adapt' itself to changing environments is merely the ability of human beings to execute actions in different environments.

### Cultural Differences in Morality

The fundamental categories that organise the description of the moral domain of other cultures arise from the describing culture. The notions of 'selfhood', the processes of learning, the experience of 'body', 'space' and 'time', and all other practices of a community support and sustain a notion of moral domain and moral practices. The basic conception of the 'agent' in Western culture is that in each human being, there is an inner core (the self or the agent) that is separate and different from everything else. In Indian culture, the actions that an organism performs (and assessed by another being) constitute an agent and nothing more. The peeling of the outer layers in Western culture reveals the 'true' agent standing independent; in Indian culture, such peeling reaches an emptiness. This has extremely profound consequences in the domain of morality in Western and Indian cultures, says Balu.

We never finish learning about the world in any field, including morality, because the universe is complex. Western culture, obsessed with moral discussions, however, never questioned the idea that learning to be moral can have a terminus. Balu says that the moral domain and contemporary ethical discussions, as consisting of rules requiring a foundation, are secularised versions of a theological belief. Christianity admits only one Sovereign, and His Will is the Law of the universe. 'Being moral' means obedience to this law because there are no other conceptions of moral Law and no other Sovereign. The terms in which Christian religion and theology framed the question have ended up as things that are "definitionally true" or "intuitively obvious" to the practitioners of secular ethics, including the 'logical' property of 'moral' statements—moral laws are universalisable.

In Indian culture, one speaks of infinitely many sovereigns while speaking about morality. Consequently, each one of us follows his 'own' morality; in this sphere, there is no one higher than the agent. The most fundamental category of 'moral judgement' in Indian traditions is that of *appropriateness*. Actions are meaningless (outside of contextual interpretations), and moral actions, as actions, become 'appropriate' within contexts. As all the Indian traditions put it, performing an action without any kind of desire, without aiming at any kind of goal, and without attaching this intentionality to human action is always the highest kind of appropriate action. It could well be an attitude that is beyond both good and evil.

Western culture obsessed with morality has been the author of deeds that 'ought' to chill any one's blood: crusades, jihads, inquisitions, witch hunts, colonisation, the genocide of the American Indians, Nazism, and transforming a continent and culture into slaves. It takes an enormous amount of goodwill to entertain the possibility that these cultures are not intrinsically 'evil', says Balu. Indian culture does know of tortures, wars, or cruelties, but they are insignificant when compared, either in magnitude or scale, to Western acts. Thus, as Balu says, the knife appears to cut both ways: against the background of the Western conception of 'ethics', Indian traditions 'chill the blood'. Against the background of Indian traditions, the West appears immoral.

### *Cultural Superimpositions and the Peculiarity of Indian Law*

Even a basic reading of the collegium system for the selection of judges in the high court and supreme courts leads one to realise the arbitrariness and opaqueness of the Indian judicial system. The unbridled powers of a select group of judges are hardly inspiring for the delivery of an efficient legal system. Balu shows in one of the essays how superimposing Western law on indigenous culture with their own ways of justice leads to the severe distortions that we face today. There is a need for further studies on how law and culture relate and how we can evolve better legal systems.

Balu thrashes to pulp the rhetoric about the great British law being a 'gift' to us. British society and law were corrupt to the core in the eighteenth and nineteenth centuries, when Britain ruled a great part of the globe. Their neighbours, allies, and cultural relatives saw them as corrupt, contemptible, hypocritical, and immoral. The British in India did whatever pleased them, but the judges and bureaucrats clothed these acts in legal language and many non-existent laws. Justice in British India was hardly equal. Local European communities did not allow Indian judges and law officers to try them, and they got away with the most brutal crimes through lenient European judges.

Balu then explains how Indians, as cultural beings, believing British law and British institutions to be the ideal, mixed them with their own ideas relating to justice, truth, persons, and so on. The notions of truth and falsity play a crucial role in Law. These notions are rooted in Christian theology. In Indian culture, there is a clear semantic distinction between lies and deception. The socialisation process in Indian culture even involves learning to lie. Deception, however, is clearly separable from lying. Thus, lying under oath loses its reasoning in law (ratio legis). Yet, 'perjury' remains a punishable offence in the Indian legal system.

As Dr. Balagangadhara explains, in Western culture, it is the fair, objective, and impartial law that judges, not the person of the judge. In contrast, the Indian judiciary sees itself as the 'embodiment' of justice dispensing 'justice', often completely independent of, or even oblivious to, legal provisions and statutes. Even for many people going to court, the judge represents justice embodied and personified. This attitude helps us understand the massive corruption of the judiciary in India. The law in Western culture tries to reduce arbitrariness and capriciousness in settling disputes. But the imposition of Western institutions in India encourages precisely that arbitrariness that the law is supposed to prevent. The figure of the 'judge' now uses the legal institution, which gives him the power to do what he does and to make arbitrary pronouncements because of the culturally specific notion of the judge. In indigenous cultural institutions, reasonableness prevails because the judge faces the community directly and owes explanations. In modern courts, such constraints on reasonableness are absent.

Politics and law in Western culture are meant to further the general interests of society but not those of any single community, group, or individual, especially corporate interests. Strikingly, Balu says, Indian culture does not have a vocabulary to understand any kind of discourse on interests, whether institutional, private, public, general, or social. If such is the case, legislation is meant to explicitly favour specific groups, which would give them votes. The Parliament's reasons for implementing the laws are not in the general interests of society but are as narrow as the reasoning of an individual who contemplates his own benefit. The

British made laws that favoured British interests but cloaked them in the language of 'general interest' and 'interest of the empire'. Protecting the British 'interests' later took the form of the 'protection of minority interests' in the Indian Constitution.

When the State promulgates laws that only favour and further narrow interests, citizens end up using such laws mostly retributively. Seeking personal vengeance (dowry, atrocity, and so on) becomes the major, if not sole, goal of the citizenry when they go to the courts. Thus, when implemented in India, the institutions of Western law encourage just the opposite of what such laws are meant to do: a vengeful, spiteful, and 'selfish' citizenry. Instead of promoting a cohesive society, such laws encourage divisiveness and conflict in society. Our legal systems are in need a lot of deep thinking, even as our judges are unleashing their extra-judicial activism and moral judgements on practically every institution in the country without first looking in the mirror.

## The Problem with Translations

In a vital chapter, Balu discusses the problems arising from translations, which Indologists, setting up powerful one-sided discourses, have been blind to in their understanding of Indian culture. Apart from the general issues of translating between two natural languages or between different domains in the same language, there are some unique problems that arise when one encounters cultural differences, especially in the domain of theology.

In theology, till now, the decision process has endorsed the following assumptions: (a) religion exists in all cultures; (b) each religion has specific ideas about 'deity', 'sin', 'salvation', etc.; and (c) these religions are rivals of each other. Consequently, people were convinced that theological languages are mutually translatable and that the difference between these theologies lay in their content alone. For centuries, the West believed that the Christian theological language was richer than the Indian theological language.

One needs to show (which nobody has ever done) that Indian culture also has religions and that 'deva', 'moksa', 'papa' are theoretical terms within Indian theologies equivalent to 'God', 'salvation', 'sin'. However, as

Balu shows, because India does not have native religions (like 'Hinduism', 'Buddhism', and 'Jainism'), the terms from the theological language (formulated in English) cannot be translated either into Hindi or Sanskrit using native words. Theological language has become such a deep part of the natural language in the West that the awareness that certain words (even words like 'truth' and 'falsity') are part of specialised theories has been lost. Consequently, when Indians learn English, they map the technical meanings of theological vocabulary to words from their native languages and distort both English and the native language in the process. Colonial consciousness, an aftermath of colonial rule and a continuing intellectual violence of contemporary times, finally generates an attitude that does not allow the transmission of native theories about various aspects of human existence unless first refracted through the prism of European reflections about 'man and society'.

Indians, having access to Indian and European languages but not to the implicit 'theories' embedded in these languages and transmitted by these cultures, reproduce Western descriptions of India when studying India and her culture. They also end up reproducing Western descriptions when attempting to understand Western culture. Thus, unlike translations between European languages, we face specific problems that emerged because British colonialism occurred within the framework of cultural differences between the West and India, says Balu. By using two important statements in English that paved the way for many important domains in European culture—"the grand book [of] the universe... is written in the language of mathematics" (Galileo); and "Man was born free, and everywhere he is in chains" (Jean-Jacques Rousseau)—Balu shows that they make sense only in the Western world when accompanied by a cluster of ideas rooted in Christian theology. Indian cultural concepts of karma, moksha, cycles of birth, death, bondage, and so on make the assimilation of these statements to Indian traditions intensely problematic, despite accurate word translations. Thus, Rousseau's statement does not make sense in Indian metaphysics, which believes that man is never born free. At birth, the past karma binds a human intensely, and the purpose of the present life is to continually break those chains.

### *The Indologists, Sanskritists, and Social Sciences: A Death Dance for Knowledge*

Indology is not a viable route for improvement in the different domains (anthropology, sociology, and political science), as some scholars propagate. Balu, in the final chapters, deconstructs the English Indologists most efficiently. Witzel, Mancur Olson, Wendy Doniger, Brian Smith, Stephanie Jamison, and Joel Brereton are some of these Indologists or Sanskritists who display profound ignorance when they comment on Indian social systems, including caste. Contemporary social scientists gleefully accept this rubbish produced by Indologists and spin sillier stories about 'Hinduism', 'the caste system', and so on. In this vast land across a timescale of at least 3000 years, it is difficult to find one single coherent 'theory' of *varna* in the indigenous texts. However, scholars have based theories on conjectures founded on fragmentary texts from 3000 or more years ago to speculate on the nature of Indian society.

The infamous Manava-dharmashastra, or 'Laws of Manu', allegedly created by Brahmin priests seeking superior and privileged positions, makes Manu a 'symbol of oppression' today. A verse from the tenth Chapter (10:24) famously articulates some of those constraints. The crucial word 'vyabhicara' translates as sexual misconduct in most English translations. However, this is a gross violation of the rules of Sanskrit grammar. In a verse with eight Sanskrit words, Balu shows how translators remove half the words present in the source, replace them with many words not present in the source, and exhibit the result as 'translation'. Interpretations appear to precede the translation of text instead of the other way around. The end-goal focus (telos) of any translation about Indian society and culture is to show a narrow caste-ridden society with wily Brahmins. Moralising talk and a normative language ('inequality', 'discrimination', 'injustice', and such other notions) define and determine the alleged talk about society, culture, rendering even intelligent too blind to see through the charade.

Balu shows how one Indologist, Mikael Aktor, gathers evidence from the texts and commentaries across two thousand years that have different historical and geographical origins to 'show' the *varna* ideology as existing across all centuries and prove that the Brahmins legitimised oppression. In any other domain, his way of working with texts would meet objections based on methodology, chronology, the ways of culling highly selective fragments, issues of translation, and problems in the nature, genre, transmission, redaction, and context of the cited texts. However, as Balu writes, "instead, one leaves the Chapter with the distinct impression that all these texts somehow represent the 'Brahmanical ideology' behind 'the Hindu social structure'."

Indologists use discredited theories from earlier social sciences to put across outlandish claims regarding a culture about which they are ignorant. Contemporary social sciences draw upon these ignorant claims to put across additional and equally outlandish claims about human societies and cultures, again in ignorance of what the Indological claims rest upon. Balu says sharply:

> The social sciences and Indology enter a death dance where neither participant dies but knowledge does without delivering anything of substance about both Ancient and Modern India. The Indologists, Sanskritists, and social scientists, depending on each other, deserve credit for accomplishing this incredible feat of making 'the' caste system synonymous with 'discrimination' and 'oppression' and so effortlessly supplanting the British 'class' hierarchy, American 'racial' inequality, the 'apartheid' policy, the Nazi ideology, and so on. Anthropologists spent about 100 years attempting to get rid of a pernicious and incoherent concept like 'tribe' only to see it sneak back in, via Indology and other social sciences, into the Indian Constitution, Indian legislation, and their administration.

Balu concludes that the sale of ignorance as knowledge captures that nation's academic philosophy and knowledge generation.

### *Personal Concluding Remarks*

The country must one day look to Balu for solutions. Maybe it is still to sink to the deepest level to finally reach a point of hopelessness, and thus preparedness, to hold the rope thrown by the Balu school. It might take many years, but it is with intense optimism that Balu and his scholars have been working tirelessly for decades for such a day. Adi Shankara finished and packaged his treatises a thousand to two thousand years ago, not for his contemporary times but for eternity. When an individual is in despair, he looks around to find Adi Shankara's literature in place, ready to receive him. Similar is the case with Balu; the only hope remains that such a state for the country does not come after a thousand years but in a few decades. But come it will.

Balu had his share of controversies, from attacks on his ideas to ad hominem attacks and even physical threats. All of them emanate from superficial reading, a lack of understanding, and a failure to seriously engage with him because most of his ideas radically kick a person out of their comfort zones of easy, safe, and sometimes lazy scholarship. There has been a repeated accusation against Balu that he attributes more than excessive power to Western Christianity, and even a laughable suggestion that he may be a covert Hindu fundamentalist. Nothing can be farther from the truth if one carefully goes through his books and articles. The alternative viewpoints are not attacks on Christ or Christians but simply arguments against secularised Christian theology determining Indian intellectual discourses, causing immense damage to the social and cultural fabric of the country.

Throughout his arguments, he never abuses the West and always insists that the West and the East stand as equals and both have something to learn from each other. The only problem comes when one exclusive framework for one culture tries to explain and understand all cultures and all humanity across time and space. Hence, he pleads for the East to develop its own paradigms and social sciences in a healthy manner to reverse the gaze—a reversal that leads to harmony rather than strife and violence, which the present discourses continually seem to generate. Hence, when he attacks the West, Christianity, or even Indian icons, it is only the ideas and their violent consequences for Indian culture against which he takes aim. Scratching the most superficial veneer of his apparently sharp language exposes an almost divine, sage-like love not only for India but for all humanity.

For a concerned citizen of the country seeing so much hate and distress, Balu offers solutions by presenting India in a different light. When a patient comes to a doctor, he may not need to know the etiopathogenesis of his disease, the pharmacological basis of the drugs, or the evolution of different surgical practices. Relief from the pain is what the patient seeks. Hence, without making any of the theories relevant to the understanding of the ideas, Balu offers immense hope to a layperson. The academics are welcome to get hold of the background theories to make their analysis. That is indeed the incredible power of Balu's writings.

## Chapter 11

# INDIA IN THE EYES OF EUROPEANS

*Martin Fárek*

Europeans have shown a great fascination for the study of India, starting with its missionary and travel reports. However, what was the understanding of the 'otherness' of Indian traditions in this scholarship that continued until the present? The Comparative Science of Cultures programme initiated at the University of Ghent by Dr. SN Balagangadhara shows that the understanding of Indian traditions is inextricably linked to the indigenous religious developments in Europe. The Roman Catholic Church after the fall of the Roman Empire, the Protestant Reformation, and the Enlightenment formed a continuum of changes that took place in Europe since the turn of the millennium. At the time of the colonial venture in India, a Protestant understanding of religions was predominant, along with Enlightenment values.

Particularly, despite all the changes in European history, the idea of India as a land of 'pagan' religions filled with superstitions, false gods, meaningless rituals, and tyrannical priests held constant sway. There were, of course, many changes in the understanding of religion per se in India. One interpretation (Vedism > Brahmanism > Hinduism) presented the degeneration of a pure religion of the Vedas in the remote past, having Biblical links to the one true religion of Christ through the manipulation of crafty Brahmins. Another story ordered religions on an ascending evolutionary scale, starting with the primitive religions (the pagans) and ending with the highest form of religion, Christianity (especially the Protestant variety).

The Enlightenment scholars apparently rejected religion, but Balagangadhara clearly shows in *The Heathen in His Blindness* that most of their ideas were simply secularisations of theological ideas. This is, in fact, a more powerful way of achieving the universal spread of Christianity than a direct conversion of subjects. The Enlightenment did not change its understanding of the nature of Indian traditions as degenerated religions in need of reforms for their many deficiencies.

Balagangadhara shows that, across centuries, there was a continuous failure of most intellectuals in both Europe and India to understand the Indian traditions (Hinduism, Buddhism, Sikhism, and Jainism) as religions. The major mistake was to persist in calling Indian phenomena (perhaps best termed traditions) as religions, despite realising that everything they were dealing with was not religion in the definitional sense. This led to many conceptual distortions and sad consequences. Balagangadhara explains that Hinduism was not a 'construction' as some scholars have alleged, but simply an *experience* of the colonials of the many practices in an alien land that they were trying to understand and rule.

Many rituals, practices, Brahmins, deities, *murtis*, scriptures, and worships existed, but the structure or meta-narrative they gave to such a conglomerate became the 'religion' of Hinduism. Their own culture, rooted in religion, gave rise to the idea that religion is a *cultural universal,* and they could not imagine that cultures could exist without a religion. There have been many scholars like Sri Aurobindo, Bankim Chandra—or more contemporary scholars such as Frits Staal—who intuitively were not comfortable with the idea of converting Indian traditions into religions of the Abrahamic mould.

Frits Staal, for example, studying Indian rituals, concluded that the Western origin of the concept of religion is inadequate in the study of Indian traditions. Staal simply says that it is impossible to consider Asian traditions to be religion. Thus, in Asia, groupings of various traditions are not only uninteresting and uninformative but also unreal, says Fárek. What counts instead are ancestors and teachers—hence lineages, traditions, affiliations, cults, eligibility, and initiation. These are concepts with ritual rather than truth-functional overtones typical of a religion.

In the present book, Martin Fárek, a brilliant scholar and presently Associate Professor (docent) in the Department of Geography, Technical University of Liberec (Czech Republic), specifically examines whether Czech Indology, while not being a coloniser, followed a similar pattern of understanding as the rest of Europe. He also examines whether the British Orientalists and European historiography, in their understanding of Indian culture, were truly free of the many theological assumptions and ideas. The Indians looked at their past in a different manner, and this did not make sense to European scholars. The Aryan theory has played havoc with the socio-political-cultural fabric of India, and Fárek shows in this book that again, theological considerations of religion, language, and the origin of humankind formed this theory. In the final chapter, the author deals with an Indian intellectual of those times, the Bengali reformer Raja Ram Mohan Roy, and shows how his understanding of Indian culture had distortions due to influences from Western narratives.

## *The European Search for Religion in India*

In the second chapter, perhaps the crux of the book, the author describes Europe's attempts, specifically Czech scholarship, to understand the religions of India. He demonstrates that the long line of pre-colonial writings (missionary reports, travelogues, traders' descriptions), the first Oriental scholarship, the later European scholarship both in India and abroad, Indian intellectuals of the colonial and post-colonial era, and finally the present-day Indologists show a remarkable consistency in their understanding of religions in general and of Indian traditions in particular.

Over a period, through repeated affirmations, the basic story is that of a *pure religion* in the remote past (the Vedic Era) brought by the invading Aryans from Central Asia/Russia in 1500 BCE. Through the handiwork of corrupt and crafty Brahmins (who introduced not only the hierarchal 'caste system' in connivance with the rulers but also many superstitions and rituals), this religion degenerated into *Brahmanism*. Then rose the many great rebellious movements (Bhakti movements, Buddhism, Jainism, and so on) against the priesthood. Along the way, the rejected Untouchables stayed out of the Hindu fourfold caste system.

Finally, through many means, both violent and nonviolent, Hinduism not only drove Buddhism away to remote lands but also managed to absorb the good teachings of Buddha into its own fold. Buddha also became an *Avatara* of *Vishnu* in this process of absorption. Thus came about the final form of present *Hinduism*. The transition from Vedism to Brahmanism to Hinduism is the overall framework of all present understanding of Indian religions, which has also permeated the standard teaching curriculum of India today—only the mechanisms of the transition vary.

However, there were huge discrepancies in the understanding of what existed in society, its practices, and what was evident in many scriptural texts. Despite realising that doctrines (as for other Abrahamic religions) did not really exist for the disparate, apparently disconnected conglomerate of rituals, philosophies, and practices, they could crystallise some common themes: 1) Hinduism as one unified socio-religious organisation; 2) The Vedas, the Upanishads, and the Manu Dharma as its central sacred texts; 3) Reincarnation, the law of Karma, and *moksha* (the goal of life) as the central doctrines; and 4) Brahmins as the priestly class.

Though invariably Buddhism was a strong contestant, its characterisation by European scholars was even more problematic: it was a *religion*, or it was a *philosophy*, or it was an *atheistic religion* because it did not speak of God, or it was a unique *religion-philosophy*, and so on. Martin Fárek methodically analyses the information gleaned from societal practices and from the various scriptures as cited by scholars across centuries. The classical work of Balagangadhara (*The Heathen in His Blindness*) forms an important starting point for his examination. He shows how each of the elements of the main story has glaring inconsistencies, untenable conclusions, contradictions, and assumptions.

Hinduism was not a unified whole; the law of Karma and reincarnation plays no role in many traditional groupings; not *moksha* but a heavenly paradise is an aim for many others; not all priests are Brahmins; not all Brahmins are priests; Brahmins hardly had a say in the internal matters of other *jatis*; there was never ever a pan-India central sacerdotal authority implementing rules and regulations and ordering the society in a hierarchal manner; hardly any Indian ever knew or knew the content of the Vedas or even the existence of a Manu Dharma, which is allegedly the source of all problems; one could visit temples or not, declare oneself as an atheist and still be a Hindu; and so on. There is neither historical nor contemporary evidence supporting the idea that the Brahmins are a powerful priestly class in Indian society.

Buddhism was even more problematic when the Buddhist original texts clearly reveal that Buddha and Buddhism never rejected either the Brahmins or the *varna vyavastha*. In fact, Buddha himself sought to define a true Brahmin, declared Rama as his previous reincarnation, placed Kshatriyas above the Brahmins in the hierarchal ordering, and conformed with most of the Upanishadic statements and yogic-meditative methods. Later Buddhist writings did not deviate much from the original Buddha messages. The whole story of Buddhism rebelling against Hinduism is simply a house of cards placed on shifting sands.

However, the most important questions now come into play. This 'construction' of Hinduism was definitely not mischief on the part of some serious intellectuals across centuries. So, how exactly did Europeans become convinced of the religious nature of Indian traditions? What was the underlying evidence? Why do they consider the Vedas, the Upanishads, etc., to be central sacred texts and their core doctrinal texts? How did Brahmins become priests of unified Hinduism? What makes Europeans think that ascetic traditions are protest movements?

The first colonial and Oriental scholars drew their theories from the observations of many missionaries, travellers, and administrators whose predominant image of India was a negative one where the priests were exploiting society with their privileged position. The author explains how, with regards to the first colonial scholars (John Zephaniah Holwell, Alexander Dow, William Jones, and Henry Thomas Colebrooke) and the later ones too (like HH Wilson, Monier Monier-Williams, and Friedrich Max Müller), a Christian theological framework explicitly postulated the existence of religion as a quest for the only true God in all cultures, although in mostly a degenerated pagan form.

The author explains how the first British Orientalists adopted the theological questions of their predecessors and how they developed them, from Holwell's speculations about the original revealed scripture of India, distorted by Brahmins, to Jones' quest for the original monotheism of India in the Vedas and the Upanishads. The supposed 'early departure' from monotheism to polytheism was in fact the starting point of the degeneration hypothesis of Indian traditions. In this specific theological framework developed by HH Wilson and Monier-Williams, Indian religion underwent three transformations: from monotheist Vedism to the extravagant ritualism of Brahmanism to Hinduism. Knowledge of Sanskrit played no role in revising this basic understanding, which strongly demonstrates the role of theory or the background web of European cultural ideas in the selection and interpretation of data on Indian traditions. Jones' linguistic and other scholarly outputs finally assumed the truth of a Biblical global chronicle and in the search for Noah's lost sons after the Great Flood.

As an example, the Europeans saw rituals as an expression of religion only and nothing else. The established conceptual structure simply did not allow consideration that *'puja'* in Indian traditions might be something other than a false or imperfect form of worship to mainly false gods. The imbibing of theological terms into natural language made the translations of many Indian concepts like *Brahman, Deva, devis, manas, buddhi* into equivalents of many exclusively theological terms like *God, idols, sin, conscience*, and so on. What was common sense in one culture became extremely problematic when used to understand alien traditional cultures.

The Protestant criticism of Catholic priests and the degeneration of society; the Christian criticism of Jewish practices and its priesthood; the absolutely alien ideas of blasphemy and heresy; and the Enlightenment values protesting against religion became the frameworks for finally understanding Indian traditions as religions. However, as Balagangadhara shows, most of the Enlightenment principles were simply secularised forms of Christianity, which showed consistency in holding up Indian traditions as religions. Whatever movements took place in Europe, the rock-like explanation for the degeneration of the 'primitive' monotheism remained the 'power-hungry' Brahmins, an answer anticipated by the Protestant-

Catholic controversies. The argument against degenerate clergy gained force by reference to similar abominations in India, says the author.

Post-independence, there was a deep colonial consciousness, which did not allow Indian intellectuals to question the narratives set by colonisers. The most amazing facet of this entire story has to be the fact that, throughout, the definition of Indian traditions remained mainly negative: *what they were not* with respect to Christianity, Islam, or Judaism. Yet, they were religions. Despite mounting evidence across centuries that the phenomena Europeans encountered in India were never religions like Christianity or Islam, they persisted with the idea that India had many religions (sometimes even fighting each other like in Europe) instead of redefining what religions may actually mean. Their culture, rooted in religion, could never accept that cultures could exist without religions.

### Religion, Historiography, and the Indian Past

In an incisive chapter, Fárek elegantly shows how Christian theology defined the way of European historiography but played havoc with the understanding of the Indian past. The combined story of the Old and New Testaments, starting with the creation of the universe and ending with Jesus Christ as the final Messiah, formed the framework for understanding history for European scholars. The imminent expectation of Christ's second coming and the end of the world became the basis for a linear concept of time that was supposed to evolve from the creation of the universe through the turning point of Christ's advent until its ending. The concept of history as a linear time with progress from a 'primitive' past to an 'advanced' future remains ingrained to this day.

The author then traces how theology receded but, in its secularised form, the framework of universal global history persisted with the linear concept of time. More chronologies of various cultures merged into the single linear chronology of the universalising framework, where European history took centre stage, and the other cultures became its appendages. Interestingly, the same historical consciousness turned back on itself and led to criticism of its own Christian legends. However, despite gradual secularisation, Christian thinking preserved its basic structures by considering history as a goal-directed process involving all of humanity. This remains the defining philosophy of the new research field called *world history.*

The history of India written by Europeans followed the same pattern. Thus, historians trapped in religious thinking and Eurocentrism, keeping a purpose and progress in mind, wrote about Hindu, Muslim, and European (or Christian) periods of the Indian past. Many influential authors eventually applied the terms 'Antiquity,' 'Middle Ages,' and 'Modernity' to the history of India corresponding to the same religious chronological periods. The religious periodisation implied a development from primitive paganism towards its highest form, British Protestantism. Colonial scholars, starting with William Jones, did not deviate from this framework of theological thinking. They forced the local narratives of native peoples' pasts, including the Indian conception of time, into the Biblical framework. Everything that did not fit the framework of the Biblical story (the universe beginning in 4004 BCE, for example), such as the enormous time span of the Puranic ages, were simply allegories, falsities, fabrications, myths, or fables.

Even today, though rejecting explicit theology, both Indian and Western scholars fail to inquire into what those narratives meant to Indians themselves. Instead, the only possible approach to the past is either as "history proper (or true)," rooted in the theological foundations of historiography, or as a "myth (thus false)." This framework does not allow for other possibilities. European and Indian scholars have continuously discussed to date why ancient Indians did not have any historical consciousness. Apart from stereotypical reasons such as predilection for 'myths, fables, and fantasy' and 'aversion to serious narrative,' it was due to a primitive religion controlling the economic and political spheres along with a rigid caste system. The cyclical conception of time is allegedly a major obstacle to developing a historical consciousness. It never occurred to the researchers and historians of both the West and India alike that there could be a very different way of dealing with the past, quite different from the European idea of history.

The section on Indian history expands on and complements a most thought-provoking essay by Balagangadhara—*What Do Indians Need, A History or A Past?* The combination of chronological genealogies mixed with stories (an important component of teaching, learning, and socialisation in Indian culture) was perhaps a unique Indian way of preserving the past. The ancestral lineage of Shri Rama traces back across 40 generations and that of Raja Janaka (Devi Sita's father) almost 20 generations in the *Valmiki Ramayana*. These genealogies remain permanently etched. Yet, for Indians, an attitude that Europeans could not fathom, the names of Shri Rama's ancestors or the existence of Shri Rama himself are of less importance than the stories of the *Ramayana*. This 'mimetic' learning using stories forms the most important aspect of Indian culture, where there is no 'primitive' past but an 'ancient' past with stories relevant across time.

The European polarised distinction of 'historical thinking' as opposed to 'myth' fails to make sense of Indian culture. Just like the Europeans, Indians too have not grasped the theoretical grounds of Western historiography. Indian theoretical interpretations in the framework of a linear progression of time from a primitive past to a golden future stay intact in their otherwise meticulous studies.

European historiography gives importance to the link between specific events and the whole religious message. When confronted with the otherness of Indian narratives, William Jones declared: "Either the first eleven chapters of Genesis are true, or the whole fabric of our national religion is false; a conclusion, which none of us, I trust, would wish to be drawn." A message can be true only if an event actually happened. Western thought, even when rejecting Christ or Christianity, gives central importance to the factuality of Jesus Christ's life and other events; no such link has developed in Indian traditions. In Indian thinking, Shri Rama, Buddha, or Shri Krishna may never have existed, but the *Ramayana*, the Buddhist teachings, and the *Mahabharata* are always true.

Indian traditions deal with the past by mingling stories with the preservation of the names and actions of their ancestors, rulers, and important figures. However, as a major difference, Indians have taken little interest in a long-term, precise chronology, and they never ordered various events in a pan-India or global chronology. They have not tried to find the purpose of history in those memories. In what way do traditional narratives become linked to memories of past events? What constitutes the 'truthfulness' of narratives in Indian culture as opposed to the status of historical factuality in European historiography? Such research can allow Western historians to draw inspiration, in reverse, from Indian thinking and understand that there are alternative ways of looking at the past, says the author.

## *Changing Interpretations of the Aryans*

The classical paradigm of Indian pre-history initiated by European scholars is that of the invading or migrating Aryans from Central Asia/ Russia, who, in around 1500 BCE, entered India through the northwest and displaced the indigenous people. Those driven south of the Vindhyas became the Dravidians; those to the forests and mountains became the 'tribals'. The Brahmin priests, in the invading foreign groups, in connivance with the rulers, created a caste system where the first three orders (the original exploiters) were Aryans. The subjugated people, as the lowest in the hierarchy, became the Sudras and the Untouchables. Thus, the mysterious Aryans became a wholesome explanation to explain many things about India.

The only scientifically established fact of the entire theory is the relatedness of Indo-European languages, noted first by Oriental scholars such as William Jones and others who predated him (like Newton or Leibnitz). This led to a vibrant area of comparative philology, which in essence arrived at the idea of a mother language (PIE, or Proto-Indian-European language), giving rise to all the languages of Europe and India. This mother language must also have a homeland from which people migrated to various areas and where each group developed a degenerated version of the original language.

The author explains how theological assumptions formed the basic structure of the first ideas of the theory and laid the basis for later nineteenth-century linguistic and anthropological research. The discussions were on three related questions: What was the primary language of humankind? How did languages come to separate from each other and spread around the world, and is it possible to find the ideal language? The basis for these questions, especially for William Jones, was Genesis and the later dispersal of Noah's descendants as the truthful account of global history. The European nations were descendants of Japheth and India—perhaps either of Ham or Japheth.

Jones' comparative project was primarily aimed at reconstructing the earliest history of humankind and discovering the original and oldest religion. It was more about speculative identifications and parallelism of Biblical and Greek-Roman characters with Indian ones than comparative linguistics. Thus, a language family originated in the quest for an original religion. A common original homeland originated in the belief of a Great Flood, in the aftermath of which Noah and his descendants moved to all parts of the world. Ironically, a truly linguistic proof of identity and European languages came from Franz Bopp, who, in turn, took his inspiration from Indian linguistics.

Later scholars rejected explicit theology. The post-flood dispersion of nations was secularised in linguistic and anthropological speculations about the noble Aryan race subjugating the uncivilised peoples of India. Thus, Aryan theories clearly have their root in theology, which presupposes the universal truth of the Biblical accounts. The prism of the presupposed invasion remained a framework for explaining even later linguistic and archaeological discoveries.

The most important source for rejecting the Aryan theory comes from archaeology. To date, there is not a shred of evidence supporting the invasion or migration scenario. Unfortunately, this Aryan theory became an established fact, and highly selective words with fancy interpretations from the Vedic corpus became their supporting evidence. Words such as *varna* became colour and *a-nas* became 'without a nose' or 'stub' nose to support many racial speculations of distinct Aryan and Dravidian races. Such interpretations laid the basis of physical anthropology studies. In a dubious interpretation of a single passage from the large Vedic corpus by Max Mueller, the promoter of anthropometry, HH Risley claimed that the Vedic Aryans referred to their enemies as *noseless*.

Archaeology remained the biggest problem even as the Indus excavations (the Harappan and Mohenjo-Daro civilisations in the 1920s and the Mehrgarh excavations later) flew in the face of the Aryan theory. All the evidence (archaeology, textual, Vedic, inscriptions, astronomical) has suggested not only an indigenous Vedic civilisation without any Aryan-Dravidian divide but even a possible reverse migration from India to other parts of Europe (the OIT, or Out of India Theory). However, as the author says, the idea of an invasion remains primary, and the question of integrating any new findings with it is merely subsidiary to all European scholars and their Indian followers.

The author mentions one scholar who says it is amazing that European scientists were convinced for a long time about an Aryan race despite there being no biological criteria that would characterise the Aryans. The author shows elegantly how Enlightenment theories (progress of civilisation from a primitive society to its supposed culmination, represented by the Western world) and Darwin's evolutionary theories (spinning of racial ideas) played a crucial role in the Aryan debate and the subsequent speculations of the caste system in India.

Selective bits of the Vedic corpus supported their preconceived theories, and *ad hoc* adjustments explained away uncomfortable archaeological findings, but the basic idea of invading Aryans remains consistent. One adjustment, on the discovery of the Dravidian *Brahui* language in the North, involves even the mysterious Dravidian race invading from the South and destroying the Harappan culture. This is the state of contemporary scholarship to this day. Both Western and Indian scholars have not discarded the noxious Aryan theory, standing without evidence but causing intense damage to the social fabric of India.

### *Did Ram Mohan Roy Understand Western Religion?*

How does it matter to Indians how Europe views India? The answer that the Comparative Science of Cultures scholars provide is that it has mattered across centuries to date because of the intellectual entrapment of Indians in colonial narratives. Believing whatever the colonials said about us and then superimposing them on our own understanding and lived experience has caused severe distortions. Dr. Balagangadhara defines this in detail as a process of *colonial consciousness*. This violence at an intellectual level is far more severe and long-lasting than the physical and material plundering of colonialism. All current understanding of Indians about India—such as caste, religion, secularism, linguistic policies, and so on—is coloured by this colonial consciousness. Martin Fárek ends the book with a brilliant analysis of Raja Ram Mohan Roy, considered one of the great reformers of Hinduism.

Jakob De Roover and Sarah Claerhout explain the concept of 'topos' (plural 'topoi') in their recent excellent book *Religious Conversion: Indian Disputes and Their European Origins*. This refers to commonplace ideas and words that occur as clusters of interrelated notions specific to a culture. For example, while discussing Christian theology the West uses words and ideas with self-evident meanings such as 'belief', 'faith', 'doctrine', 'conversion', 'religion', and so on. 'Conceptual distortion' occurs when *topoi* originating from one cultural setting interpret *topoi* from another culture. Thus, a partial understanding of Christianity and its superimpositions on Indian culture made Gandhi look incoherent and inconsistent, as Roover and Claerhout show. Here, Ram Mohan Roy has the same inconsistencies as when he was superimposing his partial understanding of Christianity on the traditional systems of India.

Fárek shows how Roy, accepting wholly the ideas of European deism and Unitarianism, reinterpreted *Vedanta* and tried to reform the society of its evil practices, such as Sati, and 'meaningless' rituals. Image worship was immoral, with Roy arguing that this type of worship did not exist in the Vedas and *Vedanta*. His descriptions of the "one true God" as the designer of the universe, of the human body, and of nature were clearly Western-Christian ideas. Believing, like the Orientalists, that the original and pure monotheism of the Vedas had degenerated into polytheism, he strived to get the degenerated *Hinduism* back to *Vedism*, cleansing it of *Brahmanism*. The criticism of a supposedly immoral Shri Krishna involving *Gopis* followed the same line of arguments as the missionaries, even as he did not show interest in understanding the *Vaishnava* view of Krishna *Bhakti*, or devotion.

Yet Roy did not condemn idolatry completely. In a contradiction of ideas, Roy still advocated that if one is not qualified to worship the "one true God", one should worship at least the idols. But worshipping by means of form would lead to only temporary bliss. However, from a Christian viewpoint, this is completely unacceptable. True worship can only be based on belief in one true God. All other gods are simply false gods, and to worship them means to perform 'idolatry.' In the framework of Christian European lenses, his reform of *Vedanta* and Hindu society was a severe distortion, and it is no wonder that traditional scholars rejected Roy's reframing. The general populace also did not accept Brahmo Samaj in any big way.

On the other hand, Roy's great esteem for Christian ethical teaching (*The Precepts of Jesus*) was also controversial. He believed in the Unitarian doctrine of Jesus Christ being a human being, not God, and his fights with the Baptists were in line with many theological debates on the nature of Christ and Christianity. A distortion appeared here again when Roy believed that historical narratives and dogmas concerning the life of Christ were not as important as the teachings of Jesus. This was clearly a distortion of Christian fundamental importance to the truth of doctrines, and here Roy was applying his Indian understanding to Western theology (*Shri Rama may not be true, but the Ramayana is always true*). Thus, the Christians also rejected his ideas.

Fárek says that Roy's works and the facts about his life make for a strong argument that he basically accepted the Western—especially the Unitarian—framework of understanding as his own. He then strove to apply them to his life and society. Fárek says: "How can any 'earnest-minded investigator of the science of comparative religion' just compare the practices of different religious groups without considering the differences between their doctrines? How can you consider principles of moral conduct to be the essence of Christianity and resign to the very possibility of finding out who Jesus was?"

Finally, despite his heart being in the right place, Roy's superimpositions of Christian theology (where he did not really understand the concepts of 'worship,' 'idolatry,' and so on) on Indian traditions failed to convince both Indians and most Christians.

### *Personal Concluding Remarks*

This is another wonderful work from the scholars of the Comparative Sciences of Cultures in Belgium, or Ghent School. Initiated by the legendary Dr. SN Balagangadhara, its scholars have taken forward his ideas to give a better understanding of India and the world. Their works are extremely important to Indians as they give real solutions to the problems we are facing presently, especially those related to religion and the so-called caste system. The research programme has a fundamental idea regarding religion, which says that the phenomena in India (Hinduism, Buddhism, Jainism, and Sikhism) are *traditions* and not religions. Traditions and religions are two different paradigms.

The configuration of Indian culture has its roots in traditions, while Western culture's roots are in religion. The cultural understanding of Indian culture has been only one-sided from the Western, mainly European Christian, perspective. Their plea to Indian scholars is to develop, as a first step, an Indian view of itself and the world. Only with an alternative view, which does not seem to exist now, can we talk about decolonisation and replace it with something else. The colonisation is most severe at the intellectual level. At the same time, the school makes strong arguments for how most Western progressive and liberal ideas have never been free of theology. They ask the West to be aware of the strong theological background of its present lenses to view itself and the world.

The finest aspect of their writings is that they never descend to abuse, polemic, or rhetoric. Both the West and the East stand as equals, facing each other with the potential to learn from each other. Only a very superficial reading and a shallow understanding can construct them as *anti-Christian* or, even worse, *pro-Hindutva*. Their extremely scholarly output, put forth in lucid language, makes sense to laypersons and ordinary concerned citizens as it connects well to their lived experiences and shows some solid solutions that the present narratives fail to provide.

Unfortunately—out of ignorance, superficial understanding, or fear—there is deep resistance to their ideas in the dominant academic scene. The ideas of this school threaten to rip out the foundational basis of well-established truths, on which rest huge monuments of discourse. The present social sciences, permeated with Western secularised theological ideas, influence thinking in almost all spheres—politics, law, bureaucracy, and media. The present path of India is on a dangerous course, and only if we reject some old narratives and take up a fresh approach can we correct the course. Fortunately, a ray of hope comes from the Comparative Science of Cultures school. Its time will surely come, even if the wait is long.

# MAGIC BETWEEN EUROPE AND INDIA: ON MANTRAS, COERCION OF GODS, AND THE LIMITS OF CURRENT DEBATES

*Martin Fárek and Pavel Horák*

### Introduction: Understanding Mantras

This is a summary of a wonderful and thought-provoking article by Martin Fárek and Pavel Horák, scholars from the Czech Republic. Martin Fárek is doing commendable work in understanding Indian traditions from an Indian viewpoint, countering the dominant narratives set since colonial times. The latter narratives continue uninterrupted in Western and Indian universities, unfortunately. Fárek belongs to a small group of dedicated scholars, the Ghent School of Dr. Balagangadhara, whose work will hopefully correct some of the disastrous discourses ravaging the country. His significant contribution includes editing a path-defining book, *Western Foundations of the Caste System*. In this paper, he and his colleague discuss the understanding of mantras from a Western scholarly perspective and how they are finally based on Christian theological frameworks.

There are three main positions concerning *mantras*, which are perceiving them as:

1) Spells (magical practices)
2) Prayers (religious practices)
3) Both at the same time (Magico-Religious)

There is a growing scholarly dissatisfaction with the explanation (especially advocated by the missionaries) of Indian mantras as spells or charms (magical practices). Yet the debate is not new, as some early Orientalists had already suggested that mantras are prayers, and some, like John Woodroffe, believed there was nothing holy or prayerful about a mantra. Over the last 200 years, scholars vacillated between the two positions: Mantras are prayers and thus religious practice; or mantras are spells and thus magical practices. There are other standpoints too, but current research on mantras remains trapped within the same cycle of ideas about spells and prayers.

The authors strive to show that there was a whole structure of interconnected ideas, deeply rooted in Christian belief in a Biblical God and fallen angels, that formulated the dominant characterisation of magical practices in modern scholarship on India. They propose a three-step scheme that explains how the originally coherent account of Christian theology gradually dissolved into a set of vague and otherwise problematic ideas that have typified discussions of Indian mantras. We need to find a way out of the entrenched framework of ideas.

This chapter may seem a little out of place in the book, but it specifically highlights a problem with western studies of Indian culture over centuries. These studies never include the practitioners of the living and thriving tradition. We may accept or even remain indifferent to scholarly debates that confine themselves to an alien land or talk about a deceased culture. Unfortunately, they easily infiltrate Indian scholarship, leading us many times to accept them as a genuine representation and a pertinent discourse on Indian culture. The western scholarly debates on Indian mantras are an extraordinary example of this phenomenon.

### Are Indians Adoring Their Gods or Manipulating Them?

Scholarship over the last 200 years has debated extensively on whether mantras are prayers, spells, sacred formulas, or charms. Some used the terms interchangeably, leading to the impression that magical and religious practices are ultimately the same thing. Both basic explanations of mantras were present in nineteenth-century European scholarship on India: for the early British Orientalists, mantras were prayers; for others, originally mainly missionaries, they were spells. A set of problems arising from those early debates remains with us to this day.

This debate also closely links to the debate about the character of Vedic mantras. The first three Samhitas (Rigveda, Samaveda, and Yajurveda) were apparently 'religious', containing prayers to gods, while the Atharvaveda Samhita became 'magical' because of its alleged spells. However, there is hardly a consensus about this, though it is widely believed. Some modern scholars think all Vedic mantras are magical. With the emergence of Tantric studies, the mantras of traditions labelled "Tantric" became *spells* or *charms*.

### The First Position: Are Mantras Prayers?

The early Orientalists—like HT Colebrooke, HH Wilson, Max Müller, Monier-Williams, and Paul Deussen—thought that mantras were a means of adoring the gods of India. They were 'prayers', 'petitions', 'thanksgiving', 'praise', or 'worshipping' a deity or god as the object. However, the British Orientalists themselves quoted instances when mantras do not address any deity at all, like the Vedic hymns addressed to kings, their wives, or even 'prayers' offered by a groom to his bride during a marriage ceremony. These raise questions about the precise meaning of prayer. Finally, British Orientalists mentioned the existence of meaningless mantras (a few syllables like *ira ayira* repeated many times) but did not know how to account for them by the standard explanations.

### The Second Position: Are Mantras Magic?

In the second position, what would make a mantra an example of magical practice? The direct use of Christian ideas about pagan idolatry, misleading worshippers and directing them towards the wrong goals in life, is obvious here, both in the books of Christian missionaries and scholars. William Ward, one of the famous Serampore Baptists, described the mantras as 'formularies' used before the images, with a tendency to corrupt the mind with a love of pleasure.

In the nineteenth-century Orientalists' view, idolatry was the result of a *degeneration* of original noble and pure Vedic monotheism into Brahmanism, and later still into Hinduism. H.T. Colebrooke (1858), an influential Orientalist, postulated a theory about the much later development of Shaktism and Tantrism, an 'ocean of sorcery', which were in their "left-handed, or indecent mode of worship" seen as "unbridled debauchery with wine and women" (*Essays on the Religion and Philosophy of the Hindus*).

The goals pursued by worshippers became an important part of discerning between spells and prayers. If mantras are for 'salvific' or other 'noble' causes, they constitute religious performance. If used for this-worldly, and especially 'selfish' or even 'harmful' goals, they are magical. This division of goals also exists in Tantric practices: spells are for attainments in astrology, medicine, or supernatural abilities, and prayers are for spiritual emancipation.

In Orientalist scholarship, the *evolutionary* model of religion was from an early stage of primitive magic to advanced religion—a characteristic shift from *this-worldly* to *other-worldly* goals. The use of mantras within the evolutionary model had two different goals—namely, 'success in gaining health, wealth, and power' and 'full enlightenment in this life' according to scholars. They identified three stages of mantra use in Buddhist traditions:

1) mantras described as spells originally aimed for worldly goals;
2) then they became vehicles of salvation; and, finally,
3) if practised properly, "there is nothing they cannot achieve" (Conze, 1953. *Buddhism: Its Essence and Development*).


## *Manipulation and Coercion of Gods*

Researchers in the twentieth century also maintained that mantras can be spells but focused on manipulation and 'coercion' of gods as their main characteristic. The idea also comes from earlier research, which pointed to the 'Hindu belief' that an able magician is superior to gods. This explanation saw a common source of magical practices for both Hinduism and Buddhism. In this scheme, the textbooks outlining the means (sadhana) of doing this were Tantras and the new cult Tantric. As the latest edition of A.L. Basham's classic *The Wonder That Was India* proclaims, "By pronouncing the right formula (mantra) in the correct manner, or by drawing the correct magical symbol (yantra), one might force the gods to bestow magical power on the worshipper and lead him to the highest bliss."

Some scholars propagate the view that these mantras were for control of hidden forces of invisible reality. Vedic ritual and the Vedic mind use the parallel experience between a human and a god, which makes humans especially qualified to act in the divine realm and manipulate the god whose experience matches his own. The efficacy of such sympathetic magic depends on *homologies*—mystical or cryptic similarities—between the human and divine realms. Hence, a human can use his weak means to control forces far more powerful than his.

### The Third Position—Both Prayer and Spell—'Magico-Religious'

The final position merges the two previous stances into one by claiming that the mantras could be prayers and spells at the same time. Expressing dissatisfaction with all the different translations for the concept of mantra, scholars sometimes concluded that it is not possible to translate the Indian term into Western languages. This can indicate that, in the traditional Indian understanding, a mantra is utterly different from prayer, spell, sacred formula, or other phenomena discussed, say the authors Fárek and Horák.

However, with the possibility that a mantra is something altogether different from prayers or spells, there is another insight from an influential scholar, Gonda, that mantras "were mainly used in magico-religious rites, for the purpose of furtherance of worldly interests and protection from danger" (*The Indian Mantra*, 1963). This claim is puzzling because it contradicts the ideas of evolutionary theory concerning the transition from magic to religion. Why cannot the scholars clearly decide that these mantras were at first used only in magical rites? Why are they 'magico-religious', despite the talk of different goals? Unfortunately, such explanations enter standard textbooks and encyclopaedias despite the contradictions.

### Problems for Understanding Mantras

There are now several problems with understanding mantras.

(a)  Magical practices should characteristically manipulate or coerce, but scholars are not clear who or what the object of manipulation is.

(b)  Typically, the goals of a mantra divide between *this-worldly* and *other-worldly* and, although disputed, several generations of scholars keep using the pursuit of *this-worldly* goals as characteristic of magical practices.

(c)  These criteria apparently allow for characterising the very same mantra as either of the two or even as 'magico-religious'.

(d)  Some mantras do not fit the characteristics at all, but they are also explained as spells, prayers, or both at the same time.

(e)  Finally, ideas about the *degeneration* of the original monotheism or *evolution* from magic to religion were theoretical frameworks of the efforts to understand mantras.

Therefore, ideas about gods, demons, or supernatural powers play some role in the debates, but it is not clear what exactly is under discussion. Is it the attitude of worshippers towards these beings? For example, mantras were *adoration* of Vedic gods according to the early Orientalists, whereas later scholars maintain that the same mantras were *manipulating* the gods.

### Does Magic Exist?

The founding fathers of comparative religion, sociology, and anthropology once formulated bold ideas and grand theories on magical practices, but they have now run into serious problems. For many scholars, magic exists as a universally shared kind of human activity, ranging from the prehistoric magic of hunters (shamanism), through various ancient traditions, early modern Hermeticism, the magic of Asian, African, Native American, and other peoples, to different modern schools of magic.

In this perspective, the concept of magic provides a useful description of mantras. However, other scholars propose to define magic for different cultures and periods differently. For example, scholars felt that clearly 'magic' in the context of a pre-industrial African tribe does not have the same meaning as it does in a Graeco-Roman context.

Yet if one needs to examine the same term 'magic' independently for each culture and period, then are the scholars studying the same phenomenon in these cases or not? If incantations of the ancient world and Indian mantras are phenomena of the same kind, what is the problem with using the same word about them? And if they are not the same kind of phenomena, why should the same word be redefined to describe them? Why do we not use some other word to indicate that we are dealing with different phenomena in the world?

Puzzlingly, some scholars have suggested that magic does not exist at all. This contradicts the standard descriptions of the magical use of mantras in some introductory courses on Hinduism and Buddhism. Yet, the authors of such claims nevertheless continued to use 'magic' and 'magical', either explicitly or implicitly. Even modern research into magic seems unsatisfactory. Would anthropology have some solutions? Earlier scholars rejected this, and later anthropologists consider magic to be a part of religion because it is associated with supernatural powers. Hence, there is a huge conceptual mess in the study of magic.

Debates about definitions of words aside, the phenomenon of practising mantras is real. They exist or existed in Vedic, Buddhist, Tantric, Bhakti, and other traditions of India. The authors of this paper write that we will not advance in understanding any phenomenon described as magic by merely arguing about the proper definition of the word. This is an important step because research should aim at explanations of real phenomena.

However, the characteristics of magical practices, as a set of clear criteria, are the opposite of the characteristics of religious practices. Scholars in different study fields dispute the very same set of characteristics for discerning between magical and religious practices. Prayers and magic differ in tone and sentiment. Prayers imply humility, but magic is a demand for power and centres on the ego.

## *What is Wrong with These Characterisations?*

Academic ambiguity aside, there is a deeper conviction that magical and religious practices are fundamentally different from each other, yet they are also of the same kind. How do we explain this? The possibility lies in a discussion of the role that Christian theological ideas play in modern attempts to explain magic. The authors quote Murray and Rosalie Wax (1963), who in their often quoted paper 'The Notion of Magic' say that "the supplication/manipulation dichotomy does not apply to non-Western peoples, but it does reveal a great deal about how Westerners conceptualize their religion and their morality." Later discussions were more about how this dichotomy did not apply to non-Western cultures.

In his recent analysis of the alleged magical characteristics of mantras, P.E. Burchett concluded that Western problems with understanding mantras are the legacy of a Protestant division between religion and magic. This somehow transformed the thinking of the Enlightenment. Often translated as 'spells' and 'magical formulas', mantras are, by implication, irrational attempts to manipulate the Divine, in contrast to the supplicative prayers of authentic 'religion'.

Keith Thomas says that the dividing line between 'magic' and 'religion' hardened by the parallel attempts of Protestant and Catholic Reformers to eliminate all popular rites of unauthorised and ambiguous status (*An Anthropology of Religion and Magic*, 1975). If both Protestants and Catholics attempted the same goal (eliminating magical practices), they must have shared some basic understanding about these 'diabolical attempts to manipulate the supernatural' as Keith Thomas writes. What was this common ground? If the Christian characterisation of a division between magic and religion became part of later Enlightenment rationalist thought, why exactly is it problematic? Answers are not self-evident.

We should carefully consider which Christian theological ideas shaped modern debates on magic and whether the emerging characterisations (such as setting coercion versus supplication as a criterion) are still dependent on the original Biblical assumptions or not. Such a precise analysis of the ideas that enabled characterising practices in India as magical was recently carried out by M. Keppens and J. De Roover. The authors showed in *The Brahmin, the Aryan, and the Powers of the Priestly Class: Puzzles in the Study of Indian Religion*, 2020 how the Early Church Fathers' understanding of magic as human 'trafficking with demons', which should have been an important part of 'heathen idolatry', became a crucial structure of later European explanations of Brahmins as pagan priests and of their powers. This is an important conceptual structure that "establishes a connection between the 'rites' and 'formulas' of pagan priests, on the one hand, and the occurrence of certain effects in the world, on the other." If Keppens and De Roover are right, the original Christian structure of ideas about demons would still be present in the academic debates because of the conviction that such ideas form the content of the beliefs of mantra practitioners.

### The Supernatural in Debates About Magic: God, Gods, and Demons

An analysis of the concept of supernatural powers (or beings) may be the crucial link to clarifying the issues raised by the recurring debates on submission-versus-coercion characterisations, this-worldly and other-worldly goals, and tying these ideas to the beliefs of practitioners. For Christians in the first centuries of the Church, the world was full of demons that seduced those of fragile faith to the wrong path. Demons were responsible for the appearance of false prophets and the creation of heresies; for the creation of pagan stories about sons of gods, which were made up in order to divert people from the only true Son of God; for teaching people magic or astrology; and, finally, for mental and physical diseases. In sum, demons were responsible not only for human physical suffering but, more importantly, for spoiling human minds and souls.

In this perspective, spells were functional means of 'trafficking with demons'. In this way, conceptualisation of the differences between prayers and spells reflects differences between true and false religion. Worship of one true God—that is, the supernatural being in the Bible—was true religion, whereas worship of beings or objects of this world was false religion. Christian ideas of God the Almighty, Perfect, Creator of the World, etc. contrast with pagan stories about gods and demons. The Church fathers amply criticised the latter. If humans desire something for their earthly life within the limits of God's commandments, they should ask Him, which is one form of prayer. Other forms of prayer are adoration of God the Almighty, thanksgiving, confession of faith, and so on.

These ideas created a coherent explanation in which prayers are a means of submissive contact between believers and a Biblical God, whereas spells are a means of coercive human communication with demons. Human beings can properly pray to the Biblical God for both the final salvation of their souls and their 'daily bread' of this world. Understandably, such attitudes are ascribed to 'magicians' to this day in Catholic theology.

Of course, this is not an absolutely clear-cut method for discerning between prayer and spell, because prayers asking for 'daily bread' could address God. Therefore, the *submissive* approach of the worshipper must compound this criterion. In this perspective, spells do fulfil some temporary wishes but, finally, all magic seduces people from the right path to God and leads to damnation.

Now we see exactly how ideas about the nature of a Biblical God, as a superhuman being who is different from all demons (or false gods), are a crucial background for the specific debates about magic being part of false religion. In this sense, they answer a question about how true religion can be the same and yet different from magic (false religion). Without these ideas, all discussions about a submissive versus a coercive approach by worshippers, this-worldly and other-worldly goals, and, by logical extension, also distinctions between spell and prayer, lose their precise meaning. These theological ideas shaped many centuries of European thinking about prayers and spells. As such, they became the conceptual source for those who began to study Indian traditions in the eighteenth and nineteenth centuries.

### *The Conceptual Mess: Development in Three Stages*

The authors propose that the structure of Christian ideas about God and demons formed the core of the explanation of mantras as either prayers or spells. The *first historical stage* of research on the religions of India kept the originally Christian idea about the *degeneration* of the pristine monotheism of nations as a guiding explanation. The consequence for understanding mantras was simple: original Vedic teaching was 'monotheism', albeit with 'the seeds of idolatry', whereas Tantras were an 'ocean of sorcery'.

In this view, a pantheon of strange gods and demons usurped the place of striving for one true God. In the nineteenth-century descriptions, if scholars were sure that Indian practitioners of mantras were basically *monotheists*, their worship of Vedic and other gods was an indirect worship of the one true God. However, if the scholar thought, as many Christian missionaries did, that Indians were simply idolaters, then all mantras were the nature of spells like European magic. Healing, harming others, igniting feelings of love in the heart of a chosen person, protection from all kinds of disasters, wealth, success in political endeavours, etc.—all these goals promised in Indian texts look very much the same as the promises of ancient magical texts. The list of goals 'typical for magic' became a necessary part of accounts on Mantra, with little change over the last 200 years.

The *second stage* of changes in the structure of explanatory ideas was formed by the rise of grand theories of magic, which understood *magic as an early stage of the development of religion*, being in this sense a reverse of the degeneration model. The originally Christian concern with the personal qualities of a Biblical God remains, but demons are not personalities anymore. Nevertheless, the difference between religious worship and magical ritual is still clearly based on the original Christian ideas, including the idea that both involve a tie with 'the supernatural powers'.

Schayer (*Die Struktur der magischen Weltanschauung nach dem Atharva Veda und den Brahmana-Texten, 1925*) maintained the general theory of the degeneration of religion into magic, of which "the development of Indian religion from the hymns of the Rig Veda to Brahmanas" should be "the classical example." His explanation of mantras is a logical outcome of this theorising: the pious prayers of the Rig Veda contrast with "ecstatic and emotional magic", "shamanic demonology", and "sexual orgies" of the Atharva Veda. However independent of the theological ideas such theorising may look, it retains the Christian focus on differences between the true God and other beings.

The *third stage* brought another change in the structure of the ideas, characteristic of attempts to describe the beliefs of mantra practitioners. Ideas about supernatural powers or beings as agents in magical practices were retained, but in a very vague form, which allowed for fundamental changes and different additions. The clearly respectful and adoring prayer to gods became 'sympathetic magic' that manipulated the same gods. Others postulated 'hidden connections' between phenomena in this world and called it 'sacred magic'. This stage of research is puzzling; although some of the main ideas from the previous theorising were retained, they were freely mixed with other concepts. Mantras could be symbols for imagining all kinds of correspondence.

For other scholars, the focus of mantras should be 'hidden connections', typically characterised as '*homologies*'. Others speculated about the 'divine power' that mantras contain and how they are identical with gods or their energy in the traditional Indian understanding. The originally central concept of Christian God and the difference between God and fallen angels was still present in the form of a search for believers' ideas about 'supernatural power'. Because the concept was not clear anymore, the general idea of 'supernatural beings' soon allowed for adding ideas about 'hidden correspondences' or homological connections. At this stage, a connection between humans and the supernatural could have different variants: between humans and gods; between human body and universe; or between human mind and 'supernatural reality'.

Coercion versus supplication does not explain anything here, because it is not clear at all who or what is undergoing coercion. As the remnants of the originally clear-cut division between transcendental God and the demons of this world dissolved, the other-worldly and this-worldly goals of Indian traditions merged. It is not clear anymore what exactly all these concepts mean or why we are still using them.

Thus, not only individual concepts but the whole structure of ideas arising from Christian theological concerns with God and fallen angels became the core of modern theorising about Indian mantras. All these concepts clarify the central Christian theme, which is the nature of supernatural God and the human relationship with Him.

### The Present State

When you remove the ideas about a Biblical God and demons, it is no longer clear to whom or to what a worshipper is submissive and what exactly such submission means. Several generations of scholars automatically assumed that there must be a magical belief, or magical worldview, which is the ground for magical practices. Indians could hardly have equivalents of Christian concepts. As theoretical concepts, they still depend on the assumptions about a Biblical God, but they do not have even the clarity and coherence of the original Christian explanation.

The power originally attributed to God, to demons, or to 'supernatural powers' is now attributed to mantras themselves. Western and Indian scholars alike talk about mantras being 'God's Creative Power incarnate in sound', or 'divine sound', which enables one to describe 'sonic theology' in Hinduism. Yet the traditional understanding hardly sees Indian mantras as divine (transcendent) or even perfect, because one can read about the complex practices that Indians developed to purify mantras, to perfect them, and to make them work.

The authors suggest an in-depth analysis of the problematic concepts of 'spell' and 'prayer' as necessary because, unless we understand what exactly is wrong with them, it will be difficult to pave new ways for understanding mantras. All new attempts should include a clear understanding of the problems caused by the transformation of Christian theological ideas about magic. Otherwise, we will be prone to sliding back to the conceptual problems outlined above.

### *Personal Concluding Remarks*

The most amazing and striking aspect of the wonderful paper, especially for an Indian Hindu, is the realisation of the complete absence of the traditional practitioners of the mantras in the debates across ages. It takes almost eight to nine years of rigorous training to master even one Veda. As most traditional scholars concede, there are perhaps only a few living individuals who would have learned all four Vedas. One human lifespan is not enough.

Sadly, there was an eerie silence among Indian traditional commentators as a response to at least two centuries of deconstruction by the West that started with German Indology. Indology has been persistently a malicious racist enterprise that managed to make translations, sometimes shoddy, of the Vedas, Puranas, Itihaasas, and a huge corpus of literature. Universities, chairs, and scholarships then thrived on a closed group of scholars with mutual give-and-take with many scholars making their careers based on translations. They did not even know the language, let alone read the texts in their originals. The Mahabharata and the Gita were two main examples of scholarship that included the racist theme of Aryan supremacy. Vishwa Adluri and Joydeep Bagchee explore this fully in their book, *The Nay Science* (2014).

Just as colonial scholarship was dissecting, disarticulating, and disembodying our traditional scriptures, our English-speaking Indians joined them in the hope of academic careers. Not one was interested in talking to the practitioners of a live and throbbing tradition. This same idea of scholarship is evident in the Western study of mantras too. Like before, the traditional scholars and the traditional practitioners are not involved in the debates and, in return, they are not even aware of these debates. Even if they do come across such discussions, the characteristic response is unfortunately that of profound indifference. This has unfortunately led to a one-sided monologue in discussing Indian traditional and cultural issues, amounting to tremendous intellectual violence against Indians.

Many times, the traditional practitioners understand the debates, but they do not have the conceptual tools of the Western academic schools and hence choose to remain silent. In this regard, the authors of the article must be hugely complimented when they defend Indian traditions by questioning the very source of the discussions. A Christian, mainly Protestant, theological framework and secularisation of such ideas laid the basis of many narratives on India, like the so-called caste system, a universality of religion in all cultures, and creating religions out of traditions. Most of the social readings of India are the result of looking at Indian systems through Western lenses.

At the root of discussions might lie the core difference between the dominant philosophical positions of the West and that of the East, especially India. Western philosophy believes in the secondary nature of consciousness arising out of matter. The relationship between mind and matter is a matter of intense debate in Western philosophy. According to the dominant view, matter evolves into the mind, which then produces consciousness.

Indian philosophy is clear about the primary nature of Consciousness and mind-matter being two sides of the same coin. The primary Consciousness in Advaita is Brahman, and it is infinite, indivisible, and the only sentience. The entire mind-matter stands separate and the dominant Advaitic idea makes mind-matter as a *superimposition* on this Brahman. These ideas are clearly embedded in the traditional Vedic understanding of mantras.

Indian philosophy thus places the Self or Consciousness as a Primary sentient entity (*purusha*) and Nature as an insentient (*prakriti*). Both mind and matter belong to the realm of *prakriti* with individual qualities. The Self is ever free but only appears to be embodied by erroneous mental cognition. The Self perceives the eternal object through two different modes of cognition. For the Self, the mind is an instrument to think about the object, while the sense organs are instruments for perception of the object. Thus, mind and matter are two conditions of the same thing, the one appearing as thought and the other as an individual object in the world. In the Advaitic tradition, it is *Maya* that makes the same object perceived through the two different modes of cognition as different.

In Hindu traditional philosophy, nouns, verbs, and all other kinds of words have four stages: *the para* (Brahman stage); *pasyanti* (incipient ideation stage); *madhyama* (effort for articulation stage); and *vaikhari* (audible stage). The first three stages are beyond an ordinary person enveloped in ignorance. The *para* stage of speech is like internal eternal light, and by its true intuition, a man attains *moksha* (loosely liberation). In the world of objects, *Turiya* is the state of Brahman, *Prajna* is that of objects in their undifferentiated, unmanifest state, *Taijasa* the sphere of ideated objects, and *Visva* is the sphere of gross physical objects. It is not difficult to see the correlation of the word to the world or the mind-matter correlation in Indian traditions.

In the Advaita Vedantic tradition, therefore, there is a rejection of the idea of language having a physical substrate. *Instead, language is coterminous with Consciousness, the Ground of the Universe.* At its most primal level—the speech stage of *Para* or the object stage of *Turiya*—it is luminous, and the same with *Brahman*. In this way, mantras that arise from the deep contemplation of the sages can be a direct route to enlightenment, or Brahman. In simple terms, mantras directly correspond with the primary Consciousness in this understanding and become a route for moksha.

Abhinavagupta (950-1015 CE) was one of Kashmir Saivism's tallest philosophers, with many important books to his credit. He shows the way to understand mantras from a non-dual standpoint. From the perspective of Indian traditional scholars, any research on mantras that ignores his texts would simply be unforgiveable. Jaideva Singh, in his book *Abhinavagupta's Para-trisika-Vivarana: The Secret of Tantric Mysticism*, writes in the preface:

> The Divine Consciousness is identical with the Supreme Word (*para vak*), and hence every letter or word is derived from and ultimately inseparable from this Consciousness. "She (the supreme *vak*) is, in the most initial stage, stationed in the Divine I-Consciousness which is the highest mantra, and which is not limited by space and time." Therefore, the analysis of language is inseparable from that of consciousness. *Mantra* and the whole metaphysics of the Word is at the center of this text.

Similarly, the first sutra of the second section of the *Shiva Sutras* says: *Chittam Mantrah* (Chittam is Mantra). Translating chittam as simply "mind" and we accepting it has been one of the distortions which Balu speaks about in his chapter on translations in *Cultures Differ Differently*. And the commentary by Kshemaraja says:

> Mantra is not merely an aggregation of sounds, but the special *chittam* and the attainment of the unity with the divinity behind a mantra by means of meditation. A mantra separated from its mantri (the shakti behind it) cannot exist....When the mantra and the repeater are seen as different, the mantra is never efficacious. The entire root of mantra practice is knowledge of their unity.

At a basic level, prayers and spells both imply a duality with man and God standing separate; however, mantras arise in a tradition where non-duality is the dominant thinking. In such a scenario, there might be a completely different meaning to the concept of mantras. The attempt to understand mantras through another cultural framework may simply mislead and not make sense. Maybe this implies a complete winding up of the concept of mantras as prayers or spells and starting fresher narratives.

Apart from mantras, which may imply "personification" of the Self or Consciousness, Indian traditions have *suktams, stotras, shlokas, and stutis* related to various rituals and with various purposes. They are both related and unrelated to the mantras. As one poojari in a temple versed in Yajurveda simply said, mantras manifest during the deeply contemplative state of a sage, and these have no origin in mind or matter. The others are products of spiritualised minds.

Perhaps fresh research needs to take place if one wants to truly understand Indian mantras in these lines of inquiry. But that would require us to shed the duality inherent in Western philosophy and think in terms of non-duality. The Buddhists talk of *Sunya* as the final state and what would be the idea of mantras in Buddhist traditions? These are indeed questions for scholarly research, especially for those who are genuinely respectful of the traditions. That would require rising above one's own biases and training, and approaching another tradition with humility and an eagerness to learn. Otherwise, all studies conducted in a Western context result in distortions. In the meantime, people need to read scholars like Martin Fárek, sympathetic to the Indian cause, who has produced outstanding work in deconstructing many distorted explanations about Indian culture.

Part V

# GENERAL: COMPILATIONS AND SUMMARIES

"This nation is not a new race raw from the workshop of Nature or created by modern circumstances. One of the oldest races and greatest civilisations on this earth, the most indomitable in vitality, the most fecund in greatness, the deepest in life, the most wonderful in potentiality, after taking into itself numerous sources of strength from foreign strains of blood and other types of human civilisation, is now seeking to lift itself for good into an organised national unity."

**– Sri Aurobindo**

"Two essentials of nationality there are, —a geographical unity, and a common historic evolution or culture. These two India possesses superabundantly, beside many lesser unities which strengthen the historical tradition."

**– Ananda Coomaraswamy**

## Chapter 13

# COLONIAL CONSCIOUSNESS – A WIDESPREAD PHENOMENON TRAPPING OUR COUNTRY

## PART 1
### THE BACKGROUND AND THE IMPORTANT NARRATIVES

We can best understand the many intellectual discourses today in the framework of 'colonial consciousness' provided by Dr. Balagangadhara. Colonial consciousness works not only at the time of colonisation but continues to make its impact long after the colonials have left by permanently altering the intellectual frameworks of the previously colonised. It makes us think and act by simply assuming the truth of whatever the colonials said about us. We fail to develop indigenous narratives about ourselves and view both ourselves and the West through the lenses (the social sciences) provided by the latter.

Where does this 'colonial consciousness' work? The Aryan story; the conversion of Indian traditions into religions and then accepting secularism as the best solution for harmony; the superimposition of caste, a Western idea, into the *Varna* and *Jatis* of India; our disdainful view of traditional medicine; the blanking out of Indian philosophy from all learning in schools by calling it 'religion'; the need for the English language to prosper and be the national language; a historical reading of our texts and scriptures, which was never an indigenous idea; accepting the idea of one *dharmashastra (Manu)* as prescriptive and authoritative for all eternity to come; making the Western clash between science and religion our own; understanding our practices and rituals from a scientific perspective and making them superstitious and irrational; our singularly linear narratives of freedom struggle, obliterating the more uncomfortable dissenting voices like those of Sri Aurobindo or Subash Bose; accepting the political ideologies of the left-right-centre; the story of the revolt of Buddhism; the disbelief in a golden period of India that attracted plunderers from across the world; the story that we were never a nation until the British united us; the discourse on corruption that makes most Indians immoral because of a faulty religion... *ad infinitum*.

The colonials and missionaries provided a narrative that Hinduism equals the caste system, which in turn equals untouchability. The solution for untouchability and the caste system thus consisted in disbanding Hinduism altogether and adopting another religion. For the colonials, it was Christianity, and for Dr. Ambedkar, with the same understanding, it was Buddhism. Today, every single topic of discussion—caste, religion, ecology, feminism, political administration, nationalism, law, and the judiciary—is heavily superimposed by Western cultural assumptions leading to distortions. The examples exist everywhere, and it is easy to see that past and present Indian intellectuals do not transcend the terms of any debate set by the colonials.

The result is, of course, a detachment of the Indian citizen from their own cultural roots and sometimes even becoming a staunch critic. There is thus an urgent need to decolonise the most vital instrument in building the country—the social sciences. The methodology of the latter remains coloured with colonial and Oriental ideas.

### Colonial Consciousness: Summarising the Thesis of SN Balagangadhara

Balu writes that, for most Indians, colonialism appears as a self-explaining phenomenon of evil and immorality, but it is not clear how or why that should be the case. The British successfully criticised Indian religions, the caste system, the education system, Sati, the dowry system, untouchability, the revolt of Buddhism against Hinduism, its Brahmanism, and so on.

Surprisingly, Indian intellectuals do not transcend the terms of the debate, making British criticisms their own.

Balagangadhara writes:

> Colonization was not merely a process of occupying lands and extracting revenues. It was not a question of us aping Western people and trying to be like them. It was not even about colonizing the imagination of a people by making them 'dream' that they, too, would become 'modern', developed, and sophisticated. It goes deeper than any of these. It is about denying people and cultures their own experiences, rendering them aliens to themselves, and actively preventing any description of their own experiences except in terms defined by the colonizers.

The coloniser actively initiates the process that prevents the colonised from accessing their own experiences, setting their own narratives, and viewing other cultures through their indigenous lenses. The colonised becomes equally responsible for the evil of colonialism as he propagates the same process but in a different period. This perception is only based on the rhetorical force of another statement: colonisation expressed the weakness of Indian society and the strength of British society. The standard and alleged causes of this weakness were many: a weak Mughal rule; no single nation-state; the caste-ridden society; constantly fighting small kingdoms; and many such, which allowed the 'divide and rule' policy of the British. The scientific, technological, and military strengths of the West are obvious. This remains implicit in contemporary discourse.

An example of a colonial consciousness thesis is the discourse on corruption in India. The widespread corruption does not involve the deviant actions of some individuals but is a widespread social phenomenon. Corruption appears to be a rational and successful social strategy in India. Now social systems are synonymous with the caste system, which in turn equals Indian ethical values. That the Indians are intellectually weak and/or immoral has been the consistent message from colonial times to the contemporary period, and this is an example of persisting colonial consciousness. The discourse on corruption in India ends up focusing extensively on corrupt social, caste, and ethical systems.

Travellers and missionaries provided the earliest descriptions of India within the specific theological framework of Christianity. Indian religions were 'heathen' religions; the people worshipped the devil; and the Brahmin priests had degenerated a 'pure' religion. This description became a common-sense view over a period of centuries. Centuries of ethnographic descriptions of India ensured that the civilisational superiority of Western culture became an empirical truth and a premise for further conclusions. These also became facts of our political and social sciences. The civilisational inferiority of India was not based on any scientific or academic study but on presuppositions of either a religious or a secular background.

As Balagangadhara writes:

> Colonialism prevents descriptions of their own culture except in terms defined by the colonizers. Hence, colonialism is immoral because it creates an immoral consciousness. Colonialism is also a supreme educational project because the belief in civilizational superiority contains messages of the ignorance and immorality of the colonized, generating shame, the conviction of backwardness, and the desire to learn from the colonizer. The differences between different cultures now become lacunae and a deficiency of human achievement in the colonized culture. Post-colonial thinkers go further on the colonial consciousness: colonized people are immoral creatures, but what is immoral about the colonizer is the regime, not the individuals.

### *Aryans and Dravidians*

The strongest example of colonial consciousness is the tight retention of the ideas of Aryans and Dravidians. We refuse to reject or even question this narrative, the fountainhead of all other divisive narratives, despite evidence to the contrary. The Aryan Invasion/Migration theory regarding ancient Indian civilisation postulates horse-riding Aryans from Central Asia invading North India around 1500 BCE. These 'fair-skinned' Aryans defeated the 'dark' racially different indigenous natives of the Harappan Civilization by either subjugating or driving them away to forests. The indigenous Harappans

(Dasas and Dasyus) were the ancestors of today's tribals (the forest-driven), Sudras and Dalits (those who stayed behind and occupied the bottom of the Varna scale), and Dravidians (those driven south).

The Aryan theory was a construction of racist German Indologists. Max Mueller speculated on the British descendants of the same Aryan race returning to accomplish the "glorious work of civilization". The British justifications portrayed their rule as one more Aryan wave. Adluri and Bagchee, in *The Nay Science* (2014), show that racism started with linguistic studies and with Indology in German universities. The narrative then proceeds with the Aryan settlers, in a remarkably brief time of three hundred years, first created the near-perfect language of Sanskrit and then composed the Rig Veda around 1200 BCE. This story, with a two-century history of propagation, started off by noting linguistic similarities between Sanskrit and many European languages. This led to the speculation of a common ancestral language (PIE, or the Proto-Indo-European language) arising from a specific geographical area and then spreading to different places.

Unfortunately, archaeology and textual/inscriptional data, especially from the Vedic corpus, categorically reject the invading Aryans scenario. And yet, post-independent Marxist historians continued with the Aryan-Dravidian story as it fitted well with their exploiter-exploited paradigm. Genetics, a new weapon for Aryan proponents, remains ambiguous.

The major repercussion has been a near-permanent fissure in relations between the North and the South, with political movements based on a 'pure' Dravidian sentiment. All narratives which are breaking India finally root in the Aryan invasions, which probably never happened in the first place. At the heart of all AIT arguments is the injection of foreign, non-existent Aryans into an existing culture, implying a discontinuity and denial of the longest civilisational continuity. Instead of accepting our common and great civilisational past, the Aryan proponents are keen to show that the Brahmins (especially), Kshatriyas, and Vysyas are foreigners who perennially exploit the Sudras (and the recently added Dalits).

Selective and convenient application of archaeological and genetic findings; torturing Vedic texts to find racially themed discourses on Aryans and Dravidians; selective linguistic analyses; a closed circle of academic scholarships disallowing alternative voices; *ad hominem* attacks; and prominent power positions have all helped in perpetuating this account of the Aryans across centuries. The political uses of the Aryan scenario are illegitimate and divisive; they are an extension of the colonial agenda. But our intelligentsia stays rigidly fixed on this theory.

### Colonial Rule and its Advantages

It is an effort even today to convince many intellectuals and apologists that colonial rule was a disaster for India. Angus Maddison, in his research on world economics, shows clearly that India was an economic powerhouse of the world until the colonials landed. Yet his research and findings have not been able to permeate the general conscience of the country.

In 1750, India and China were contributing 75% of the world's GDP. In 1600, Britain was contributing 1.8% of the world's GDP (Angus Maddison). When Britain left India in 1947 after 200 years of rule, Britain was contributing 10% of the world GDP, and India was reduced to a pathetic 1.8%. The British left a society with 16% literacy, a life expectancy of 27 years, and over 90% living below the poverty line. India's rich maritime trade, banking systems, agriculture, cloth and steel industry, and traditional handicrafts suffered a brutal assault under colonial rule. The high taxation system continued despite the famines. Huge lands cultivated opium, which further impacted the agrarian systems.

The British could subvert all the state machinery (armies, censuses, bureaucracies, railroads, hospitals, telegrams, and scientific institutions) and liberal norms (individual rights, freedom of thought and speech, artistic and political expression, equality under the law, and political democracy) to their own advantage. Educated Indians became clerks, interpreters, or maximally lawyers, destroying the entire indigenous educational system. Indian soldiers formed the backbone of the British army during the two World Wars. In the 107 years from 1793 to 1900, an estimated 5 million people died the world over in all the wars combined. But, in just ten years (1891–1900), 19 million people died in India due to famines alone, arguably the biggest colonial holocaust. The regular famines right till the second world war in Bengal were the result of careless planning, Malthusian ideas, and leaders with racist views (like Churchill) sitting in England looking the other way.

The pro-British groups argue that the British gave us political unity, democracy, a free press, a parliamentary system, and the rule of law, along with the railways, tea, the telegraph, and the English language. But many of these would have just evolved without the need for colonisation, as has happened in many countries because of globalisation and the internal needs of trade. The railways were more for the British exploitation of Indian resources than for Indians. The unity that the British are said to have given us is the biggest myth. They thrived on the policy of divide and rule, which became more so after the 1857 mutiny. All these policies led to the partition of the country in 1947. The horrors of the partition, in which millions died, are another sad saga.

Karl Marx (1853) wrote:

> Indian society has no history at all… What we call its history is the history of the successive intruders who founded their empires on the passive basis of that unresisting and unchanging society. The question, therefore, is not whether the English had a right to conquer India, but whether we are to prefer India conquered by the Turk, by the Persian, by the Russian, to India conquered by the Briton. England has to fulfil a double mission in India: one destructive, the other regenerating the annihilation of old Asiatic society, and the laying the material foundations of Western society in Asia.

However, we tend to deify Marx rather than Will Durant who wrote in *The Case for India* (1930):

> The British conquest of India was the invasion and destruction of a high civilization by a trading company utterly without scruple or principle, careless of art and greedy of gain, over-running with fire and sword a country temporarily disordered and helpless, bribing and murdering, annexing and stealing, and beginning that career of illegal and 'legal' plunder, which has now gone on ruthlessly for one hundred and seventy-three years, and goes on at this moment while in our secure comfort we write and read.

### *English as a Medium of Instruction*

Language in post-independent India took on a peculiar form. In a linear historical view, the Indian past became 'primitive'. Sanskrit and the local languages became redundant, and the state policies went for an exclusive English-based education, especially in institutes of higher learning and civil services. Now, we have a clear-cut social hierarchy, placing a select few who know English fluently above those who are not comfortable with it.

As Sankrant Sanu says in *The English Medium Myth* (2018), arguing for a vernacular language would be either regressiveness or a false sense of 'nationalism'. English language-based class separation privileges a foreign culture over the native culture; disconnects the general population from the intellectual and policy discourses; and creates a ceiling for progress in academia for those educated in the native languages. Only 4 of the top 20 richest countries have an English-based education system, while 19 out of the 20 poorest countries were colonies of European powers, and more than half of these countries do not even recognise the common spoken language as an official language.

Regarding its role in facilitating communication, there is no problem with any language. However, alien languages can be destructive as carriers of culture. English, as a medium of instruction, destroys culture and deracinates its citizens. Kenyan writer, Ngũgĩ wa Thiong'o calls English a "culture bomb" for other cultures because it annihilates a people's belief in their names, languages, environment, heritage of struggle, unity, and ultimately in themselves.

In a crucial parliamentary debate, Sanskrit lost to English as a medium of instruction by only one deciding vote. A near-perfect language carrying all our intellectual, academic, cultural, and artistic heritage receded into the background; with newer Indological narratives, Sanskrit has even become 'exploitative', 'patriarchal', and 'oppressive'. The social sciences simply rehashed old colonial theories without providing a better understanding of India, causing immense damage to our social fabric. Our state policies, in their inclination and deep fascination towards English, do not allow an Indian to reach the highest levels of arts and sciences in a vernacular language. This is only hastening the demise of the great Indian culture, something that even our colonials could not do.

Ananda Coomaraswamy famously said about English: *"A single generation of English education suffices to break the threads of tradition and to create a nondescript and superficial being deprived of all roots—a sort of intellectual pariah who does not belong to the East or the West, the past or the future. The greatest danger for India is the loss of her spiritual integrity. Of all Indian problems, the educational is the most difficult and most tragic."* This is unambiguously still relevant to India, with its acceptance of both the English language as the major medium of instruction and secularism as the guiding principle of our curricula.

### Political Ideologies

The hard right-left divide in the West is confusing, as we are a mix of both. Hyrum Lewis in *The Myth of Left and Right* (2022) shows that 'left' and 'right' are the biggest false narratives embedded in our collective minds. There is no 'essence' in the terms; it is simply a social (or 'tribal') phenomenon where one is simply identifying with a group of people. The political positions of both have flipped many times to radical opposites. In India, the Marxists, even more imaginative, appropriated the term 'left' to themselves and clumped everybody else not agreeing with them as 'right', which necessarily became 'bad'. Their peculiar language continued the previous Islamic, missionary, and colonial attacks on Indian culture and heritage.

'Right-wing' conjures up images of extremely conservative US Republicans and xenophobic European right-wing parties, which is hardly descriptive of traditional India. The left in India, sticking to the image of atheism and state control, developed a brand of secularism and liberalism that meant appeasing the minorities and abusing the majorities, respectively. The best 'conservative' and 'liberal' ideals evolved over centuries into a unique Indic thought, and the tragedy came with independence when we rejected our past.

There are two narratives. One is the colonial narrative which says that, before the colonists came, India was an unmitigated disaster. The superstitious religion of Hinduism was the cause of the evil caste system, which in turn was synonymous with exploitation, deprivation, and poverty. It was a nation divided between warring kings. Religion, caste, sect, and language divided the people without any unity as a proper nation. The primitive and unscientific India had to seek solutions from the West to improve itself. The colonials also gave India much-needed unity. Post-independent academia propagated this linear version of history: past equals primitive equals India; future equals advanced equals the West. The other narrative places traditional India with its diversity, a decentralised polity, enlightened Dharmic monarchy as a standard, free citizens, and absence of extreme cruelties (crusades, jihads, inquisitions, witch hunts, colonization, the genocide of the American Indians, Nazism, and transforming a continent and culture into slaves) associated with the West. Which could be true?

The best evidence comes from Angus Madison's research into world economics, which shows that India was one of the two largest economies in the world in the first millennium CE until the colonials landed. We had the highest philosophical insights and an impressive intellectual heritage, with a huge corpus of texts. India had contributions in the fields of astronomy, mathematics, linguistics, logic, physics, metallurgy, shipbuilding, bricks, agricultural technology, dyes and pigments, civil engineering, town planning, sanitation, medical and biological sciences, and vaccination, leading to many early Europeans remarking that it was the West that needed to learn from the East.

Our indigenous systems had some worth, as their outcomes attracted thousands from Central Asia, the Middle East, and Europe. An inferior, poor, and barbaric individual invades and robs a superior, rich, and cultured person according to all common sense. As for individuals, the same is true for countries. All and sundry came to India to become rich; India produced its material and spiritual riches through its own efforts; India went to alien countries purely for trade and philosophical interactions and never to invade physically, rule people, or take slaves. And yet, Indian culture and ways of organising life were 'primitive' before the colonisers came. Strangely, collectively, we Indians believe the colonial story.

India had evolved as a decentralised polity, enlightened monarchy, and free citizenry ages ago. The bedrock of Indian polity was the three quartets, as Sri Aurobindo explains: the four *Varnas*, the four *Ashramas* (brahmacharya or student, grihastha or householder, vanaprastha or forest dweller, and sannyasa or renunciate), and the four *Purusharthas* (dharma, artha, kama, and moksha). Our texts focused on *qualities* and *duties* at all levels, from the king to the ordinary citizen, unlike Western *rights-based* traditions. The wars fought in Europe in medieval times were unusual in the Indian context, which left mostly the agricultural lands and the temples intact. People freely moved across kingdoms for pilgrimages and access to knowledge without charges of treason.

Our traditions are uniquely non-dogmatic, non-predatory, evolving, and self-reforming without claims of exclusivity. The hallmark of Indic traditions has been an *"indifference to differences"* and this is the solution to most social problems in a multicultural world. Hence, alternatives to Western models thrived across the country without affecting trade, agriculture, literature, or the sciences. However, modern social sciences, with a great colonial hangover, have a strong antipathy for the traditional systems of India. Western traditions search for maximal individual liberty under the umbrella of minimal state interference and maximal state security and create *isms* of the most bewildering variety. Colonial consciousness allowed narratives of Western political philosophies to permeate Indian thinking, even though many of the ideas did not make sense.

### Tribals: The "Original" Inhabitants

The neologism *Adivasi* (*adi*, original; *vasi*, inhabitant) of the nineteenth century became the most successful disinformation campaign by the colonials and missionaries of modern times. In settler colonies (like Australia), 'aboriginal' made sense to distinguish the European settler from the natives. However, in non-settler colonies like India, 'aboriginal' became a pure colonial construct, which placed the 'majority' as simply the pre-European colonisers of the 'tribal minorities'.

Many tribes of North-East India migrated *much later* from the surrounding countries after the indigenous non-tribal peasant population.

Historical data does not support the division of India's population into 'aboriginal tribals' and 'non-tribal' invaders. International organisations (like the ILO) strengthened this distinction by introducing *internal* coloniality and a permanent faultline. Hinduism, dating back to pre-Aryan times, is as 'aboriginal' as the tribal populations. The similarities between Hindu traditions and the tribal traditions in their fundamental polytheistic nature and paganism (deifying the feminine, nature, and animals) show them clearly distinct from the prophetic-monotheistic religions. The 'tribals' and other 'mainstream' Vedic-Sanskritic traditions have many elements in common through mutual interactions.

The impossibility of defining and the broad usage have relegated the concepts of 'race' and 'tribe' into disuse. 'Tribe' is a key but obsolete concept from anthropology's early history that usually served colonial, administrative, and ideological purposes to call the indigenous groups primitive. As Balu says, strangely, anthropologists spent decades trying to get rid of a pernicious concept like 'tribe', only to see it sneak back into the Indian Constitution, Indian legislation, and its administration.

### Hindus, Hinduism, Hindutva

The standard liberal elite discourse is: "Hinduism is good and Hindutva bad." However, have we understood the meanings of the words Hindu, Hinduism, and Hindutva? For the Islamic invaders and the later colonials, all Indians on the other side of the Indus River who were not Abrahamic were collectively 'Hindus'. A West rooted in religion saw religions in all the colonised cultures. The experience of alien practices came together in the meta-narrative explanatory framework of a religion called Hinduism. The subsequent religions of Buddhism, Sikhism, and Jainism were further explanations of Indian society.

The colonial intellectuals did not realise that Indian 'traditions' behaved differently from a phenomenon called 'religion' as exemplified by Christianity, Islam, and Judaism. With a few exceptions, generations of intellectuals since colonial times have not questioned the understanding of Hinduism as a religion. The widely diverse traditions with still wider beliefs go against the definition of religion, yet our understanding of

Hinduism as a religion stays intact despite all the inconsistencies and contradictions.

Similarly, Balagangadhara shows that colonial consciousness in Hindutva manifests as a repetition of Orientalist discourse. Whether it was Francis Xavier, Grant, or James Mill, the description of degraded and condemnable Brahmins was a standard Orientalist discourse. Reformist movements like Arya Samaj swallowed this and did not pause to check the Orientalist discourse of Western education 'removing the accumulated filth produced by Brahmins' in its reformist strategies. Acceptance of Orientalist discourse as a *true* description of Indian society leads to repetition of the same discourses. India is thus corrupt, immoral, idolatrous, and has a false religion in desperate need of reform. This is precisely colonial consciousness. The colonial and 'post' colonial experiences of Indians remain the same.

The similar rhetoric of the Sangh Parivar and Orientalism with regards to denouncing the caste system, eradicating superstitions, and searching for a 'pure' Hinduism for a 'Hindu' nation shows that the Sangh has been unable to discover a non-colonial, non-Western framework to understand India. Colonisation (both Islamic and European) broke the access that Indians had to their own traditions; post-independence, colonial consciousness maintains this barrier. Balu stresses that, today, the Hindutva movement continues a tendency to 'reform', which ironically becomes Orientalism 2.0 in terms of the damage it causes to Indian culture.

### Buddhism vs. Hinduism

A disruptive colonial narrative that we fail to reject is the supposed antagonism between Buddhism and Hinduism. Thus, Buddha broke away, rebelling against the caste system and the Vedas. However, Buddha himself described Rama as his previous incarnation. He may have said the Vedas were unnecessary for enlightenment, but his messages were Upanishadic in nature. The subtle differences between Advaita and Buddhism are hardly a reason for violent or unpleasant encounters.

Orientalists started treating Buddhism as a separate religion because they discovered it outside India. With clearer origins, Buddha became

Martin Luther, and Buddhism was a Protestant-like attack on Hinduism. An exclusive belief in Buddha over the rejection of any other god is unbelievable in traditional cultures like India. Buddhist buildings, temples, rituals, and mantras follow established Hindu Vedic patterns and Vastu Shastras. The image of Buddha sits happily in many Hindu homes and temples.

Buddha, contrary to popular narratives, never rejected the varnas. He, in fact, put the Kshatriyas at the top of the hierarchy. The conversion of Dr. Ambedkar, along with thousands of his followers, in 1956 strengthened the anti-Hindu programme of Buddha in a retrospective manner. Buddha was simply a beneficiary of an established Hindu pluralistic tradition.

Koenraad Elst simply says, "Buddha was every inch a Hindu." One of the most profound intellectuals of the twentieth century was Ananda K. Coomaraswamy, who made a deep study of almost all the faiths in the world. He begins his introduction of Buddhism in *Hinduism and Buddhism* (1943) by writing:

> The more superficially one studies Buddhism, the more it seems to differ from the Brahmanism in which it originated; the more profound our study, the more difficult it becomes to distinguish Buddhism from Brahmanism, or to say in what respects, if any, Buddhism is really unorthodox.

### *Secularism and Writing History*

Secularism was a solution for European Christendom at a specific time in its history when the various denominations were fighting each other. The separation of the Church from the state was never a universal solution for all cultures across time. Today, the secularism model is severely stressed with the influx of Islam into Europe. Paradoxically, in India, as Jakob De Roover shows, secularism is generating a hardening of stances on all sides. Our post-independent political thinkers, heavily influenced by Western thought, in a classic example of colonial consciousness, applied secularism to dealing with the 'communal' problem in India.

The unclear understanding of Hinduism, the different nature of the clash between Hinduism and Islam, and the intricate intertwining of the 'secular' and the 'sacred' in Indian cultural life not allowing a separation, finally amounted to secularism exerting intense violence on Indian culture. Gradually, secularism degenerated into an appeasement of the minority.

The distorted writing of history resulted from these ideas of secularism. Our history books turned indigenous figures into footnotes, while we imbued Delhi-centric history with great passion and vigour. The Indian past became 'primitive' even as the vision was to a 'golden' future represented by Europe. The left-liberal thinking and powerful Marxist academicians writing our textbooks, in a great symbiotic relationship, completely distorted the historical narrative.

At Independence, when we were at our lowest in confidence and self-respect, there was a need to teach something positive about ourselves without needing to lie. The lesson should have been that we were one of the richest and most culturally advanced countries in the world, with wonderful achievements in various domains. We, on the other hand, just grew up being ashamed of our country, its religion, its culture, and its arts. Today, there is a disconnect among the youth with the idea of India. In fact, a twisted ideology is out to convince people that any idea of patriotism is fanatical. Sanskrit became an exploitative language; the Ramayana and Mahabharata were trivialised; and Indians, of course, became misogynistic, casteist, and socially exploitative. Of course, India did not 'really exist' before the colonials. Hinduism was a template to show that everything was wrong in Indian culture.

History writers used every trick in the book for brainwashing, like lies, appealing to authority, prejudice, cherry-picking, generalities, assumptions, thought-terminating clichés, and so on. At least two crucial generations built their lives believing that nothing good came from our country. Our history became a history of invaders (the mythical Aryans, Islamic rulers, the Europeans, and the British in succession) instead of the land and its people. There was no discussion on why greedy rulers needed to come to India in the first place when the reverse never happened. To please or protect, our thinkers in all relevant fields inappropriately associated the present-day Muslims with past Islamic invaders, when it was quite unnecessary. The invaders became benign and benevolent, which went against a huge body of contemporary descriptions by chroniclers and historians of the Islamic period.

## PART 2
## COLONIAL CONSCIOUSNESS: CONSEQUENCES FOR THE NATION AND THE WAY FORWARD

### *Ignoring Indian Philosophy*

Philosophy deals with the most engaging questions for humanity related to the purposes of life and the universe, the reality of the world, the presence of God, the matter-mind relationship, and so on. Philosophers equate philosophy only with Western thought which, in turn, is either ignorant or dismissive of Indian thought. Surprising, because any person, irrespective of time and place, can have philosophical insights applicable to humanity. The West puts philosophy between theology and science. Like theology, it speculates on matters of indefinite knowledge; like science, it appeals to human reason rather than to the authority of a tradition.

Indian *darshanas* have a different view. Karl Potter says, "To understand the philosophy of a culture, we must come to some understanding of its ultimate values." Greek and European philosophers affirmed that morality, the highest value, lies in the exercise of reason and the subjugation of passions. In contrast, the ultimate value in Indian *darshanas* is not morality but *freedom* and *control*. It is not rational self-control in the community's interest, but complete control over one's environment. Freedom consists of complete liberation from the karmic chains of cause and effect and the achievement of complete peace in this present life. This freedom is possible for every human being, and there is a route for every human, not necessarily the same route. The supreme practical value is renunciation, as Krishna tells Arjuna: giving up the fruits of the acts that one is capable of performing successfully.

There were many great philosophers and many individual schools, broadly divided into orthodox (Nyaya, Vaisesika, Yoga, Samkhya, Mimansa, and Vedanta) and non-orthodox (Charvakism, Buddhism, and Jainism), with many debates, expositions, commentaries, and criticisms. The extensive corpus seeks answers to most of the existential questions much before Western philosophy took its roots in the Age of Enlightenment during the sixteenth and eighteenth centuries. The pre-Socratic philosophers, Socrates, and the later Greeks (like Plato and Aristotle) showed many similar thoughts, like Indian philosophers, giving credence to the idea that there might have been an interaction. Western philosophy considers itself an inheritor of Greek philosophy, but it might have just distorted the views to confirm the scientific developments.

Karma and rebirth are an extremely integral part of Indian thought. The lower and higher truths and the absence of antagonism between them are important in understanding Indian traditions with their rich variety of customs, rituals, and gods. The entire corpus of Indian thought strives to tell human beings that freedom is possible for everyone; freedom comes by many routes; freedom does not involve stopping any 'secular' activity; and freedom is never a pressure to convert. Any human being with an unfinished purpose of total freedom points out that philosophy can never be dead.

The sense of 'I' is the 'consciousness' that allows us to participate in the world and gives us a sense of 'doership'. Consciousness, in Western paradigms, is the state of awareness that begins after waking up from a dreamless sleep and continues until going back to sleep again, slipping into a coma, or dying. It excludes deep, dreamless sleep. Dreams and 'self-awareness' are special forms of consciousness. The overwhelming scientific-philosophical view is that consciousness is a product of the mind.

Indian philosophy has a different paradigm. Consciousness is the primary entity, and matter-mind (two sides of the same coin) stands separate from it. In the Indian tradition, the cogniser (Purusha) and the cognised (prakriti) belong to two distinct categories. The essential characteristics are sentience or consciousness (chaitanya) and inertness (jadatva), respectively. Consciousness is One, both immanent, and transcendental. Different schools of Vedantic thought have slightly different ideas about how the individual (Jiva) and the Brahman (Paramatman) relate to each other. Atman (Jiva) and Paramatman (Brahman) are one, according to Advaita, the most popular school of thought. Matter and mind are superimpositions on top of the one *Brahman* (Consciousness, Self, Purusha).

The Self is ever free but only appears embodied as an individual by erroneous mental cognition. The erasure of this cognition leads to Self-realisation and freedom. The potential for freedom exists in every individual, irrespective of time, place, sex, religion, caste, creed, ethnicity, culture, or any personal identity. And the means are only self-effort. The universe has a purpose, and this is to help the individual attain liberation. It is thus easy to see that the paradigm of Indian philosophy directly challenges Western thought with its alignment with contemporary science. The amazing aspect of Indian arts, music, poetry, sciences, cultures, and philosophies is an intense 'spiritualisation' of its activities. Every single path—grammar included—can be a means to liberation. In his classic work, *The Word as Revelation: Names of Gods*, Ram Swarup elegantly demonstrates this.

Regarding perception, the standard Western paradigm is that light falls on an object first. This reflected light enters the eyes and falls on the retina, from where neural impulses travel to the brain. Here, the image undergoes a reconstruction, and the person 'sees' the object. The same sequence is true for all the other senses too. This is the 'stimulus-response theory of perception'—a stimulus of some sort evoking a response inside our brains through an intermediate causal chain. There is a difficulty, however, in explaining how an internal image inside the brain projects to the outside world.

Hence, what we perceive in the external world is not as it really exists, but how the interpretation occurs in our brains through our endowed senses. It is an indirect form of reality. In Kantian philosophy, the original unknown is the 'noumenon' and the known constructed reality is the 'phenomenon'. This forms the basis of both philosophy and neuroscience. However, this is incoherent in explaining the ontological status or reality of the world. If there is an unknown 'noumenon' and a representative 'phenomenon', then every object in the causal chain from the external world to the perceiver, including the intervening medium (even the brain), is unknowable.

A strictly materialistic or 'scientific' view of the process of perception has caused deep troubles in the Western philosophical world to date. Indian thinkers and philosophers had a far better understanding of the process of perception. All perception, whatever we see or hear, is direct, immediate, real, and in its true form—*Direct Realism.* Perception involves a *transparency* between the Self and the object, with contact between the two. There is no time lag in perception. The physical organs are only to enable this transparency and work as seats of experience too.

The perceiver goes out and reaches the object in the world—an inside-to-outside process. It is, thus, a composite process in which the self, the mind, and the sense organs together participate to establish contact with the object. This is the contact theory of perception of Indian philosophy. Contact with the object by the perceiver gives direct information about the world as it exists. Hence, the external world, as seen or heard, is an actual world in its reality and not a construction. Perception is never a valid source of knowledge in Western traditions, but it is the most important source of knowledge in Indian traditions.

It is a tragedy of our education systems after independence, in a continuation of the colonial legacy, that they ignored teaching the growing generations the richness, depth, antiquity, and sophistication of Indian philosophy. The separation of theology and philosophy did not happen in Europe itself until the Reformation. Hegel, the German philosopher, made Indian philosophies into religion and largely fashioned the Western image of India. Proving Indian thought from a Western perspective, and the other way around too, remains difficult due to the incommensurability problem and differing presuppositions. However, Indian philosophy seems to give far better explanations of reality and the world than Western philosophy. Unfortunately, our schools never teach us anything about the rich Indian philosophical systems, an old European idea that everything related to philosophy in India is religion.

### *Educational Policies of Modern India*

Ananda Coomaraswamy, one of the greatest intellectuals of modern India, put forth ideas about Indian education more than a century ago that are relevant even today. He wrote that education, as devised by the English, was a striking blow to "almost every ideal informing the national culture." According to Coomaraswamy, it is crucial to preserve essential elements from an Indian perspective for education. Some of these were:

1.  The almost universal philosophical attitude of Indians.
2.  The sacredness of all things (the antithesis of the European division of life into "sacred" and "profane"). In India, this was never so; religion idealises and spiritualizes life itself rather than excludes it.
3.  The true spirit of religious toleration, as illustrated continually in Indian history.
4.  Special ideas in relation to education, such as the relation between teacher and pupil (*guru-shishya* parampara or traditions); *memorizing* great literature; *music* as an important carrier of individual and national culture; learning not to become a mere road to material prosperity; and the extreme importance of the teacher's personality.
5.  The principle of altruism—founded on the philosophical truth "Thy neighbor is thyself"—serving as the basis of ethics.
6.  Control of action and thought, concentration, and capacity for stillness.

For Coomaraswamy, national culture was the only vantage point from which a person could take a wider view of other cultures. Education should not separate the "educated" from their past, nor from the "uneducated." The two Indian epics (*Mahabharata and Ramayana*) and *Puranas* have been the great medium of Indian education for the transmission of national culture and the basis of real character building. He wrote that modern English education ignores and destroys this. "*The story of Arjuna focusing on the bird's eye embodies the culminating ideal of the nation,*" says Coomaraswamy. Education should aim to cultivate good Indian citizens by using national culture and national languages (literary, musical, and artistic) as the medium of instruction.

After independence, as Dr. Bhikhu Parekh writes, ignoring primary education and focusing instead on higher education led to a huge variety of schools with little coordination, limited relevance to Indian conditions, and poor attempts to ground pupils in Indian history and culture. The future citizens of India grew up with little in common, sometimes sharing the minimum of memories and values with their parents. Secularism also damaged our education greatly. Classifying the most wonderful philosophies and metaphysics available in our *Vedas, Upanishads, Darshanas, Mahabharata, Ramayana, Bhagavad Gita, Puranas,* and countless other texts as 'religion' and then excluding them from study at the school level has been the single most important cause of the lack of pride in our culture. The profound and basic Upanishidic message of "the same Self in All" is, in fact, the basis for all humanism, ecology, environmentalism, and even feminism. However, anything from our traditions became a part of non-secular instruction, leading to sad consequences for the country.

### *Nations and Nationalism*

The British consolidated India politically to some extent but they were not the first to do so. The British divided us politically into two countries using religion; caused social disruptions by their caste system narratives and Aryan theory frameworks; converted traditions into religions; stripped us economically; dragged us into two World Wars in which we had no stakes; caused the worst famines; fed their industries with raw material produced in India; made India a market for their finished products; destroyed agriculture by converting large tracts of land for cash crops or for their opium trade; levied heavy taxes; and many more… And yet apologists credit the British for uniting India as 'one nation' politically.

India as the West's creation has a significant intellectual history in both colonial and post-colonial thinking. Standard Western theories (Hobsbawm, Gellener, and Anderson) trace the origins of nations through institutional, economic, and technological transformations. These scholars only enlighten us on the emergence of modern 'governmentality' to attain greater efficacy. The modern understanding of a state-nation cannot imagine a nation as a 'civilizational continuity' based on traditions, culture, and rituals.

Cultural or linguistic *homogenisation* is the basis of modern nation-states; however, spiritual places, holy rivers, and important texts like the Mahabharata and Ramayana have defined Bharat's geography. India is an ancient 'felt community', as Saumya Dey argues, because it does not emerge through deliberate cultural or linguistic systematisation. It functions and forms through a sense of belonging to the land disseminated through symbols. The swastika, the lotus, the Devatas of temples, the tirthas (pilgrimages), and the Sanskrit language are some examples that evoke and collectively assimilate Indians into the same matrix of meanings.

India has diverse social, linguistic, and spiritual practices. The cultural heritage acts as an overall cement that accommodates Vedic, Jain, Buddhist, Tantric, Puranic, Sikh, folk, and tribal concepts, forms, attitudes, customs, and practices. Our diversity and acceptance of diversity hold the key to defining a civilisational India transcending historically the idea of political unity. Tagore, Sri Aurobindo, and Swami Vivekananda, stressing the spiritual and cultural aspects of India, recognised the recentness of and the possible evils nationalism in the European sense could generate. Sovereign independent states became the norm, but the consequences were aggressive nationalism, colonialism, and world wars leading to global plunder and the extermination of local populations.

Our nationhood was never a homogenisation from the top but a decentralised polity bound by a common culture. States, nations, sovereignty, and nationalism are clearly rooted in European history and Christian theology. Our nationalism was about absorption and not invasion. The forcible application of Western theories to the Indian context led to the division of our country first on a *religious* basis, followed by the states on a *linguistic* basis. An artificiality in cultural identities leading to stress is now the result of such policies. Our ancient kingdoms had multiple languages without disputes amongst the native speakers.

Our best definition as a people (or *nation*) would be where diversity was the norm and the essence of nationalism was protecting the diversity of the country. Political unity was of lesser importance. India has been the longest-continuing civilisation for at least five thousand years. Colonial scholarship had to claim that India had nothing by way of literature, arts, religion, or the sciences. Compared with the other civilisations, India appeared to be singularly lacking in political unity and, therefore, in history.

The colonials had a clear mission in showing the political disunity of India, but why do we need to repeat this story? 'Colonial consciousness' makes its presence again.

Bharat is a cultural unit with a federation of sub-identities, preserving their individuality and equally contributing to the evolution of a common culture. Radhakumud Mookerji (*The Fundamental Unity of India*) shows how both the foci and loci of religious and cultural identities lay within the same sacred geography, which was proof of civilisational unity. India is a dynamic cauldron of many physical, spiritual, and social components (*sampradayas or paramparas*). India could absorb a multitude of religions without any issues, so long as they subscribed to the idea of a multi-traditional land. For reasons we do not understand, even Abrahamic religions took the form of traditions in our country. In this paradigm of mixing traditions without friction, there would be more space to understand and encourage syncretism with Abrahamic faiths.

Western ideas to mould political unity through homogenisation using language or common economic ideals do not simply apply to India. The facts of India do not match the Western theories of nations and nationalism, but typically, the theories stay intact while denying the data. Can we not look at India through our own lenses?

## Freedom Struggle and the Story of Independence

We are mainly aware of Gandhi and the Congress in our independence story, which makes a good narrative for the British too. We refuse to acknowledge revolutionary movements and individuals like Sri Aurobindo, Savarkar, or Bose in the freedom struggle. Critics have attacked Bose for seeking support from Hitler and Japan. Hitler initially had good relations with Russia and England. Later, he attacked Russia, and England turned against Germany. Incidentally, India's Communists changed their attitudes towards the British when England became an ally of Russia. They were initially opposed to British rule but, when Britain became an ally of Russia, the Communists switched sides and allied with the British. They even opposed the Quit India movement of 1942 and generally started taking orders from the English.

Post-war, the winners became the good people, and the losers (specifically Hitler) became the bad. The Nazi regime murdered six million Jews and more than five million non-Jews on racist lines. However, in just 10 years (1891–1900), 19 million people died in India due to famines alone. The recurrent famines were the result of the colonials mismanaging Indian agriculture, a holocaust of no less proportion. In the last holocaust of 1943-44, during the Second World War, the British rulers under Churchill, with Australian complicity, starved to death up to 3 million Indians for strategic reasons. For India, perhaps Winston Churchill and the British were equally cruel and brutal as Hitler. But we exonerate the former. Madhusree Mukerjee documents this aspect of Churchill during the Second World War in her book *Churchill's Secret War: The British Empire and the Ravaging of India during World War II.*

Subhash Bose had an equal role, arguably even more than Gandhi, in gaining our independence. We do not critique the European power dynamics during the World Wars but find great trouble when Bose approaches the "enemy of an enemy" to gain independence. Possibly, Bose found no difference between the British and Nazis in terms of their cruelties. A colonised attitude prevails when we draw up our heroes and villains of the freedom struggle. In popular accounts, we make Gandhiji and Nehru our sole heroes, as we brush aside the contributions of the many other revolutionaries and people like Subash Bose. The British declared Bose a war criminal and the Indian government was extremely grudging in honouring his contribution for a long time after independence.

### *Science and Technology*

Extraordinarily, the assessment of a 150-year colonial rule of at least a five-millennium-old civilisation became a benchmark for us. That a self-sufficient country stood strong for such a long time without any scientific or technological achievements is hard to believe, yet it is the firm idea of most Indians. Everything we had was either fake or borrowed from the Greeks, Chinese, Babylonians, Mesopotamians, or Arabs.

We can be legitimately proud of our ancient sciences without outside validation. There are apparently 30 million manuscripts in Indian repositories related to science and technology. Ancient Indian science had an interface with the ordinary world (*loka parampara*) in the best of Indian traditions. Macaulay (1835) said that Indian knowledge systems were a public waste "for giving artificial encouragement to absurd history, absurd metaphysics, absurd physics, and absurd theology." Similar observations continued over centuries. Beginning as a grudging admiration for Indian science and technology, especially in astronomy and agriculture, the colonial writings in the seventeenth, eighteenth, and nineteenth centuries progressively made sure that Indian society had nothing in comparison to superior European thought.

Unfortunately, few have heard of Dharampal's *Indian Science and Technology in the Eighteenth Century*. Beginning in 1964–65, and over the next decade, Dharampal meticulously reconstructed from the British archives the colonial descriptions of Indian sciences. The conclusions undermine the legitimacy of colonial-dominated perceptions about Indian society. Contrary to the standard teaching, Indian society was functioning well and was extremely competent in the arts and sciences of its day when the British started their rule. Its interactive grasp over its immediate natural environment demanded praise.

India's huge corpus of texts (the broad five groups—*Vedas, Upavedas, Vedangas, Puranas,* and *Darshanas*) covering all fields of human activity testifies to the capacity of Indians to create knowledge without any foreign influences. As a practical culture, technology came before the theoretical sciences many times. However, we did develop some of the most advanced mathematical and geometrical theories in the form of verses. Indian historians of science (like Prof. K. Ramasubramanian) convey that ancient Indians had advanced arithmetic, algebra, geometry, trigonometry, combinatorics, astronomy, and calculus but these were many times in the form of terse and succinct verses. There was a tradition of detailed commentaries that explained the formulas. These proofs in commentaries were an important component of Indian mathematics, but the critics conveniently ignored them. Modern mathematics evolved a notational and equational form like a+b=c which did not seem to exist in the original verses of Indian mathematicians.

Bhaskar Kamble describes the deep contributions of ancient Indian mathematicians, especially the Kerala School, in his recent book *The Imperishable Seed* (2022). The disrupting colonial rules (Islamic and European) forced us from creating knowledge to just protecting it from annihilation. Independence could have been a break, but the ideology-driven academia was intensely inimical to Indian traditions. Their view of a linear history was clear: a primitive Indian past for steering to a golden future (like modern Europe). In a few crucial generations, our education system could deracinate most Indians successfully. India has a deep intellectual history of many ideas and technologies. However, the general belief remains of an unscientific India before the colonials came.

### *Medicine: The Charaka Oath Controversy*

That India has a great intellectual heritage and a huge corpus of texts covering all fields of human activity is testimony to Indians' ability to create knowledge indigenously. Ayurveda, a 5000-year-old tradition, has two main schools: *Charaka* and *Sushrutha*. *Charaka Samhita* (likely 500 BCE) with 120 chapters had Persian, Arabic, and Latin translations; the Arabic translation was Al-Beruni's chief source of medicine.

A medical college dean suspended for allowing his students to deliver the 'Charak Shapath' points to a deep colonial consciousness. The oath is simply a tradition and a broad reiteration of some ethical principles that are not binding (least of all legally) in any respect. The Hippocratic oath (original or modified) is equally, if not more, inadequate to address the realities of a medical world that has witnessed huge scientific, economic, political, and social changes.

Does the traditional oath even have relevance in modern times? The answer would be affirmative for a traditional society like India. Traditions are simply handed down from one generation to another, and unless they positively harm society, a traditional society would not question them. There are rarely answers to the 'why' of traditional practices. "Why do you wear bangles?" "Why do you wear a bindi?" These questions do not make sense, and the only answer is that they are traditions, an answer that fails to satisfy people demanding scientific explanations.

As Balagangadhara's thesis goes, India is a traditional culture where the 'how' question is important. Such cultures are rooted in rituals, which, in turn, bring people together. The Western culture, which has roots in religion, has the 'why' as its most important question. Science, atheism, and the division of people are natural outcomes of such cultures. The colonials, coming from a Western culture, took a 'scientific' view and developed a deep antipathy to Indian traditions, including its medicine, notwithstanding some of its great developments.

Unfortunately, post-independent thinkers shared the same view of traditional India. The past as primitive, the future as golden, and the present as a stepping stone were straight-line historical narratives derived from the West. Hence, colonial consciousness believes that somehow the Hippocratic oath makes more sense than the Charaka oath.

### Shiv Shakti and Rocket Scientists/Engineers Going to Tirupati

Indian philosophy concerns itself with *para vidya* and *apara vidya*, the knowledge of the 'higher Self' and the knowledge of the 'external material world', respectively. It is one of the fundamental tenets of Indian knowledge systems that these two are not antagonistic to each other and are manifestations of a single unity in the form of *Brahman*. In such a stance, there is an intense spiritualisation of every single aspect of *apara vidya* (all 'secular activities') dealing with the material world.

As Indian intellectuals like Sri Aurobindo or Ananda Coomaraswamy argue, the separation of the 'sacred' and the 'profane' profoundly fails to make sense in our culture. Science and most other secular activities can also be a route to the divine. Most of the secular activities finally seek the unity that binds the *para* and the *apara*. In contrast, science, as popularised in Western culture, also seeks unity, but only in the *apara*, or material realm.

The divine goddess could inspire the highest poetry and mathematics of Kalidasa and Ramanujan, respectively. Ramanujam attributed his deepest insights into mathematics to the grace of his village deity. This irritated his atheist mentor in England, who could not understand the proofs of theorems on many occasions. Ramanujam simply skipped many intermediate steps and explained that it was intuitive at a certain level. It used to be a challenge for Hardy, who spent hours trying to understand Ramanujam's proofs. The most important point here is that the clash between 'science' and 'religion' (the problematic conversion of Hindu traditions as religions is another matter) never existed in Indian culture. There is no dichotomy when a rocket scientist breaks a coconut in the temple.

The clash between the 'word of God' and 'the word of science', typically seen in Abrahamic cultures of the West, never existed in India. Every secular activity, including science, is intensely 'spiritualised' and can be a way to *moksha*, the ultimate ideal of our culture. Even asking a scientist why they go to a temple exposes ignorance on the part of the questioner about the nature of Indian culture. The answers also fail to convince because they do not make sense in Abrahamic frameworks. Science must be in opposition to spirituality, and the idea that they are two aspects of the same unity seems to escape our collective thinking. Nothing is a better name for the recent landing point on the dark side of the moon than *Shiv Shakti*, because that represents the philosophy of the entire culture for thousands of years—the union of the primordial Consciousness and energy.

### Feminism

The initial waves of Western feminism achieved victories in voting rights, political participation, equal pay, and emancipation for women. However, the subsequent waves led to a confrontation with strong narratives of 'patriarchy', 'toxic masculinity', and a general distrust of males and the institute of marriage. Our intellectuals transpose Western narratives onto Indian soil without realising that our familial, societal, cultural, marital, and economic factors are different.

Indian feminists taking Western theories simply wash out the divine component of women in Indian culture. India's huge body of texts and traditions were about women working as equals in maintaining the family and society. Indian ideas of *Ardhanareshwar*, women in Bhakti traditions achieving gender equality and equal respect; women protesting patriarchy, kings, caste divides, and oppressive social norms; and hundreds of inspiring women in history and literature do not figure in discussions of Indian feminism.

There are problems, of course, like the low respect for women voicing out choices in lower socio-economic classes and the struggle of an urban woman to balance work and home. Western feminism, when applied to Indian culture, leads to anti-Hinduism as the blame finally falls on the traditions and texts, cherry-picking from a huge corpus. The ridicule of 'patriarchy' and 'regressive nature' extends to many Indian festivals, customs, and symbols like *Mangalasutra* and *Sindoor*. They unsettle the Hindu family and the marriage system.

Finally, the Western utilitarian approach lost understanding of the exclusive value of birthing, motherhood, and lactation. Feminism is a modern expansionist creation of the West based on patriarchy and liberal secularism. Our traditions seek harmony, deify women, and ask women to be just women, true to their physical, mental, and intellectual natures. They may have better solutions for not only us but for the world.

### *Concluding Remarks*

The German Indologists of the eighteenth and nineteenth centuries, who laid the basis for all future Indology, damaged and distorted Indian culture with their poor understandings and interpretations of our texts. The method for reading the texts was a *historical-critical* approach, a reading of the Mahabharata and Gita through the prism of time and history. From a historical perspective, the Indologists could use the texts to construct a history of ancient India and how, finally, the Germans were related to the mythic Aryan race.

Adluri and Bagchee in *The Nay Science* (2014) show how this approach to analysing Sanskrit texts caused immense epistemic violence to the philosophical perspectives transcending time and place. The scripture reading needs a lot of grounding in language, grammar, logic, meter, faith, and humility, which the Indologists were obviously deficient in. There was a whitewashing of the traditional commentarial approach of Indian scholars. It is sad that post-independent Marxist scholars, and many non-Marxist scholars too, read these texts using a historical-critical approach.

The colonial consciousness pervades perhaps every framework for understanding our culture. It is an idea of decolonisation to rename India Bharat. Maybe it is a small, big, or irrelevant step. But a step it is. The important thing for decolonisation is to replace a colonial story with an indigenous story, as Dr. Balagangadhara says. But how many indigenous stories do we have? Do we have alternative explanations for all the colonial narratives for replacing and decolonising ourselves? The answer is a big no. After independence, our social sciences, the most important field in rejuvenating a country, simply built upon and provided more data to strengthen the colonial narratives.

Our social sciences wore European lenses and looked at India. The Brahmins remained villains. The point of criticism, instead of towards the colonials, remained on the Hindu religion and the evil caste system. This was perhaps the greatest colonial achievement, as today we blame ourselves for all our problems, including the fact of our colonisation. Thus, we urgently need to decolonise the social sciences. Of course, one should not reject the hard-won previous insights of the social sciences, and the task involves transcending beyond the 'us' versus 'them' binary.

Balagangadhara says:

> Indologists use discredited theories from earlier social sciences to put across outlandish claims regarding a culture about which they are ignorant. Contemporary social sciences draw upon these ignorant claims to put across equally outlandish claims about human societies and cultures, again in ignorance of what the Indological claims rest upon. The social sciences and Indology enter a death dance where neither participant dies but knowledge does without delivering anything of substance about both Ancient and Modern India. The Indologists, Sanskritists, and social scientists, depending on each other, deserve credit for accomplishing this incredible feat of making 'the' caste system synonymous with 'discrimination' and 'oppression' and so effortlessly supplanting the British 'class' hierarchy, American 'racial' inequality, the 'apartheid' policy, the Nazi ideology, and so on.
>
> (*Cultures Differ Differently*)

Modern sociology simply describes the ills of the Indian cultural systems, presuming the truth of the Orientalist descriptions of non-Western cultures. This permeates politics, media, civil services, and the general conscience of the country. The damage to India from colonial consciousness runs deep and requires a collective effort, which might take decades. The roots are in the social sciences departments, and decolonisation must start *there.*

## Chapter 14

# THE UNITY OF INDIA

India, even after 75 years of independence, remains in the grip of dangerous and divisive narratives. It is unfortunate that our academia, legal luminaries, and politicians have been unable to correct many narratives initiated by the colonials. The most dangerous of these has to be the Aryan Invasion Theory. The hegemonical Western academia does not allow any resistance to the idea of invading Aryans coming from Russia or Central Asia to India around 1500 BCE and driving away the indigenous inhabitants of the land.

Archaeology, linguistics, textual sources, and genetic studies are all invoked in this theory, even though the first completely rejects the Aryan invasion (or migration), and the others conclude, equally or even more plausibly, that there was a reverse migration from India to different parts of Europe. However, despite all evidence to the contrary, Indians seem to have simply internalised the Aryan invasion/migration narrative and even built a huge edifice of conclusions based on its assumptions. It is irrelevant to us whether Aryans existed or not according to some scholars. That may be true, but it is a fact that most of the divisions propagated in the country depend to some extent on the mysterious Aryans.

The indigenous people of India driven south became the Dravidians. Those pushed into forests became the tribals, and the people who stayed back became subjugated as the lowest in the hierarchy of the caste system (*Shudras,* and especially the 'untouchables'). In the 'Breaking India' narrative, the Dravidians, tribals, and the Dalits (Scheduled Castes or ex-untouchables) are in opposition to the majority dominant, upper-caste,

'Hindus'— the latter always trying to exploit and subsume the former into a Vedic-Sanskritic-Brahmanical culture.

Hinduism stands in opposition to the non-Vedic cultures just as Sanskrit, a language of the oppressive Brahmins, is in opposition to the Dravidian languages. Into this colourful and vibrant narrative enters the story of Buddhism rebelling against the oppressive practices of Hinduism. In a Martin Luther-like Protestant attack on the Catholic Church, Buddha attacks the Brahmanical practices of a decadent Hinduism. The conclusion drawn by this narrative is that India had never been a nation and that it was simply the British who united us. A similar explanation of a disunited India ruled by a bunch of warring kings allows for the success of Islamic rulers too. The scholars who follow this line grossly ignore the fact that, despite having such a decentralised polity and no unity in the modern definition of a nation-state, we were far advanced in the fields of economics, art, literature, architecture, engineering, sciences, medicine, philosophy, and spirituality, to name a few. Did it not occur to them that we never needed to invade countries around us but did attract a huge number of plunderers from Europe and the Middle East across centuries who needed us for their survival?

Why did our intellectuals, academia, and politicians fail? Are all these misrepresentations indicative of a deeper phenomenon at an intellectual level, thanks to the invasions? Colonial consciousness may explain this phenomenon.

### Aryans, Dravidians, Tamilians, and The Rest

The Dravidian movement, initiated by E.V. Ramaswamy Naicker (Periyar), has strong views about the ancient history of Tamil Nadu. The Aryan Invasion Theory turns most North Indians and Brahmins into descendants of the invading Aryans and Tamils as the indigenous Dravidians. The other claims are that Tamil is older than its deadly rival Sanskrit and that the Dravidian culture is wholly separate from the so-called Aryan culture.

Archaeology, epigraphy (study of inscriptions), numismatics (study of coins), and literature (the Sangam literature) disprove all the above theories. Archaeology has so far fixed the emergence of urban civilisation in Tamil Nadu two and a half millennia after the appearance of Indus cities. Inscriptions and coins dating back to the second and third centuries BCE confirm the names of cities, kings (Chola, Pandya, and Chera dynasties), and chieftains mentioned in the Sangam literature. The present evidence from all sources suggests that the earliest Tamil kingdoms were established around the fourth century BCE, and urban developments were a century or two later.

The material evidence in the excavations clearly shows that, culturally, the people of the South shared many beliefs and practices with builders elsewhere in the subcontinent. The Southern culture attached great importance to the cult of the dead and ancestors, which parallels that in Vedic culture. The Pandya-era coins show extensive evidence of Vedic sacrifices and Vedic-Puranic symbols related to Vishnu and Shiva, both.

The rich Sangam literature (300 BCE to 300 CE) — in texts like *Tolkappiyam, Kural,* and *Purananaru* — shows not only extensive references to Vedic sacrifices but a complete absence of any mention of a great clash between Aryans and Dravidians. Scholars have shown by innumerable examples that knowledge of Sanskrit literature from the Vedic period to the Classical period is essential to appreciating Tamil literature. Vedic and Puranic themes inextricably weave into the most ancient culture of the Tamil land known to us. Sangam literature shows evidence of the fourfold varna system too. Today, the Tamil language has assimilated and uses between 20% and 40% of the commonly used vocabulary from Sanskrit.

Surprisingly, there are no references to the word 'Dravida' in *Tolkappiyam,* the oldest surviving work on Tamil grammar, literature, and linguistics. The first use in Tamil was by the sage Tayumanvar in the eighteenth century. In the Vedic-Puranic-Itihaasic literature, 'Arya' denoted a noble person, and 'Dravida' was used in a purely geographical sense. As one scholar shows, 'Dravida' is not of Tamil origin at all because Tamil grammar neither provides for a word beginning with a sonant (hence cannot begin with *d*) nor with a half-syllable. The word has most likely Prakrit or Sanskrit roots.

The historical period of the great Pallava, Chola, and Pandya temples and the overflowing devotional literature by the Alwars, the Nayanmars, and other seekers show a clear integration of Vedic-Sanskritic elements into

Tamil. Without conflict, there was every sign of a deep cultural interaction between the North and South. In reverse, the Tamil genius has contributed extensively by way of temple architecture, music, dance, and literature to the North and other South Asian countries too. 'Dravidian' has a meaning in both the old geographical sense or in the modern linguistic sense; racial and a totally different cultural meanings are unscientific and irrational and are simply a manifestation of a colonial mindset. As Michel Danino says, every region of India has developed according to its own genius, creating its own bent while remaining faithful to the central Indian spirit.

### Dalits and Untouchables

Chapter 7 dealt with this in more detail. The distinction between 'Caste Hindus' and 'Untouchables' was never an age-old division within Hindu society. The Commissioner for the 1901 Census in India sent to every Census Commissioner, as a part of his standard scheme, four Sanskrit-named 'Shudra' categories, of which the last was *Asprishya Shudra*, explained as "castes whose touch is so impure as to pollute even Ganges water." This system failed. Basically, the census research revealed that the structure of Indian society did not correspond to the conception of the caste hierarchy it had started out with. In the process, officials and scholars could neither provide a coherent hierarchical classification of castes nor identify the 'Untouchables' or 'exterior' castes in any consistent way. The colonials divided society into *Caste Hindus* and *Depressed Classes*. Later, the *Government of India Scheduled Castes Order* of 1936 ordered the division of the people of India into *Scheduled Castes and others*, and we continue to follow the legacy of caste legislation to this day.

In 1950, the Constitution passed a Scheduled Castes Order to include a set of groups for special benefits. Today, the government has transformed more than one thousand two hundred communities (jatis) and 64.5 million people at the last census into a single category of Scheduled Castes. In view of the many provisions given to them, the Supreme Court insists on guidelines for "intelligible differentiae" distinguishing the persons inside and outside the groupings. Surprisingly, the decisive factors are not social or economic backwardness, age, income, or disability but a single tenuous characteristic of 'untouchability'. With a wide range of social practices, never uniform but variable in different parts of the country, the list was never exhaustive, and other practices were added to it.

As Jakob De Roover writes (*Scheduled Castes vs. Caste Hindus: About a Colonial Distinction and Its Legal Impact*):

> On the one hand, the term 'untouchability' was used to refer to a variegated series of practices and situations. Sometimes, it was used to refer to situations where members of some group were not allowed into a temple. At other times, it pointed to the fact that some groups refused to take water from the hands of persons belonging to other groups or to the custom of providing separate cups for people from different groups. It could also refer to situations where members of one group would take a bath after having physical contact with members of another group or where people would clean their house after a member of a particular group had entered it. It could also indicate the fact that a group lived in separate quarters at the borders of a village. The list was never exhaustive and other practices could be added to it. During the censuses and in the committee reports, it turned out that some such practices existed in certain parts of India but not in other parts. In other words, the word 'untouchability' appeared to be a label that covered a set of actions or practices, whereas it remained unclear which common trait those practices shared.
>
> On the other hand, the British believed that the actions and practices referred to as 'untouchability' expressed the fact that certain caste groups were considered impure and polluting by the rest of the Hindu population. Empirically, however, it was not clear which groups were the victims at the receiving end of such practices. The members of different groups classified as 'Untouchables' or 'Depressed Classes' also engaged in actions and practices that were designated as 'untouchability'; and they did so towards each other. Several of these groups seemed to consider each other impure and polluting. How then could these groups be distinguished as a separate class because they were the victims or objects of untouchability?

The situation became even more complicated, once one considers the fact that practices labelled as 'untouchability' are also visible in the interaction among so-called 'high-caste Hindus'. One of the criteria to identify untouchable castes was that Brahmins would not accept water from these castes. However, it turned out that some Brahmin groups and even 'lower' castes refused to take water or food from certain Brahmins. For instance, Lingayats and Peasant castes in Karnataka refused food and water from the hands of specific Brahmin groups. Similarly, some would clean their house after a member of a Brahmin group had entered it. In other words, high-caste groups could also be victims of 'untouchability'.

It remained unclear then to which phenomena the term 'untouchability' referred. Inevitably, this confusion undermined the 'test' of untouchability, which was supposed to function as the intelligible differentia for the colonial classification of Depressed Classes. Undoubtedly, this classification seemed easier to make in some regions of India than in others. Going by the statements made by the officials, however, even the agreement on the question of identifying the depressed classes in the 'easier' regions was tenuous.

The Constituent Assembly never clearly defined 'untouchability' despite its decisive role in formulating caste legislation. The Committee for caste legislation of contemporary India took what they called two "generally accepted tests of untouchability" from the previous 1911 Census Superintendents: *"Those who are denied access to the interior of ordinary Hindu temples"* and *"cause pollution, (a) by touch, (b) within a certain distance."* This was confusing, filled with circular logic, and begging questions right at the beginning. Many of the 'exterior' castes considered polluting by 'interior' Hindus also had strong caste organisations and included numerous individuals of substance and education. Many *jatis* in both the 'interior' and 'exterior' groups practiced many forms of untouchability internally amongst themselves too.

Basically, the claim is that if one human being refrains from touching or approaching another human being, this becomes caste-based untouchability when the former belongs to the Caste Hindu and the latter belongs to the Untouchable Caste. And how can one recognise these Untouchable Castes? Well, they are the ones who are subject to caste-based untouchability. This route leads us into a vicious circle. Members of the Assembly in 1949 conceded that the term "Scheduled Castes" may be a fiction and that it was impossible to give a cut-and-dry definition of untouchability.

This evolved into a common indication of "an internal feeling of odium" expressed in a variety of practices and which denies political rights to certain groups. This also become vague and subjective as inward feelings of odium, aversion, and contempt exist among all kinds of people towards all kinds of other people. There are basic cognitive problems confronting the currently dominant account of Indian society with no intelligible differentia that distinguish all the persons grouped together as SCs from others excluded from that group. Indeed, the class of Scheduled Castes exists, but only in the Indian legal and political system.

## Tribals Versus The Rest

The continuing debate on the status of tribals of India and how they connect to 'mainstream' Hinduism has a single purpose of breaking India. The neologism *Adivasi* (*adi*, original; *vasi*, inhabitant) of the nineteenth century, a Sanskrit word and hardly a self-description of the tribals, became the most successful disinformation campaign of modern times by the colonials, Christian missionaries, and Indian secularists. In settler colonies (America, New Zealand, Australia), 'aboriginal' made sense to distinguish the European settler from the natives. However, in non-settler colonies like India, the term 'aboriginal' became a pure colonial construct.

A strong narrative now pits the majority dominant Hinduism (as the original foreign invaders) against the 'original' inhabitants (now the minorities — Dravidians, non-Hindu tribals, lower castes, and Hindu untouchables). This notional division of Indians into 'natives' and 'invaders' is a permanent colonial legacy. Susana Devalle, while talking about Jharkand tribes, says, "This colonial categorization as 'tribal' is at best out of place and, at worst, ahistorical and sociologically groundless." Interestingly, many tribes of Jharkhand and North-East India migrated *much later* from the surrounding countries after the indigenous non-tribal peasant population. Hence, the historical data do not support the division of India's population into aboriginal tribals and non-tribal invaders.

In the post-colonial era, other international forces (like the International Labour Organization) strengthened the distinction between dominant national communities and indigenous/tribal peoples, introducing an *internal* coloniality and a permanent faultline where the minority tribal communities became racially and culturally distinct from the majority national communities. The majority, by implication, are simply the pre-European colonisers of the tribal minorities. The now distinctly separate people have become the focus of intense evangelical activity. Such conversions in certain communities have severely disrupted the social and cultural fabric of coherent societies. Such disruption has never happened in the interaction between the 'mainstream' and the 'minor' traditions, as is usual in a traditional pagan land.

The impossibility of accurately defining combined with the broad usage have relegated the concepts of *race* and *tribe* to the dustbin of social sciences academia. Scholars feel that 'tribe' is a key but obsolete concept from anthropology's early history that usually served colonial, administrative, and ideological purposes to mainly paint the local groups as 'primitive' or 'backward'. The ancientness of the Hindu religion itself from "pre-Aryan times" makes it as 'aboriginal' as the tribal populations. The similarities between Hindu traditions and the tribal traditions in their fundamental polytheistic nature and paganism (deifying the feminine, nature, and animals) show them clearly distinct from the prophetic-monotheistic religions.

The tribals and other "mainstream" Vedic-Sanskritic traditions have many elements in common: partly by way of distant common roots; partly by way of the integration of tribal elements in the Sanskritic civilisation; and partly by the adoption of elements from the Vedic-Puranic Tradition into the tribal traditions. Balu (in *Cultures Differ Differently*) observes that, strangely, anthropologists spent decades trying to get rid of a pernicious and incoherent concept like 'tribe', only to see it sneak back, via Indology and other social sciences, into the Indian Constitution, Indian legislation, and its administration.

### Buddhism Versus Hinduism

A disruptive narrative that spread in India, starting with the colonials and continuing in post-independent India, is the story of Buddhism and its supposed antagonism with Hinduism. Thus, Buddha at some point in his life broke away, rebelling especially against Hinduism, the 'caste system', and the Vedas to form his own religion. Prince Gautama (563 BCE–486 BCE), a Kshatriya of the Ikshvaku dynasty following his enlightenment, became the Buddha, who himself described Rama as his previous incarnation. His liberal use of Upanishadic terminology shows no break or rebellion against an existing system.

There are only a few differences in the philosophies of Advaita and Buddhism. The concepts of Ignorance, Reincarnation, Karma, Moksha or Nirvana, the lower knowledge related to the world, and the higher transcendental knowledge show a remarkable similarity in both Advaita and Buddhism. The final state of enlightenment is merging in the Brahman for Advaita, whereas Buddhism speaks of *Sunyata*, silence, and nothingness. Hardly a reason for violent or unpleasant encounters with the background of Indian traditions.

Orientalists started treating Buddhism as a separate religion because they first discovered it outside India — without any conspicuous link with its original home, India. When its origins became clearer, writers made Buddha a Martin Luther and Buddhism a Protestant-like protest and successfully converted a branch of an Indian traditional tree into a religion called Buddhism. It now supposedly rebelled against another branch called Hinduism. European authors and their Indian followers imaginatively superimposed the medieval European religious wars on the supposed Hindu-Buddhist encounters. An exclusive belief in Buddha — to the complete rejection of any other god or saint — is quite simply an unbelievable proposition in traditional cultures like India. Buddhist buildings, temples, rituals, and mantras follow established Hindu Vedic patterns and Vastu Shastras. Buddhist monks who went to China and Japan took the Vedic gods like the twelve Adityas and Saraswati (River Goddess Benzaiten) with them.

Buddhist texts reveal that Buddha, contrary to popular narratives, never rejected the varnas. Buddha accepted the Varna Vyavastha; he, in fact, put the Kshatriyas at the top of the hierarchy. Everyone in their position in the Varna could follow the eight-fold path in their quest for enlightenment. The conversion of Dr. Ambedkar, along with thousands of his followers, in 1956 strengthened the anti-Hindu programme of Buddha in a retrospective manner. Conversion, implying a rejection of all previous beliefs, is a typical religious concept prevalent in Christianity and Islam. In traditional cultures devoid of such demands, one can embrace another tradition, keeping the old view perfectly intact. The twenty-two pledges of Ambedkar and his Neo-Buddhism are almost a polemic against all the Hindu Gods, Brahmins, and Hindu rituals, further radicalising the Buddhist religion.

Buddhism was just another tradition in the Hindu land, where new traditions, sects, and gurus evolve all the time, showing many paths to the final enlightenment. Buddha was showing another path and was simply a beneficiary of an established Hindu pluralistic tradition. Koenraad Elst says simply, "Buddha was every inch a Hindu."

### *Muslims, Christians, and Sanatana Dharma*

SN Balagangadhara's thesis holds the solution to religious harmony in the country. His claim about religions at the most basic level goes like this: *India is a land of traditions and not religions.* If Christianity, Islam, Judaism, and Zoroastrianism are religions in their true definition (consisting of *A Book, A God, A Doctrine, A Temple*), then there are no indigenous religions in India. As a corollary, if what we have are religions, then Christianity, Islam, and Judaism are not religions. The standard understanding has only given us wars, strife, conversions, and inquisitions, even as the biggest problem across all ideologies is the continuous understanding of traditions as religions.

Prof. Balagangadhara shows that—both "metaphysically" and "sociologically —it is an impossibility that indigenous phenomena (Hinduism, Buddhism, Jainism, and Sikhism) in the country are religions.

Hinduism was an *experiential entity* for the colonials. They united the different practices and narratives into a *meta-narrative*—a broad framework of explanation—a single entity called Hinduism. Their own cultural background, rooted in religion (specifically Christianity), which could not comprehend that cultures could exist without religion, guided this exercise.

'Traditio'—as the Ancient Romans used it—referred to ancestral practices transmitted over generations. India is a land of traditions. Calling oneself a Hindu for the sake of convenience is a continuation of ancestral traditions. The notion of 'practice' is widespread: from stories through visits to temples to performing rituals. Balagangadhara attributes two important properties to traditions: (a) the enormous flexibility in belonging to a tradition and the sharpness with which the boundaries are drawn between traditions; (b) the possibility that any element could be absent from a tradition and yet it could maintain identity and distinction.

How do we then understand Christianity and Islam in India? Balagangadhara says that the simple answer is that when these religions entered India, they met with an already-formed culture. These religions adapted to the existing culture to survive. They held their beliefs and practices by adapting to Indian uses of the resources of socialisation. Thus, Indian Christianity and Indian Islam remain Indian irrespective of their religious beliefs and practices, which have the space to flourish as one of the many diversities present in Indian culture. In this process, these religions undergo modifications in how the believers live their daily lives, which do not affect the content of their beliefs or their places of worship. It is exactly this kind of adoption and adaptation to Indian culture that many *madrassa* schools and evangelical Christians militate against, says Balu.

Traditions, when they become religions, lose their flexibility and absorptive power. Traditions with rituals at their foundation unite people; religions with *My One True God* against *Your False Many Gods* disrupt societies. India's practical solution was to traditionalise the religions so that they lost focus on proselytization and made some genuine attempts at cultural syncretism. In reverse, our thinkers are trying hard to convert our traditions into religions, with a resultant and not surprising rise in intolerance and fundamentalism.

## Nationhood Of India

Ill-informed Indians follow post-colonial scholars who use the modern definition of a nation-state, an outcome of the intra-Christian Religious Wars and the Treaty of Westphalia, and assert that India was somehow a creation of the West and that we were "never a nation." Standard Western theories, mainly Marxist-influenced, trace the origins of nations in institutional, economic, and technological transformations. Apparently, the democratic state and its elite create nations through *cultural homogenisation* by invoking symbols and inventing traditions like a national anthem or a national language.

Marxist models tend to look upon India's history as a history of invasions and invaders, largely ignoring the military, social, and cultural ways in which India resisted the invasions to preserve her original genius. Thus, Marxist scholars at Jawaharlal Nehru University (JNU) believe that India is incoherent, fragmented, and marked by foundational differences. Other dangerous indigenous narratives include Kerala not really belonging to India, Tamil nationalism resting on linguistic pride and official antipathy for Hinduism (though 88% of Tamil Nadu called themselves Hindus in the 2011 census), and so on.

India's greatest feat is her cultural integration through a long organic interaction between Vedic culture and local traditions, resulting in Hinduism as we know it. 'Nation' does not do justice to India's expression of oneness. India, as a civilisational entity, has been an ancient 'felt community' for thousands of years because it did not emerge through deliberate systematisation. It functions and forms through a sense of belonging to the land disseminated through symbols. This process manifests itself as 'culture' autonomous of the state. Thus, people could belong to the same set of meanings and land, despite differences in languages, by perceiving the same symbols (swastika, the lotus, the temples, the pilgrimages, the Sanskrit language, and so on) as a great unity.

*Bharatvarsha* exists in the oldest scriptures as the land south of the Himalayas and north of the oceans. India was *Sapta Sindhu*, the land of seven rivers in olden times. The Greeks called the land India, or *Indika*, which also derives from the word *Sindhu*. The Mahabharata, Ramayana, and Vishnu Purana describe Bharata Varsha with clarity in the various travels of its characters across the land. The Ramayana and Mahabharata, in fact, became the major tools for integration. The references to the great epics are all over the country and even in places like Indonesia, where local traditions link in some way to the two great epics.

A united India based on multiple traditions, rituals, mythology, and customs existed for thousands of years. A dense network of holy places and temples created a sacred geography of the country and a strong tradition of pilgrimages. The 12 Jyotirlingas, the 52 Shakti Mahapithas, and the 26 Upapithas spread over the Indian subcontinent and became the defining points for drawing the boundaries of the country. There was perhaps no political unity in the European definition of nation, though there was early political unity, like in the Mauryan Empire. However, a united geo-cultural India existed for thousands of years, making India a continuously surviving civilisational state despite constant attacks.

## Colonialism and Colonial Consciousness

We can best understand the many intellectual discourses today within the framework of 'colonial consciousness', as provided in detail by Dr. Balagangadhara. As he says:

Colonization was not merely a process of occupying lands and extracting revenues. It was not a question of us aping Western people and trying to be like them. It was not even about colonizing the imagination of a people by making them 'dream' that they, too, would become 'modern', developed, and sophisticated. It goes deeper than any of these. It is about denying people and cultures their own experiences; of rendering them aliens to themselves; of actively preventing any description of their own experiences except in terms defined by the colonizers.

In the previous chapter, we observed that colonial consciousness not only operates during the colonization process but also persists long after the colonizers have departed, permanently transforming the intellectual frameworks of the colonized people. We remain trapped in colonial narratives and fail to look at ourselves and the west through indigenous lenses.

As noted in the previous chapter, 'colonial consciousness' encompasses a vast number of prevalent narratives about India amongst Indians, not only in the country but around the world. Despite evidence to the contrary, most educated Indians refuse to believe alternative versions. The decolonization project is indeed a monumental effort. Decolonization requires more than just rejecting colonial narratives, as we also need to replace them with indigenous narratives. Unless we develop our own views instead of simply parroting western theories and stories, decolonization would only mean an empty nest.

According to Dr. Balagangadhara, this perception stems from the rhetorical force of the statement that colonization is an expression of strength. The strengths of the West are obvious: its scientific, technological, and military might. This implicit consensus about colonialism is omnipresent in contemporary times, too. Today, the problems regarding India and the language tools remain remarkably the same for both Western and Indian intellectuals. The result, of course, is a detachment of Indian citizens from their own cultural roots, sometimes even leading them to become staunch critics. Post-colonial Indian intellectuals continue to employ the same European social science methodology to understand India. Hence, their results simply reflect colonial and Oriental thought.

## Concluding Remarks: Academic, Political, and Legal Impositions of Disharmony

Sanatana (Eternal) Dharma defines and permeates the land of India. The words Hindu and Hinduism remain undefined in unambiguous terms even today, giving rise to many controversies. However, 'Hinduism' has the strongest correlation with Sanatana Dharma. Whether Hinduism is synonymous with or is a subset of Sanatana Dharma, the only understanding of India can come from within the framework of this Dharmic philosophy. Only Sanatana Dharma, a huge conglomerate of traditions, has the immense capacity to absorb alien ideas and religions if they go on the path of becoming traditions. The key to harmony in a traditional world comes from its fundamental philosophy of an *indifference to differences,* which far transcends the classical paradigms of *tolerance, acceptance,* and *mutual respect.*

The only social reality in India is its *jatis; varna* is perhaps an ideal. Untouchability was a weed, and we have rightly taken steps to remove it from society. However, we have made untouchability a permanent legacy. An 'ex-untouchability' status, which is only a political and legal reality, has spilled over into socio-cultural life, causing great distress and division. Such a policy repeats the same mistakes of the preceding centuries. By retaining the term 'caste' we are continuing the colonial legacy and the baggage of the improper understanding of our *varnas* and *jatis.* How wonderful would it be if the *jatis* and the *varnas* became *equal categories* with no institutionalised segmentation of society based on hierarchical gradings? Successive governments, by creating hierarchies, are instilling false notions of superiority, inferiority, guilt, anger, and shame in various proportions while paradoxically wanting to create an equal society. One of the most important aspects of our ancient, medieval, and contemporary times is that *jatis* belonging to the *Shudra varna* were the most powerful in the social, political, and economic sense.

There is never a denial of discrimination of all kinds in Indian society. Discrimination exists in all societies, and India is no exception. But to conceive of a system in which it becomes almost *morally obligatory to become immoral* is an extremely poor understanding of India. Unfortunately, for a host of intellectuals, any attempt to resist or correct becomes an example of 'Brahmanism'. For example, Jalki and Pathan elegantly show that the data for Dalit exploitation is methodologically faulty, has plenty of cherry-picking, and is riddled with selective interpretations. Yet the intellectual dishonesty regarding the figures and the generalisation of prominent anecdotal reports do manage to give a massive negative image of India on national and international platforms.

The various groups across the country, the diverse *jatis,* and the traditions with all kinds of practices are an array of flowers in the same garden of India. Indian culture and traditions have been an unbroken continuity for thousands of years, a melting pot of all three purported human groupings (Caucasoid, Mongoloid, and Negroid); six language families (Indo-European, Dravidian, Austric, Sino-Tibetan, Burushaski, and Andamanese); many traditions (Vedic and non-Vedic interacting either in a syncretic mode or remaining indifferent to each other without violence); and many religions configuring in the traditional mould.

We are one people and one land. Every person on this land is a part of and an inheritor of this great culture, irrespective of what faith they may be following, what *jati* they may belong to, or what language they are speaking. As Sri Aurobindo insisted, a true understanding of our traditional past is not only important for India's future but for the future of all of humanity. He says, *"The greatness of the ideals of the past is a promise of greater ideals for the future. A continual expansion of what stood behind past endeavour and capacity is the one abiding justification of a living culture."*

The solutions to multiculturalism and harmony can only come from India. We absorbed and assimilated every culture from across the world for thousands of years, and yet we are in the dock for the 'ugly caste system' and 'Hindu fundamentalism'. The anger is only increasing, and the fissures are deepening for all the wrong reasons. We need to urgently dissipate the anger and show hope to the world.

# REFERENCES AND ADDITIONAL READINGS

## Chapter 1

1. *The Heathen in His Blindness: Asia, the West and the Dynamic of Religion* (2015) by Dr. S.N. Balagangadhara.
   A classic text in which Dr. Balagangadhara explains his notions of religions and traditions in detail. It shows clearly how the entire process of converting our traditions into religions is at the root of all 'religious' frictions in India.
2. *Do All Roads Lead to Jerusalem? The Making of Indian Religions* (2015) by Divya Jhingran and S.N. Balagangadhara.

A simplified version of the above book.

## Chapter 2

1. *Religious Conversion: Indian Disputes and Their European Origins* (2022) by Sarah Claerhout and Jakob De Roover.
2. "Conversion of the World Proselytization in India and the Universalization of Christianity" (2008) by Sarah Claerhout and Jakob De Roover, *Academia.edu.*

## Chapter 3

*Europe, India, And the Limits of Secularism* (2015) by Jakob De Roover.

### Chapter 4

*Western Foundations of the Caste System* (2017) edited by Martin Fárek, Dunkin Jalki, Sufiya Pathan, and Prakash Shah.

### Chapter 5

1. "Evolution of the figure of the Brahmin in early Muslim writings" (2022) by Dunkin Jalki, *Oñati Socio-Legal Series*, vol. 13 (1).
2. "Caste, race, and slavery: On comparisons between race in the United States and caste in India, and to forgotten assumptions behind the legal categories" (2022) by Martin Fárek, *Oñati Socio-Legal Series*, vol.13 (1).
3. "Caste in a New Light: Jati in British Multiculturalism" (2022) by Prakash Shah, *Oñati Socio-Legal Series*, vol. 13 (1).
4. "On the explanatory adequacy of the Hindutva-as-Brahmanical model" (2023) by Garima Raghuvanshy, *Oñati Socio-Legal Series* vol.13 (1).
5. "The enigma of caste atrocities: Do scheduled castes and scheduled tribes face excessive violence in India?" (2023) by Nihar Sashittal, *Oñati Socio-Legal Series* vol.13(1).
6. "Violence Against SCs: How Absence of Reliable Data Leads to Disaster" (2018) by Sufiya Pathan, *Academia.edu*.

### Chapter 6

"The Impossibility of Refuting or Confirming the Arguments about the Caste System" (2015) by Sufiya Pathan and Dunkin Jalki, *Academia.edu*.

### Chapter 7

1. *The Beautiful Tree: Indigenous Indian Education in the Eighteenth Century* (1983) by Dharampal.
2. "The Plight of Brahmins" (1990) by Meenakshi Jain, *The Indian Express* (Sep 18).
3. "The Brahmin, the Aryan, and the Powers of the Priestly Class: Puzzles in the Study of Indian Religion" (2020) by Marianne Keppens & Jakob De Roover, *Academia.edu*.
4. "Scheduled Castes vs. Caste Hindus: About a Colonial Distinction and Its Legal Impact" (2017) by Jakob De Roover, *Socio-Legal Review* vol. 13 (1).

## Chapter 8

*Reconceptualizing India Studies* (2012) by Dr. S.N. Balagangadhara.

## Chapter 9

*What does it mean to be 'Indian'?* (2021) by S.N. Balagangadhara and Sarika Rao.

## Chapter 10

*Cultures Differ Differently: Selected Essays of S.N. Balagangadhara* (2022) edited by Jakob De Roover and Sarika Rao.

## Chapter 11

*India in the Eyes of Europeans: Conceptualization of Religion in Theology and Oriental Studies* (2022) by Martin Fárek.

## Chapter 12

"Magic between Europe and India: On Mantras, Coercion of Gods, and the Limits of Current Debates" (2021) by Martin Fárek, *Academia.edu.*

## Chapter 13
### Aryans and Dravidians

1. *The Nay Science: A History of German Indology* (2014) by Vishwa Adluri and Joydeep Bagchee.
2. *Breaking India: Western Interventions in Dravidian and Dalit Faultlines* (2012) by Malhotra Rajiv and Arvindan Neelakandan.
3. *The Problem of Indian History* (2012) by Michel Danimo.
4. *The Lost River: On the Trail of The Sarasvati* (2010) by Michel Danimo.
5. *The Rigveda: A Historical Analysis* (2004) by Shrikant Talgeri.
6. *Still No Trace of an Aryan Invasion: A Collection on Indo-European Origins* (2018) by Koenraad Elst.
7. "Vedic Roots of Early Tamil Culture" by Michel Danimo in *Saundaryashri: Studies of Indian History, Archaeology, Literature and Philosophy* (2009) edited by P. Chenna Reddy.

8. "The A of ABC of Indian chronology: Dimensions of the Aryan problem revisited in 2017" by Manogna Sastry and Megh Kalyanasundaram in *Land of Dharma: Studies in Tamil Civilization* (Proceedings of the Swadeshi Indology Conference Series) edited by Shrinivas Tilak and Sharda Narayanan.

9. *The Secret of the Veda* by Sri Aurobindo.

He completely trashes the idea of invading Aryans and invaded Dravidians with detailed explanations.

### Colonial Rule and its Advantages

1. *The World Economy: Vol. 1: A Millennial Perspective & Vol. 2: Historical Statistics* (2007) by Angus Maddison.

2. *An Era of Darkness: The British Empire in India* (2016) by Shashi Tharoor.

3. *The Theft of India: The European Conquests of India, 1498–1765* (2016) by Roy Moxham.

### English as a Medium of Instruction

1. *The English Medium Myth: Dismantling Barriers to India's Growth* (2018) by Sankrant Sanu.

2. The English Class System (2007) by Sankrant Sanu.

### Political Ideologies

1. "The Poverty of Indian Political Theory" (1992) by Bhikhu Parekh in *History of Political Thought* vol. 13.

2. "Nehru and The National Philosophy of India" 1991 by Bhikhu Parekh in *Economic & Political Weekly* vol. 26.

3. *The Indian Conservative: A History of Right-Wing Indian Thought* (2019) by Jaithirth Rao.

4. *The Myth of Left and Right: How the Political Spectrum Misleads and Harms America* (2023) by Hyrum Lewis and Verlan Lewis.

5. "It's Time to Retire the Political Spectrum" (2017) by Hyrum Lewis in *Quillette* [online magazine].

6. "John Locke, Christian Liberty, and the Predicament of Liberal Toleration" (2008) by Jakob De Roover and S.N. Balagangadhara in *Political Theory*, 36(4), 523-549.
7. *The Social Political Thought of Sri Aurobindo* (2019) by Dr. Debashri Banerjee.
8. "The Bugbear of Democracy, Freedom, and Equality" (1977) by Ananda K. Coomaraswamy in *Studies in Comparative Religion* vol.11 (3).
9. *Spiritual Authority and Temporal Power in The Indian Theory of Government* (2013) by Ananda K. Coomaraswamy.
10. *Perversion of India's Political Parlance* (2016) by Sita Ram Goel.

## Tribals vs. The Rest

1. "Are Tribals Hindus?" in *Who is a Hindu? Hindu Revivalist Views of Animism, Buddhism, Sikhism, and Other Offshoots of Hinduism* (2002) by Koenraad Elst.
2. *Decolonizing the Hindu Mind: Ideological Development of Hindu Revivalism* (2016) by Koenraad Elst.
3. *India that is Bharat: Coloniality, Civilisation, Constitution* (2021) by J Sai Deepak.

## Hindus, Hinduism, Hindutva

1. *Letters on Hinduism* (1940) by Bankim Chandra Chatterjee.
2. *Who is a Hindu? Hindu Revivalist Views of Animism, Buddhism, Sikhism, and Other Offshoots of Hinduism* (2002) by Koenraad Elst.
3. *Hindutva: Origin, Evolution, and Future* (2022) by Aravindan Neelakandan.

## Buddhism vs. Hinduism

1. "How Buddha was turned Anti-Hindu" (2019) by Koenraad Elst, *Indica Today*.
2. *Fundamentals of Indian Philosophy* (1997) by Ramakrishna Puligandla.
3. *Presuppositions of India's Philosophies* (1963) by Karl H. Potter.
4. *Hinduism and Buddhism* (1999) by Ananda K. Coomaraswamy.

A fantastic resource for understanding the non-antagonism between Hindu and Buddhist traditions.

### *Secularism and History Writing*

1. *Brainwashed Republic: India's Controlled Systemic Deracination* (2017) by Neeraj Atri and Munieshwar Sagar.
2. *Eminent Historians: Their Technology, Their Line, Their Fraud* (1998) by Arun Shourie.
3. "What Do Indians Need, a History or the Past? A Challenge or Two to Indian Historians" (2014) by S.N. Balagangadhara, *Academia.edu.*

### *Indian Philosophy*

1. *Essentials of Indian Philosophy* (1963) by M. Hiriyanna.
2. *Natural Realism and Contact Theory of Perception* (2019) by Chittaranjan Naik.
3. *On the Existence of the Self: And the Dismantling of the Physical Causal Closure Argument* (2021) by Chittaranjan Naik.
4. *The Nyaya Theory of Knowledge* (2017) by Satishchandra Chatterjee. A wonderful book examining the Indian systems of logic that strive to explain the reality of the world around us. It shows how Indian logical systems differ significantly from Western logical systems, which focus more on rules and constructions of sentences than on explaining the world.
5. *Methods of Knowledge: According to Advaita Vedanta* (2001) by Swami Satprakashananda. A classic text in a surprisingly lucid and easy style explaining the Advaitic position on the means of acquiring knowledge.

### *Educational Policies of Modern India*

1. Education in India; Memory in Education; and Music and Education in India in *Essays in National Idealism* (1909) by Ananda K Coomaraswamy.
2. Nehru and the National Philosophy of India (1991) by Bhikhu Parekh

### *Nations and Nationalism*

1. *Indian Culture and India's Future* (2022) by Michel Danino.
2. *The Fundamental Unity of India* (1914) by Radha Kumud Mookerji.
3. *Narrativizing Bhāratvarṣa & Other Essays* (2021) by Saumya Dey.

## Freedom Struggle

1. *Savarkar: A Contested Legacy from a Forgotten Past* (2019) *Vol. 1, and* (2021) *Vol. 2.* by Vikram Sampath.
2. *Bose: The Untold Story of an Inconvenient Nationalist* (2022) by Chandrachur Ghose.
3. *History of the Freedom Movement in India* (1962) *Vol. 1,* (1963) *Vol.2,* and (?1964) *Vol.3* by R.C. Majumdar.
4. *Sri Aurobindo & India's Rebirth* (2018) by Michel Danino.
5. *Churchill's Secret War* (2018) by Madhusree Mukerjee.

## Science and Technology

1. *Science and Technology in Ancient Indian Texts* (2012) edited by Bal Ram Singh, Girish Nath Jha, Umesh Kumar Singh, and Diwakar Mishra.
2. *Indian Science and Technology in The Eighteen Century* (2021) by Dharampal.
3. *Essential Writings of Dharampal* (2022) by Gita Dharampal.
4. *The Man Who Knew Infinity: A Life of the Genius Ramanujan* (1991) by Robert Kanigel.
5. *The Imperishable Seed: How Hindu Mathematics Changed the World and Why this History was Erased* (2022) by Bhaskar Kamble.

## Feminism

1. *The Madness of Crowds: Gender, Race and Identity* (2019) by Douglas Murray.
2. *Indigenous Roots of Feminism: Culture, Subjectivity and Agency* (2011) by Jasbir Jain.
3. "Feminism in India: The Tale and its Telling" (2019) by Maitrayee Chaudhuri, *Tiers-monde 209.*
4. *The Sabarimala Confusion: Menstruation Across Cultures: A Historical Perspective* (2019) by Nithin Sridhar.

## Chapter 14
### Introduction and the Section on Tamils

1. *Breaking India: Western Interventions in Dravidian and Dalit Faultlines* by Rajiv Malhotra and Aravindan Neelakandan.
2. "The Problem of Indian History" (2012) by Michel Danino, *Academia.edu.*
3. *The Lost River: On the Trail of The Sarasvati* by Michel Danino.
4. *Genetics and the Aryan debate: "Early Indians" Tony Joseph's Latest Assault* by Shrikant G. Talageri.
5. *Still No Trace of an Aryan Invasion: A Collection on Indo-European Origins* by Koenraad Elst.
6. *The Aryans and the Ancient System of Caste* by Marianne Keppens (in *Western Foundations of the Caste System,* edited by Martin Fárek, Dunkin Jalki, Sufiya Pathan, and Prakash Shah).
7. "Vedic Roots of Early Tamil Culture" (2005) by Michel Danino, *Academia.edu.*
8. *Land of Dharma: Proceedings from the Swadeshi Indology Conference Series,* edited by Shrinivas Tilak and Sharda Narayan.
9. *Dravidianism with Language Equaling Race — The Third Wheel in Tamil-Sanskrit Interactions* by Ravi Joshi and Yamuna Harshavardhana (*In Land of Dharma: Proceedings from the Swadeshi Indology Series*).
10. "The A of ABC of Indian chronology: Dimensions of the Aryan problem revisited in 2017" by Manogna Sastry and Megh Kalyanasundaram (*In Land of Dharma: Proceedings from the Swadeshi Indology Series*).

### The Section on Tribals

1. *Are Tribals Hindus? (In Who is a Hindu? Hindu Revivalist Views of Animism, Buddhism, Sikhism, and Other Offshoots of Hinduism)* by Dr. Koenraad Elst.
2. *Decolonizing the Hindu Mind: Ideological Development of Hindu Revivalism* by Dr. Koenraad Elst.
3. *India that is Bharat: Coloniality, Civilisation, Constitution* by J. Sai Deepak.

### The Section on Buddhism

1. "How Buddha was turned anti-Hindu" (2018) by Koenraad Elst, *Pragyata.*
2. "Were Shramana and Bhakti Movements Against the Caste System?" (2017) by Martin Fárek in *Western Foundations of the Caste System* edited by Sufiya Pathan and Prakash Shah, Martin Farek, Dunkin Jalki.

### The Section on Christianity and Islam in Indian Traditions

"How to Speak for the Indian Traditions: An Agenda for the Future" (2005) by S. N. Balagangadhara, *ResearchGate.net.*

### The Section on Nationhood of India

*Narrativizing Bhāratvarṣa & Other Essays* by Saumya Dey.

### The Section on Colonial Consciousness

hipkapi.com.
A one-stop site that gives access to many of the key ideas of Dr. Balagangadhara. It is a storehouse of articles and covers many important points about the widest variety of subjects comparing cultures in his almost four decades of extraordinary work at the University of Ghent in Belgium.

### Concluding Section

"Is India Civilised?" Aurobindo's three-part essay in *The Foundations of Indian Culture and the Renaissance in India.*

# ABOUT THE AUTHOR

Dr. Pingali Gopal, MS, MCh, FRCS, is a Paediatric and Neonatal Surgeon based in Warangal. Dr. Gopal was born in Assam and later, because of his father's work as an oil company geophysicist, moved successively to Calcutta (now Kolkata), Dehradun, Jammu, Ahmedabad, and Mumbai. He belongs to a Telugu-speaking family.

He completed a major part of his schooling and medical education in Ahmedabad. After qualifying as a general surgeon in Ahmedabad, he moved to Wadia Hospital, Mumbai, to become a Paediatric Surgeon. He obtained his speciality degree from the University of Mumbai in 1995. Following a two-year stint at Birmingham Children's Hospital in the United Kingdom and obtaining FRCS (Glasgow), he returned to India and settled in Warangal (now split into Warangal and Hanamkonda) in Telangana. He writes on matters concerning Indian culture in various online magazines such as Pragyata, IndicaToday, Bṛhat, and Indiafacts.

In trying to understand Indian culture, he is a follower of stalwarts like Sri Ramakrishna Paramhansa, Swami Vivekananda, Sri Aurobindo, Sri Ramana Maharishi, Anand Coomaraswamy, and—in more recent times—Michel Danino, Vishwa Adluri, Chittaranjan Naik, and SN Balagangadhara. He also dabbles in short stories and has recently published a collection of stories, *From Here to the Stars*. He has been living and practicing in Hanamkonda-Warangal, Telangana, since 1999.

9 798889 610959 4